A LITERARY PILGRIM
IN ENGLAND

BY

EDWARD THOMAS

Oxford New York Toronto Melbourne
OXFORD UNIVERSITY PRESS
1980

Oxford University Press, Walton Street, Oxford OX2 6DP

OXFORD LONDON GLASGOW
NEW YORK TORONTO MELBOURNE WELLINGTON
KUALA LUMPUR SINGAPORE JAKARTA HONG KONG TOKYO
DELHI BOMBAY CALCUTTA MADRAS KARACHI
NAIROBI DAR ES SALAAM CAPE TOWN

A Literary Pilgrim in England *was first published in 1917*
This edition first published as an Oxford University Press paperback 1980

British Library Cataloguing in Publication Data
Thomas, Edward, b. 1878
A literary pilgrim in England.
1. Literary landmarks — Great Britain
2. Great Britain — Description and travel — 1971
I. Title
941   PR109   79–41287
ISBN 0-19-281291-2

Printed in Great Britain by
Cox & Wyman Ltd, Reading

6·95

A LITERARY PILGRIM

IN ENGLAND

To
C. AND F. HODSON

CONTENTS

CONTENTS

LONDON AND THE HOME COUNTIES

BLAKE
LAMB
KEATS
MEREDITH

*

BLAKE was born and bred in London, lived there for all but three years of his life, and died there. Nor can I discover that he ever went farther out of London, except on that one excursion to Felpham, than he could walk in a day. And he was not a walker. 'He never took walks,' says Gilchrist, 'for walking's sake, or for pleasure; and could not sympathize with those who did.' Pictures, statues, and books seem to have had more reality for him than for any other man. Merely out of books and prints, and out of his strong feeling about 'the Druid Temples which are the patriarchal pillars and oak groves,' he could probably have drawn Stonehenge so as to impress us as we are ready to be impressed after hearing about it, yet seldom are. That was one of his principal gifts, to translate into visible and chiefly human forms what would in other minds remain vague, scattered notions and fragmentary blurred images. For example, at the beginning of the French Revolution he was a Republican, and wore a red cap in the streets of London, and in 1791 wrote the first book of a poem called 'The French Revolution.' He paints the notables – the King, Necker, the Archbishop of Paris, Aumont, Bourbon, Orleans and a Duke of Burgundy, Mirabeau, and La Fayette. The Duke of Burgundy's portrait shows how readily and sublimely Blake's mind would work upon a hint. His materials were chiefly three: the grandeur of the idea in the title of Duke, the solid mass and dignity expressed in the sound of the word 'Burgundy,' and connected with this the thought of blood-red wine. Thus he created a Duke of Burgundy (the title was then extinct), a colossal Bacchic emanation from these three sources:

'Then the ancientest peer, Duke of Burgundy, rose from the
    Monarch's right hand red as wines

From his fountains; an odour of war, like a ripe vineyard,
    rose from his garments,
And the chamber became as a clouded sky; o'er the Council
    he stretch'd his red limbs,
Cloth'd in flames of crimson; as a ripe vineyard stretches over
    sheaves of corn,
The fierce Duke hung over the Council; around him crowd,
    weeping in his burning robe,
A bright cloud of infant souls: his words fall like purple
    autumn on the sheaves. . . .'

It could hardly have mattered to such a man where he lived
after his youth. Yet he gives as one reason for returning to
London that he 'ought not to be away from the opportunities
London affords of seeing fine pictures, and the various im-
provements in works of art going on in London'; moreover,
London, and in particular South London, suited him. Towards the end of his life he complained of Hampstead air, saying that it always had been bad for him: 'When I was young,
Hampstead, Highgate, Hornsey, Muswell Hill, and even
Islington, and all places north of London, always laid me up
the day after.' Accordingly, in London, and for much of the
time near the river, he dwelt all his life, and avoided the
northern heights. London was still a town, or not more than
two towns, with country borders, when Blake was born in
1757, at 28, Broad Street, Golden Square. Gilchrist says that
'as he grew older the lad became fond of roving out into the
country. . . . On his own legs he could find a green field
without exhaustion. . . . After Westminster Bridge – the
"superb and magnificent structure" now defunct, then a new
and admired one, – came St. George's Fields, open fields, and
scene of "Wilkes and Liberty" riots in Blake's boyhood; next,
the pretty village of Newington Butts . . .; and then, un-

sophisticate green field and hedgerow. . . . A mile or two further through the "large and pleasant village" of Camberwell, with its grove (or avenue) and famed prospect, arose the sweet hill and dale and "sylvan wilds" of rural Dulwich. . . .' The tree that he saw filled with angels was on Peckham Rye. 'Another time, one summer morn, he sees the hay-makers at work, and amid them angelic figures walking.' Here, too, he must have found suitable dens and bowers for the wild beasts, virgins, shepherdesses, of his books. What he saw and read to any purpose made equal and similar impressions on him, and he combined the two with beautiful freedom. No wonder he declared afterwards that the whole business of man was in the arts – that the man or woman who was not poet, painter, musician, or architect, was not a Christian – that they must leave fathers and mothers and houses and lands if these stood in the way of Art. These free and astonishing remarks were written round his engraving of the Lacoon. Their meaning is not clear except to his peers, but certain it is that in Blake's view life should be a poem, a free and astonishing thing. The innocence of life he loved; everything done and said at liberty from the mere reason or from the self-conscious, 'self-righteous' virtues, as he considered them, of pagans, deists, and agnostics. His own life and work proclaim his own enjoyment in a great measure of this innocence.

He saw life whole. An unlearned man, who can only be understood completely by the very learned, he had made for himself out of the streets of London, the churches and shops, the fields of Dulwich, and out of ruminations among all sorts of books and pictures, a system of the world. The Bible, Shakespeare, Milton, the mystics, newspaper reports of the American War and the French Revolution, popular songs, Westminster Abbey, pictures and sculptures and engravings,

London streets, provided the elements of this world. He had no need of crying:

> 'What do we here
> In this land of unbelief and fear?
> The Land of Dreams is better far
> Above the light of the morning star.'

For this land and the Land of Dreams were one. Books were, if anything, stronger than direct sensuous experience, or he could not have mingled eyesight and memory of books about foreign lands as in 'To the Evening Star':

> 'Let thy west wind sleep on
> The lake; speak silence with thy glimmering eyes,
> And wash the dusk with silver. Soon, full soon,
> Dost thou withdraw; then the wolf rages wide,
> And the lion glares thro' the dim forest:
> The fleeces of our flocks are covered with
> Thy sacred dew: protect them with thine influence.'

He wrote of England as if her poets played on harps and wore 'laurel wreaths against the sultry heat.' He could write as beautifully by accepting the conventional idea, let us say, of a shepherd, as others by refusing it altogether. It would be impossible for him to think of a shepherd without thinking of Christ, so that he writes:

> 'How sweet is the shepherd's sweet lot!
> From the morn to the evening he strays;
> He shall follow his sheep all the day,
> And his tongue shall be filled with praise.
> For he hears the lamb's innocent call,
> And he hears the ewe's tender reply;
> He is watchful while they are in peace,
> For they know when their shepherd is nigh.'

It is doubtful whether three years by the sea added anything to his geography. He had always that crystal cabinet and its world and 'little lovely moony night':

> 'Another England there I saw,
> Another London with its Tower,
> Another Thames and other hills,
> And another pleasant Surrey bower.'

The only poems that might have sprung from the recollection of actual times and places are those in a small class of poems like the 'Echoing Green,' 'Laughing Song,' and 'Nurse's Song.' In all three there is an echo, and in two a most real sense of the last half-hour of child's play in the evening. Childhood, also, may perhaps have lent him the memory of a folk-song in the words of —

> 'As I walk'd forth one May morning
> To see the fields so pleasant and so gay, . . .'

and in the tone of 'My Pretty Rose-Tree,' which is like 'The Seeds of Love':

> 'A flower was offer'd to me,
> Such a flower as May never bore;
> But I said, "I've a pretty rose-tree,"
> And I passèd the sweet flower o'er. . . .'

When he was only ten, Blake was put to a drawing-school in the Strand, and is said not long afterwards to have written the verses, 'How sweet I roam'd from field to field.' Out of school he used to frequent print-dealers' shops and picture sales. He was apprenticed at fourteen to the engraver Basire, at 31, Great Queen Street, Lincoln's Inn Fields. So he came to discover, what must have been a large part of London, of history, of the earth, to him, Westminster Abbey. For he was sent there and left alone to make drawings of the structure and monuments, Basire having to make engravings of them for Gough, the antiquary. He looked into the faces of the Kings and Queens of England and learnt history. In his old age he drew 'visionary heads' of the Kings.

Still living with his father in Broad Street, Blake began to engrave for publishers, and to meet fellow-artists, such as Stothard and Flaxman. By 1782 he was able to marry Catherine Boucher of Battersea — Battersea, 'the pleasant village of the St. John's' — and take lodgings at 23, Green Street, Leicester Square. He used to go to Mrs. Mathew's *salons* at 27, Rathbone Place, and meet the Bluestockings and their friends, and, as J. T. Smith said, read and sang several of his poems to airs of his own. His father died in 1784, and he moved to 27, Broad Street, and opened a shop with a partner as printseller and engraver, his favourite younger brother Robert living with him, his brother James keeping on the hosier's business at No. 28, next door. Robert died in 1787, and the poet and his wife moved to 28, Poland Street. There he published 'Songs of Innocence' in 1789, having printed it in the manner revealed to him in a vision of the night by his brother Robert. 'On his rising in the morning, Mrs. Blake went out with half a crown, all the money they had in the world, and of that laid out 1s. 10d. on the simple materials necessary for setting in practice the new revelation,' the reproduction in facsimile of the songs and their designs. The 'Book of Thel' and the 'Marriage of Heaven and Hell,' reproduced in the same way, also came out of Poland Street. And there he wrote the 'French Revolution,' which was to have been published by John Johnson, and worked at designing and engraving plates for the same publisher. Blake sometimes sat at Johnson's table at 72, St. Paul's Churchyard, in a company that included, at one time or another, Priestley, Godwin, Holcroft, Tom Paine, Fuseli, and Mary Wollstonecraft. He

16

was then, in Mr. John Sampson's opinion, writing some of the 'Songs of Experience' and 'A Song of Liberty.'

In 1793 he moved to 13, Hercules Buildings, in Lambeth, a one-storied house, with 'a narrow strip of real garden behind, wherein grew a fine vine.' It was here that he produced the 'Gates of Paradise,' 'America,' 'Visions of the Daughters of Albion,' 'Europe: a Prophecy,' the 'Book of Urizen,' the 'Song of Los,' 'Ahania,' the 'Four Zoas,' and the plates for Stedman's 'Narrative of a Five Years' Expedition against the Revolted Negroes of Surinam,' and for Young's 'Night Thoughts.' And here he saw the vision of the 'Ancient of Days' and his one ghost:

'When talking on the subject of ghosts, he was wont to say they did not appear much to imaginative men, but only to common minds, who did not see the finer spirits. A ghost was a thing seen by the gross bodily eye, a vision by the mental. "Did you ever see a ghost?" asked a friend. "Never but once," was the reply. And it befel thus. Standing one evening at the garden-door in Lambeth, and chancing to look up, he saw a horrible grim figure, "scaly, speckled, very awful," stalking downstairs towards him. More frightened than ever before or after, he took to his heels and ran out of the house.'

In September, 1800, Blake and his wife and sister were at Felpham, near Bognor, neighbours of William Hayley. Flaxman had introduced him to this man, Cowper's friend and biographer, and a poet whom people visiting Bognor went out of their way to see, 'as if he had been a Wordsworth.' Blake was to illustrate his ballads and the additional letters to his life of Cowper, and to engrave Maria Flaxman's designs for his 'Triumphs of Temper.' What is more important, Blake here conceived, and possibly wrote, his 'Milton' and 'Jerusalem,' and certain shorter poems. He had at first high spirits at Felpham. Being now away from all his friends, he wrote a few letters; but it would be rash to conclude that he had not equally high spirits at Hercules Buildings, where he had no occasion to write long letters. 'Felpham,' he said, 'is a sweet place for study, because it is more spiritual than London. Heaven opens on all sides her golden gates; her windows are not obstructed by vapours; voices of celestial inhabitants are more distinctly heard, and their forms more distinctly seen; and my cottage is also a shadow of their houses.' The hyperbolical next sentence where he speaks of his wife and sister bathing – 'Courting Neptune for an embrace' – should warn us that Blake sometimes used grand words loosely or lightly. Another letter shows how open he was to the suggestion of words like 'father' – he seems to take it almost as if it were 'Our Father which art in heaven':

'The villagers of Felpham are not mere rustics; they are polite and modest. Meat is cheaper than in London; but the sweet air and the voices of winds, trees, and birds, and the odours of the happy ground, make it a dwelling for immortals. Work will go on here with God-speed. A roller and two harrows lie before my window. I met a plough on my first going out at my gate the first morning after my arrival, and the ploughboy said to the ploughman, "Father, the gate is open." I have begun to work, and find that I can work with greater pleasure than ever.'

This was written soon after his arrival. On his first visit in August to look for a house he had been taken with the place, and sent an invitation to the Flaxmans:

'Away to sweet Felpham, for Heaven is there;
The Ladder of Angels descends through the air;
On the turret its spiral does softly descend,
Through the village then winds, at my cot it does end.'

18

He wrote other verses a few days after his arrival, on a vision by the sea, as he tells his patron, Mr. Butts, which showed him all he had ever known and left him as a child — verses 'such as Felpham produces by me, though not such as she produces by her eldest son [Hayley].' A later poem, composed 'while walking from Felpham to Lavant to meet my sister,' contains an interesting piece of introspection:

> 'What to others a trifle appears
> Fills me full of smiles or tears,
> For double the vision my eyes do see,
> And a double vision is always with me.
> With my inward eye 'tis an old man grey,
> With my outward a thistle across the way.'

He strikes the thistle or 'the old man' on his path, and straightway he sees a sun spirit 'outward a sun — inward, Los in his might,' and he speaks:

> 'This earth breeds not our happiness,
> Another sun feeds our life's streams;
> We are not warmèd with thy beams.
> Thou measurest not the time to me,
> Nor yet the space that I do see:
> My mind is not with thy light array'd;
> Thy terrors shall not make me afraid.'

This agrees with his note to Wordsworth: 'Natural objects always did and do weaken, deaden, and obliterate imagination in me!' and with his practice. 'Throughout life, he was always, as Mrs. Blake truly described him, either reading, writing, or designing. For it was a tenet of his that the inner world is the all-important; that each man has a world within greater than the external. Even while he engraved, he read, — as the plate-marks on his books testify. He never took walks for mere walking's sake, or for pleasure; and could not sympathize with those who did. During one period he, for two years together, never went out at all, except to the corner of the Court to fetch his porter.'

Mr. John Sampson finds that 'Milton' 'recounts in all their freshness Blake's first spiritual experiences at Felpham,' that 'the poem is indeed – a thing rare in Blake – redolent of the countryside and its new images, the plough and harrow, insect life, the scent of flowers, the song of birds, and the aspects of the sky, conceived in the same spirit of exaltation which characterizes the letters to Butts and Flaxman.' But I have been less fortunate. There are two beautiful passages, 'Thou hearest the Nightingale begin the Song of Spring,' and 'Thou perceivest the Flowers put forth their precious Odours,' but for me they do not scent the poem, being in it, not of it. There is no more of Felpham in it than of Hyde Park and the Almshouses of Mile End and old Bow and Tyburn's awful brook. And then the harrow and 'the servants of the Harrow!' It is another thing of the same name. It 'cast thick flames.' It never lay outside his door at Felpham. Luvah's bulls that 'each morning drag the sulphur Sun out of the Deep, Harnessed with starry harness black and shining, kept by black slaves, That work all night at the starry harness!' – these are magnificent, but not Sussex. As to the insect life, 'the Grasshopper that sings and laughs and drinks. Winter comes: he folds his slender bones without a murmur' – he is exquisite, but could he not have come from anywhere except Felpham? Could not 'the Flea, Louse, Bug, the Tape-Worm, all the Armies of Disease' who precede him and the slow Slug? Walking in his cottage garden, Blake 'beheld the Virgin Ololon, and address'd her as a daughter of Beulah'; but I believe he might have beheld her at Hercules Buildings or even at South Molton Street. For Blake gave up Felpham for London, having found Hayley intolerable, and having been put out by a trial for high treason at Chichester. He had beheld a soldier in his garden at Felpham and turned him out. The soldier retaliated by accusing him of uttering seditious and treasonable expressions. Blake was acquitted, but he left Felpham soon after, and Hayley, and Lord Egremont of Petworth, and Lord Bathurst of Lavant, and Mrs. Poole of Mid-Lavant; and early in 1804, took lodgings at 17, South Molton Street, where he dwelt nearly seventeen years. He was often 'reduced so low as to be obliged to live on half a guinea a week,' but he made the drawings for Blair's 'Grave,' and Phillips' 'Pastorals,' and the 'Canterbury Pilgrims'; he wrote and drew unceasingly. 'Strange,' says Gilchrist, 'to think of Blake shut up in dingy, gardenless South Molton Street designing such pastorals! His mind must have been impregnated with rural images, enabling him without immediate reference to Nature to throw off these beautiful suggestions, so pastoral in feeling, of Arcadian shepherds and their flocks under the broad setting sun or tranquil moon.' There have been stranger things. Thus Blake used to sit at night with John Varley the artist and astrologer, and make pencil sketches of historical personages, kings, Wat Tyler, the man who built the Pyramids, as he summoned them before him at midnight or after in 1819 or 1820. Varley was a new friend, met through John Linnell, one of the young artists who gathered round Blake, stored up his sayings, bought his pictures, and assembled at his grave in 1827.

In 1821 he made his last move, to 3, Fountain Court, Strand. He designed the 'Inventions to Job' there, being paid two or three pounds a week for them by Mr. Linnell while they were being done. One room sufficed for Blake and his wife to sleep in, cook and serve meals, and work; another for receiving guests. 'There was an air of poverty as of an artisan's room; but everything was clean and neat; nothing sordid.' It had a 'divine window' looking between walls on to the river. Blake himself got down first to light the fire and boil the kettle, and fetched his pint of porter from the public house at the corner of the Strand. His wife could cook. She could draw at times uncommonly like him. 'When he, in his wild way, would tell his friends that King Alfred, or any great historical personage, had sat to him, Mrs. Blake would look at her husband with an awestruck countenance, and then at his listener to confirm the fact.' If his work was not going right, the two knelt down and prayed. In his last days, when she was nursing him, he suddenly said: 'Stay! Keep as you are! You have been ever an angel to me. I will draw you!' Tatham said the drawing was 'highly interesting, but not like.' He went out very little, but occasionally on a Sunday up to Collins's Farm, North End, Hampstead, where Linnell lived. Mulready and Varley and Samuel Palmer also visited there. To the end he was working hard. He was doing a series of drawings for Dante, and learning Italian too, and he took this work up to Hampstead with him. From time to time, to order, he executed fresh copies of the 'Songs' or the 'Ancient of Days.'

At the end of the period when there was a Merry England he was one of the best of Londoners. But it does not appear in his work, where he used 'Primrose Hill and Saint John's Wood,' 'Pancras and Kentish Town,' 'The Jew's Harp House and the Green Man,' in some sense now hidden from us. He had perhaps seen their spirits, but had not been able to put them down in words as he had the tiger's and the lamb's. Even South Molton Street is but three words in his writing, and not a reality of any sort. Nobody as yet has discovered even what he meant by 'Albion.' The multitudes of London are represented in his poems practically by two suffering types.

Everywhere he hears 'the mind-forg'd manacles,' but over all
two voices, of the chimney-sweeper and the harlot:

> 'How the chimney-sweeper's cry
>   Every black'ning church appals,
> And the hapless soldier's sigh
>   Runs in blood down palace walls.
> But most thro' midnight streets I hear
>   How the youthful harlot's curse
> Blasts the new-born infant's tear,
>   And blights with plagues the marriage hearse.'

'Songs of Innocence' include a picture of 'children walking
two and two, in red and blue and green . . . multitudes of
lambs, thousands of little boys and girlings raising their innocent hands,' in charge of 'grey-headed beadles, with wands as
white as snow . . . wise guardians of the poor'; 'Songs of Experience,' a contrary picture of 'babes reduced to misery, fed
with cold and usurious hand.' His England, then, is just this:
meadows and streets and cold churches, with children playing
in twilight or weeping, lions and lambs mingled, birds singing,
angels clustering in trees, venerable, seraphic old men pacing,
harlots and soldiers plying, mighty figures descended from
those in Westminster Abbey and the Italian churches and
galleries, peopling the clouds and a misty mid-region of
'Where?' and Blake himself, a sturdy, half-Quakerish revolu-
tionary, with rapt forehead carrying home his pint of porter.

*

LAMB was old-fashioned in nothing so much as in this: that he thought London a very good place to live in, and at the same time loved the country – in fact, loved both without giving either a cause for jealousy. When he was planning to live in King's Bench Walk in 1800 – as a matter of fact, he and his sister moved to 16, Mitre Court Buildings in the Temple in March, 1801 – he rhapsodized to Manning:

'I shall be as airy, up four pair of stairs, as in the country, and in a garden in the midst of enchanting (more than Mahometan paradise) London, whose dirtiest drab-frequented alley, and her lowest-bowing tradesman, I would not exchange for Skiddaw, Helvellyn, James, Walter, and the parson into the bargain. O! her lamps of a night! her rich goldsmiths, printshops, toyshops, mercers, hardware men, pastrycooks, St. Paul's Churchyard, the Strand, Exeter Change, Charing Cross, with the man *upon* a black horse! These are thy gods, O London! . . . All the streets and pavements are pure gold, I warrant you. At least, I know an alchemy that turns her mud into that metal – a mind that loves to be at home in crowds.'

At that moment he was suffering (cheerfully) under an egotistic letter from the Lake poets. Two years later, when he saw the mountains, spending three weeks with Coleridge at Keswick, he called them 'glorious creatures, fine old fellows.' He admired them, but it was not his native air. His father had been a Lincolnshire man, his mother a Hertfordshire woman. He himself was as much at home between the Temple and Ware as Wordsworth in the mountains, and less conscious of being so.

Crown Office Row in the Temple was his birthplace, and, having passed the first seven years of his life there, he had such

a liking for the Temple church, the halls, the gardens, the
river, that when he came to write about them he declared he
repeated no verses with kindlier emotion than Spenser's:

'There when they came, whereas those bricky towers,
The which on Thames' broad aged back doth ride,
Where now the studious lawyers have their bowers,
There whilom went the Templar knights to bide,
Till they decayed through pride.'

'The most elegant spot in the Metropolis,' and doubly so to
a poor boy whose first school looked into 'a discoloured dingy
garden in the passage leading from Fetter Lane into Bartlett's
Buildings.' There the boys sat wedged into uncomfortable
sloping desks endeavouring after 'a free hand,' and writing out
'Art improves Nature.' When he left the Temple in his
eighth year, in 1782, it was for Christ's Hospital.

'In his yellow coats,
Red leathern belt, and gown of russet blue,'

he became a travelled Londoner. Summer excursions to the
New River near Newington, visits to the Tower, 'where, by
ancient privilege, we had free access to all the curiosities,' and
'solemn processions through the City at Easter, with the Lord
Mayor's largess of buns, wine, and a shilling' – these stirred
up town and country for him for ever in a delicious mixture.
Thus he was from time to time driven to break out on provocation from some extreme rustic, and cry up the streets, markets, theatres, churches, Covent Gardens, shops, shoppers,
lights, coaches, bookstalls . . ., and exclaim: 'O city abounding in whores, for these may Keswick and her giant brood go
hang;' or again: 'I was born, as you have heard, in a crowd.
This has begot in me an entire affection for that way of life,
amounting to an almost insurmountable aversion from soli-

tude and rural scenes.' He could even in a way enjoy, from the very intensity of its significance, the 'delicate suburban' home of Sir Jeffery Dunstan, where the atmosphere was made up of 'a strong odour of burnt bones . . . blended with the scent of horse-flesh seething into dog's meat, and only relieved a little by the breathings of a few brick-kilns.' His country scenes have a peculiar brightness of grass and water, as if he had emerged out upon them from the dark Temple or the 'delicate suburban' wilderness. In his longer holidays he got out far beyond Newington, to Blakesware, between Widford and Ware in Hertfordshire. His grandmother had been housekeeper for half a century in the old house. Widford Church is the church of the poem, where 'the grandame sleeps':

> 'On the green hill-top,
> Hard by the house of prayer, a modest roof,
> And not distinguished from its neighbour barn
> Save by a slender tapering length of spire.'

She died in 1792, but Lamb revisited the place from time to time. As early as 1799 he writes to Southey of 'an old house with a tapestry bedroom, the "Judgment of Solomon" composing one panel, and "Actæon spying Diana naked" the other . . . an old marble hall, with Hogarth's prints and the Roman Cæsars in marble hung round . . . of *a wilderness*, and of a village church, and where the bones of my honoured grandam lie.' But, he adds, 'these are feelings which refuse to be translated, sulky aborigines, which will not be naturalized in another soil.' Thirty years later he wished he were buried 'in the peopled solitude' of such a house, 'with my feelings at seven years old.' Nothing, he said, 'fills a child's mind like a large old mansion; better if un- or partially occupied.' The marble hall, the twelve Cæsars, the Hogarths, the family portraits, the tapestry hangings 'full of Bible history,' appear in Margaret Green's story of 'The Young Mahometan' in 'Mrs. Leicester's School'; the garden south wall ('can I forget the hot feel of the brickwork?') in the letter on 'The Last Peach.' House and gardens reappear in the essay on 'Blakesmoor in H – shire.'

He had other connexions with Hertfordshire, near Wheathampstead. 'The oldest things I remember,' he wrote in one of his best-known essays, 'is Mackery End; or Mackaree End, as it is spelt, perhaps more properly, in some old maps of Hertfordshire; a farmhouse, delightfully situated within a gentle walk from Wheathampstead.' He recalled going there with Mary to see a great-aunt, a sister of his grandmother's. They were Brutons, but the grandmother at Blakesware married a Field, the great-aunt a Gladman. A Bruton, says Mr. E. V. Lucas, still lived at Wheathampstead in 1904. The letter already quoted, speaking of an 'aversion' from the country, admits that it was suspended in his younger days 'during a period in which I had set my affections upon a charming young woman.' This was presumably the 'Alice W – n' of the essays; the Anna of the early sonnets, who made him declare himself

> 'well content to play
> With thy free tresses all a summer's day,
> Losing the time beneath the greenwood shade.'

She must have helped him to the 'truant love of rambling' which made this sonnet (of 1795):

> 'The Lord of Light shakes off his drowsyhed;
> Fresh from his couch up springs the lusty sun,
> And girds himself his mighty race to run.
> Meantime, by truant love of rambling led,

I turn my back on thy detested walls,
Proud city, and thy sons I leave behind,
A selfish, sordid, money-getting kind
Who shut their ears when holy freedom calls.
I pass not thee so lightly, humble spire,
That mindest me of many a pleasure gone,
Of merriest days of love and Islington,
Kindling anew the flames of past desire;
And I shall muse on thee, slow journeying on,
To the green plains of pleasant Hertfordshire.'

Alice was Ann Simmons, a girl he had met at Blakes-ware.

1795 was the fourth year of Lamb's service with the East India Company; the year when the family moved from the Temple to 7, Little Queen Street, Holborn; the year when Coleridge left Cambridge; and the last or one of the last when he and Lamb supped and talked at the Salutation and Cat near Smithfield. In 1796 Mary Lamb was the death of her mother; the father died soon after, and the aunt Hetty followed. Lamb and his sister were left alone together at Little Queen Street. For a short time they were at 45, Chapel Street, Pentonville. At Pentonville he used to see the Quaker Hester. Then the brother and sister moved to 34, Southampton Buildings. For nine years from 1801 they lived at 16, Mitre Court Buildings. Now, in 1802 he was writing 'The Londoner' and private letters which show with what a zest he was tasting London. He transcribes 'The Londoner' in a letter to Manning:

'Every man,' he says, 'while the *passion* is upon him, is for a time at least addicted to groves and meadows and purling streams. During this short period of my existence, I contracted just enough familiarity with rural objects to understand tolerably well after the *Poets*, when they declaim in such passionate terms in favour of a *country life*.

'For my own part, now the *fit* is long past, I have no hesitation in declaring that a mob of happy faces crowding up at the pit door of Drury Lane Theatre just at the hour of five give me ten thousand finer pleasures than I ever received from all the flocks of *silly sheep* that have whitened the plains of *Arcadia* or *Epsom Downs*.

'This passion for crowds is nowhere feasted so full as in London. The man must have a rare *recipe* for melancholy who can be dull in Fleet Street. . . .'

But apart from the crowd, Lamb had the advantage of more select company – Wordsworth, Coleridge, Hazlitt, and others – on Wednesday evenings. The 'passion' was not up-set – it may have been sustained – by occasional holidays in Hertfordshire, at Oxford, or Cambridge, or Brighton, in the Lakes, or with Hazlitt at Winterslow. Mary could walk fifteen miles a day in 1817, and at this rate she and her brother must have explored far round Brighton.

In 1809, after a brief interval at 34, Southampton Buildings, Chancery Lane, the Lambs entered 4, Inner Temple Lane. When they left in 1817, they had been seventeen years in the Temple. They were now in Russell Street – the part then known as Great Russell Street, between Covent Garden and Catherine Street – 'at the corner of Bow Street, and the site where Will's Coffee House once stood.' They had been transplanted from 'our native soil,' said Lamb to Dorothy Wordsworth, but to 'the individual spot I like best in all this great city,' on account of the theatres and Covent Garden, 'dearer to me than any gardens of Alcinous, where we are morally certain of the earliest peas and 'sparagus.' Mary calls it a cheerful place, and quite enjoys 'the calling up of the

carriages and the squabbles of the coachmen and little boys'
in November; but new chairs and carpets and the absence
of the Hogarths (now all bound in a book) from the wall
cause her misgivings. Lamb dates his next letter from 'The
Garden of England': a few weeks later he was for examin-
ing the bumps of the Comptroller of Stamps at Haydon's
dinner-party, if Keats and the host had not hurried him
away.

In May, 1819, Lamb was writing to Manning, then at
Totteridge in Hertfordshire, to inquire after his cousins, 'the
Gladman's of Wheathampstead, and farmer Bruton.' Probably he was then fresh from revisiting them, and about to
write his essay on 'Mackery End in Hertfordshire.' He was
comparing the dead wood of his desk unfavourably with the
living trees of Hertfordshire. – Of one thing at least he was
tired in London, and that was the India House.

Already for some years he and his sister had begun to slip
away at times to 'a rural lodging at Dalston,' 14, Kingsland
Row, 'to divide their time, in alternate weeks, between quiet
rest and dear London weariness.' There Lamb could take a
seventeen-mile walk in fields, and could write without fear of
interruption; but presently he resolved to move entirely out
on to the country margin of London. – He took a cottage at
Colebrook Row, Islington, in 1823:

'A cottage, for it is detach'd; a white house, with six good
rooms. The New River (rather elderly by this time) runs (if a
moderate walking pace can be so termed) close to the foot of
the house; and behind is a spacious garden, with vines (I
assure you), pears, strawberries, parsnips, leeks, carrots, cab-
bages, to delight the heart of old Alcinous. You enter without passage into a cheerful dining-room, all studded over and
rough with old books, and above is a lightsome drawing-room,

three windows, full of choice prints. I feel like a great lord, never having had a house before.'

The 'London Magazine,' he fears, is falling off, but he has pears to gather and a vine to sit under. It was at the end of this autumn that George Dyer, 'staff in hand, in broad open day, marched into the New River,' and suggested the essay 'Amicus Redivivus,' and the rebuke to that mockery of a river. Lamb had known the New River high up at Ware and low down at Newington. That the poet had to be rescued by ordinary means proved, however, that the river was no true river, with 'no swans, no naiads, no river-god.' A year and a half later, in March, 1825, he left this note for Henry Crabb Robinson:

'I have left the d – d India House for ever! Give me great joy. – C. LAMB.'

He walked twenty miles one day; next day wrote to Wordsworth and Bernard Barton. They were four years at Islington. 'My house-deaths,' wrote Lamb to Hood, 'have generally been periodical, recurring after seven years, but this last is premature by half that time.' Life at Islington had not agreed with him, even mitigated by daily work at the British Museum; so he took a step which brought him half-way to Ware and Blakesware – i.e. to Enfield – yet not so far but that he could 'occasionally breathe the *fresher air* of the Metropolis.' He could still say – to Wordsworth that is:

'O let no native Londoner imagine that health, rest, and innocent occupation, interchange of converse sweet, and recreative study, can make the country anything better than altogether odious and detestable. A garden was the primitive prison till man with promethean felicity and boldness luckily sinn'd himself out of it. Thence followed Babylon, Nineveh,

31

Venice, London, haberdashers, goldsmiths, taverns, play-houses, satires, epigrams, puns – these all came in on the town part, and the thither side of innocence.'

To Bernard Barton he could say he dreaded Summer with his long days. 'No need of his assistance to make country places dull. With fire and candle light I can dream myself in Holborn. With lightsome skies shining in to bedtime, I cannot. . . .' But London was not what it was. Friends had gone; clubs had crumbled away. Even more than at Enfield he could be lonely in London, after seeing off Emma Isola, 'our adopted young friend,' at the end of the holidays. And there was that 'dear London weariness.'

Much of his country lives now only in his letters, particularly in one to Charles Cowden Clarke written in December, 1828:

'The way from Southgate to Colney Hatch through the unfrequentedest blackberry paths that ever concealed their coy branches from a truant citizen we have accidentally fallen upon. The giant tree by Cheshunt [Goff's Oak] we have missed, but keep your chart to go by, unless you will be our conduct. At present I am disabled from further flights than just to skirt round Clay Hill, with a peep at the fine back-woods, by strained tendons, got by skipping a skipping-rope at fifty-three – *heu mihi non sum qualis*. But do you know, now you come to talk of walks, a ramble of four hours or so, there and back, to the willow and lavender plantations at the south corner of Northaw Church by a well dedicated to St. Claridge, with the clumps of finest moss rising hillock fashion, which I counted to the number of two hundred and sixty, and are called "Claridge's covers," the tradition being that that saint entertained so many angels or hermits there, upon occasion of blessing the waters ? . . . A sweeter spot is not in ten counties round. You are knee-deep in clover — that is to say, if you are not above a middling man's height. From this paradise, making a day of it, you go to see the ruins of an old convent at March Hall, where some of the painted glass is yet whole and fresh. . . .

'I shall long to show you the "clump meadows," as they are called; we might do that, without reaching March Hall. When the days are longer, we might take both, and come home by Forest Cross. So skirt we Pennington, and the cheerful little village of Churchley, to Forty Hill. . . .'

He put some of this country into the sonnet on his walks with Mary Lamb and Emma Isola:

'By Enfield lanes and Winchmore's verdant hill. . . .'

But his sister was too often and too long absent, ill; and soon, in 1829, they gave up their house and moved into lodgings next door, at the house now known as Westwood Cottage, in Enfield Chase Side. From here he wrote the letter to Wordsworth on man's 'promethean felicity' in sinning himself out of gardens and the country. He could no longer have written that letter on 'Mrs. Gilpin riding to Edmonton,' Mrs. Gilpin having climbed up on to the top of one of 'the high awkward styles' of Edmonton. But to Edmonton they went in 1833, Mary to a private asylum, Lamb to rooms in the same house, in Church Street. He was now 'three or four miles nearer the Great City, coaches half-price less, and going always, of which I will avail myself.' Sixteen miles a day was still not too much for him: he could not read much in summer-time. Emma Isola was getting married to Edward Moxon. He dined with an old school friend 'at Johnny Gilpin's' — i.e. at The Bell at Edmonton — and 'talked of what old friends were taken or left in the thirty years since we had met.' In his writing he had always looked back too much, but in these last years it was no literary artifice. At long intervals he struggled to London. Mary, when she was well, walked 'always up the road, dear Londonwards.' Coleridge died, and then Lamb died, five months later, in December, 1834, at Church Street, Edmonton. He was a good Londoner, but a good Hertfordshireman too, a lover of pure, gentle country – cornland, copse, and water – and of gardens refined out of it. What he saw he put down almost exactly, a little enriched, perhaps, certainly a great deal touched by the pathetic that comes of looking backward, and never more so than when he wrote of the country, because he had never known it except as a place deliberately resorted to for rest and change of air, since he was a child at Newington, at Blakesware, near Widford, at Mackery End, near Wheathampstead.

KEATS lived the greater part of his life in London and in the country on London's northern borders. His father was a West-Country man; where his mother came from, whose maiden name was Jennings, is unknown and unconjectured. The poet, their eldest son, was born at a livery stable in Finsbury Pavement. When he was nine or ten he went to live at Church Street, Edmonton, at the house of his mother's mother. His schooldays were passed at Enfield, under the father of his friend, Charles Cowden Clarke. Leaving school on his mother's death, he went, when he was fifteen, as apprentice to a surgeon at Edmonton. There he began to read Spenser and write verses. A quarrel caused him to quit the surgeon and study at St. Thomas's and Guy's Hospitals; and he divided the next three years of his life, 1814 to 1817, between lodgings at 8, Dean Street, Borough, in St. Thomas's Street, in the Poultry, and at 76, Cheapside, sometimes alone, sometimes with other students or with his two younger brothers.

In 1816 Keats had an August holiday at Margate. Otherwise these twenty-two years seem to have been spent in the middle of a city or in the gentle garden country adjacent.

The city, unless by provocation, gave him no impulse to writing. When he was just twenty he said, in the epistle to George Felton Mathew, that he was beckoned away by his work from poetry, and that, even if he could give all his time to the 'coy muse,'

> 'with me she would not live
> In this dark city, nor would condescend
> 'Mid contradictions her delights to lend.'

Nevertheless, with poetry and his friends he was very happily alive. It was at his lodgings in the Borough, after a night with his friend Clarke at Clerkenwell, that he wrote

35

the sonnet 'On First Looking into Chapman's Homer.'
Other poems and letters record his enjoyment of the talk,
the reading, the music, the card-playing, that filled long
nights with his friends. He writes while

> 'lovely airs
> Are fluttering round the room like doves in pairs,'

or while his solitude is still thrilled by memories. On his way
homeward, probably from Leigh Hunt's in the Vale of Health,
he composed the sonnet:

> 'Keen fitful gusts are whispering here and there
>   Among the bushes, half leafless and dry;
>   The stars look very cold about the sky,
> And I have many miles on foot to fare;
> Yet feel I little of the cold bleak air,
>   Or of the dead leaves rustling drearily,
>   Or of those silver lamps that burn on high,
> Or of the distance from home's pleasant lair:
> For I am brim full of the friendliness
>   That in a little cottage I have found;
> Of fair-haired Milton's eloquent distress,
>   And all his love for gentle Lycid' drown'd;
> Of lovely Laura in her light green dress,
>   And faithful Petrarch gloriously crown'd.'

Verses were, in fact, his compliments to the pleasures of life.
He stuffed them with what had just come to his eye or to his
mind. From Margate, for example, he wrote to his brother
George:

> 'These things I thought
> While, in my face, the freshest breeze I caught.
> E'en now I am pillow'd on a bed of flowers
> That crowns a lofty cliff, which proudly towers

Above the ocean waves. The stalks and blades
Chequer my tablet with their quivering shades.
On one side is a field of drooping oats,
Through which the poppies show their scarlet coats.'

Dwelling so much in a country of small fields and many
gardens, and among artistic town-dwellers like Leigh Hunt,
who regarded the country as a picture-gallery and pleasure-
resort, Keats began by rhyming pretty catalogues of the pretty
things in Nature. Seldom does he approach or aim at a picture even as complete and proportioned as that just quoted; a
score or so of tiny details, each separate and self-sufficient, can
do nothing to remind us of the actual scenery from whose
myriad elements these were chosen. How little Keats cared
so long as nothing ugly or mean entered the catalogue is
shown by his picture of the 'flowery spot' where he thinks the
'coy muse' might condescend to him. He mingles Druid oaks,
laburnum, and cassia, adding nightingales and 'a ruin dark
and gloomy.'

In April, 1817, when he had given up the hospitals and
published his first book of poems, Keats took the coach to
Southampton and crossed to the Isle of Wight. He all but
filled the letter written to his brother from Southampton with
a list of things seen by the way. The island, St. Catherine's
Hill, Shanklin Chine, the white cliffs, Carisbrooke Castle,
the copses, the primroses and cowslips, and the sea, delighted
him; he stopped at 'Mrs. Cook's, New Village, Carisbrooke';
he wrote the sonnet 'On the Sea,'

'It keeps eternal whisperings around
    Desolate shores,'

and he began 'Endymion'; then fled from solitude and un-
wholesome food, and a nervous poetic mood, 'a continual

burning of thought,' which made sleep almost impossible. Margate, in spite of its lack of trees, attracted him. Having his younger brother for company, he went on with 'Endymion,' borrowing from his surroundings, perhaps, such things as the comparison of the shouts of Pan's worshippers to

> 'dying rolls
> Of abrupt thunder, when Ionian shoals
> Of dolphins bob their noses through the brine.'

The two moved on together to Canterbury, and afterwards to lodgings, which the three brothers shared, at Well Walk, Hampstead. Here Keats was writing the second book of 'Endymion.' Walking on the heath in the summer of 1817, he repeated selections from it to his friends. The third book was the task of a holiday at Oxford, where he was the guest of an undergraduate at Magdalen Hall, Benjamin Bailey. It was September, and the friends boated on the Isis and read Wordsworth among the rushes, or sat up over 'The Matchless Orinda' or Hazlitt's 'Round Table,' or took a trip to Stratford-on-Avon. Keats wrote 1,000 lines in three weeks, excluding his parody of Wordsworth, a description of Oxford in this style:

> 'The Gothic looks solemn,
> The plain Doric column
> Supports an old Bishop and crosier;
> The mouldering arch,
> Shaded o'er by a larch,
> Lives next door to Wilson the hosier. . . .'

After a few weeks at Hampstead again, he retired from the squabbles of Hunt, Haydon, and Horace Smith, and the noise of his landlady's children, to get 'a change of air' and 'a spur to wind up' his poem at Burford Bridge. There he read Shakespeare's Sonnets and 'Venus and Adonis,' and finished 'Endymion.' He liked the place for its 'hill and dale and a little river,' and one of his letters from there tells how he went up Box Hill after the moon, came down again, and wrote some lines. I seem to see the influence of that late autumn and of Box Hill in several parts of the fourth book of 'Endymion' — in details like the 'hazel cirque of shedded leaves,' but above all in this passage:

'Where shall our dwelling be? Under the brow
 Of some steep mossy hill, where ivy dun
Would hide us up, although spring leaves were none;
And where dark yew-trees, as we rustle through,
Will drop their scarlet-berry cups of dew!
O thou wouldst joy to live in such a place!
Dusk for our loves, yet light enough to grace
Those gentle limbs on mossy bed reclined:
For by one step the blue sky shouldst thou find,
And by another, in deep dell below,
See, through the trees, a little river go
All in its mid-day gold and glimmering.
Honey from out the gnarled hive I'll bring,
And apples wan with sweetness gather thee, —
Cresses that grow where no man may them see. . . .'

At Hampstead that winter he was correcting 'Endymion' and exchanging verses with his friend John Hamilton Reynolds. Reynolds sent him two sonnets on Robin Hood. Keats replied with

'No, those days are gone away,'

and, inspired by the metre, wrote also the lines on the Mermaid Tavern. A Hampstead thrush sang well in February, and the poet enjoyed a 'delicious diligent indolence' in obedience to the thrush's words:

> 'O fret not after knowledge — I have none;
> And yet my song comes native with the warmth.
> O fret not after knowledge — I have none;
> And yet the evening listens.'

March, April, and part of May, 1819, he spent at Teignmouth, where he wrote most of 'Isabella' and the prefaces to 'Endymion,' and some doggerel, but had too much rain to like Devonshire. Already he was planning a Northern tour with his friend Charles Armitage Brown. He wanted to gain experience, rub off prejudice, enlarge his vision, load himself with finer mountains, strengthen his poetry, make his 'winter-chair free from spleen,' escape literary disquisitions, and 'promote digestion and economize shoe-leather.' Starting in June from Lancaster, they zigzagged through August and part of September to Cromarty, where Keats had to take ship home with a bad cold and toothache. They visited Wordsworth's, Scott's, and Burns's country. — They climbed Skiddaw and Ben Nevis. They crossed to Ireland, and to Mull, Iona, and Staffa. They saw mountains and mountaineers, cataracts, great waters, and eagles. Keats wrote poems on Burns at Kirk Alloway, on Meg Merrilies at Dumfries, on himself at Kirkcudbright:

> 'There was a naughty boy,
> A naughty boy was he;
> He would not stop at home,
> He could not quiet be;'

on Ailsa Craig, on Fingal's Cave, and on Ben Nevis, while he was fresh from the first impression of them. The basalt pillars of Fingal's Cave made him think of the Titans who rebelled against Jupiter. When he came to write 'Hyperion,' he remembered the eagles, the mountains, the cataracts, the sea-creeks, as he described Thea guiding Saturn:

'Through aged boughs, that yielded like the mist
  Which eagles cleave, upmounting from their nest . . .'

the Titans groaning, but inaudible,

              'for the solid roar
Of thunderous waterfalls and torrents hoarse,
Pouring a constant bulk, uncertain where.
Crag jutting forth to crag, and rocks that seem'd
Ever as if just rising from a sleep,
Forehead to forehead held their monstrous horns . . .'

or Saturn at the approach of Hyperion:

                'Whose hoar locks
Shone like the bubbling foam about a keel
When the prow sweeps into a midnight cove.'

Thus Keats became 'an old stager in the picturesque,' as he said himself. Thus he learned to 'hate descriptions,' so that his poems thereafter contained no mere details verified from a notebook, but only broad noble features as suitable for heaven or hell as for the earth. 'Hyperion' was begun in the winter of 1818–19, after the Northern tour, when he was living with Brown at Wentworth Place, Hampstead. There, too, he began 'The Eve of St. Agnes'; and both have a stormy and mountainous setting, harmonizing with the dethroned and dejected Titans, contrasting with the happiness and luxury of the lovers, Porphyro and Madeline.

The next year, Keats's greatest poetic period, was spent, half at Hampstead, half in Sussex, Hampshire, and the Isle of Wight. He stayed at Chichester in January, 1819, with the

Dilkes, and at Bedhampton in that neighbourhood with the Snooks, relatives of the Dilkes. There he wrote down part of 'The Eve of St. Agnes.' Chichester may also have suggested to him 'The Eve of St. Mark,' which, he thought, as he was writing it later on at Winchester, gave 'the sensation of walking about an old country town in a coolish evening.' The spring and early summer at Hampstead produced 'La Belle Dame sans Merci,' most of the odes, and the sonnets on Fame, to Sleep, on the Sonnet, and others. But in July he was at Shanklin, in the Isle of Wight, with James Rice and afterwards Charles Brown. He was, as he put it, 'at the diligent use of his faculties.' He had been moulting, and had, he believed, 'a pair of patient sublunary legs' in exchange for wings. His judgment was now more deliberate, and when he got into 'a train of writing' the greatest things came of it. 'Lamia' was soon half finished. 'Otho the Great,' with Brown's collaboration, progressed at a great pace. 'Hyperion' began to grow again. But though he admired Bonchurch and Steephill Keats was dissatisfied with Shanklin, saying: 'The neighbourhood of a rich, enclosed, fulsome, manured, arable land, especially in a valley and almost as bad on a flat, would be almost as bad as the smoke of Fleet Street. Such a place as this was Shanklin, only open to the south-east, and surrounded by hills in every other direction. From this south-east came the damps of the sea, which having no egress, the air would for days together take on an unhealthy idiosyncrasy altogether enervating and weakening as a city smoke.' Moving to Winchester early in August, he found the air of St. Catherine's Hill 'worth sixpence a pint.' By the beginning of September 'Lamia' and 'Otho the Great' were finished, 'The Eve of St. Agnes' was being revised, 'The Eve of St. Mark' and 'King Stephen' begun. 'Hyperion' was looked at and thrown over. The beauty of the stubble-fields on a fine late September

Sunday – 'I never liked stubble-field so much as now – ay, better than the chilly green of the spring,' he says – moved him to write the stanzas 'To Autumn':

'While barred clouds bloom the soft-dying day,
    And touch the stubble plains with rosy hue. . . .'

Keats left Winchester early in October, meaning to settle in Westminster and make a living at journalism. But Fanny Brawne drew him to Hampstead. He settled again at Wentworth Place. Between Fanny Brawne and 'Cap and Bells' and the recast of 'Hyperion,' which he called a vision, he divided himself down to the last drop of life. When he coughed blood in February, 1820, he was a doomed man. He wrote no more, except some frantic verses to Fanny Brawne, and the last sonnet, which Sir S. Colvin attributes to the September night following a day spent, apparently, at Lulworth in Dorset, when the poet landed for a few hours from the steamer which was carrying him to his Roman grave.

*

In one sense Meredith is a Londoner's poet, for his country is
the Londoner's par excellence — Hampshire, Surrey, Kent,
Sussex — and in him the London rambler, exulting in the
wind over a land of gorse and pine on a Saturday or Sunday,
seems to reach godlike proportions. The beauty of his country has something almost hectic, violent, excessive, about it,
caused, perhaps, by contrast with the city. Meredith was
eminently a writer of books and a lover of such society as
cannot be had often outside of London. What wonder, then,
that in his poems we so often feel that we have come out of
London into the fields, as in that early 'Invitation to the
Country'! —

> 'Now 'tis spring on wood and wold,
> Early spring that shivers with cold,
> But gladdens and gathers, day by day,
> A lovelier hue, a warmer ray,
> A sweeter song, a dearer ditty;
> Ouzel and throstle, new-mated and gay,
> Singing their bridals on every spray —
> Oh, hear them, deep in the songless city!
> Cast off the yoke of toil and smoke,
> As spring is casting winter's grey,
> As serpents cast their skins away:
> And come, for the country awaits thee with pity,
> And longs to bathe thee in her delight,
> And take a new joy in thy kindling sight. . . .'

When Meredith was not in London, or travelling, or
visiting friends, he was, for the greater part of his life, reading
and writing in some cottage not very far from London, and
taking exercise on the surrounding heaths and hills. At Portsmouth, his birthplace, he spent most of his first fourteen years.

Then he had two years at the Moravian school at Neuwied on
the Rhine. At sixteen he was in London, his mother being
dead, his father at the Cape. As a recreation from the study of
law and literature he took 'long walks through the market-
gardens of Chelsea into Surrey and Middlesex.' In 1849, at
the age of twenty-one, he married, and 'the next few years
were spent chiefly on the Continent.' He was, however, at
Weybridge in 1850, and for some time boarded there at a
house called 'The Limes.' 'Love in the Valley' is dated Weybridge, May, 1851, and dedicated to T. L. Peacock, his wife's
father, then living at Chertsey. He was also much at Seaford
– in 1856 and 1857, for example – and invites his friend Eyre
Crowe to share the 'fishing, bathing, rowing, sailing, lounging, running, picnicking, and a cook who builds a basis of
strength to make us equal to all these superhuman efforts.'
These were the years when he was writing his early poems
and 'The Shaving of Shagpat, Emilia [sic] Belloni,' and the
story of 'The House on the Beach.' He was inquiring for a book
of Hampshire dialect, planning 'Richard Feverel.' Esher was
his next home. He moved there with his boy, aged five, but
without his wife, in 1858, first to a cottage in the village,
afterwards to Copsham Cottage, between Esher and Oxshott.
For neighbour, and companion in walking, he had William
Hardman, afterwards editor of the 'Morning Post,' and original
of Blackburn Tuckham in 'Beauchamp.' Meredith showed
him the place where he wrote the fifth pastoral:

'Now from the meadow floods the wild-duck clamours,
  Now the wood-pigeon wings a rapid flight,
Now the homeward rookery follows up its vanguard,
  And the valley mists are curling up the hills.

'Three short songs gives the clear-voiced throstle,
  Sweetening the twilight ere he fills the nest;

While the little bird upon the leafless branches
Tweets to its mate a tiny loving note.

'Deeper the stillness hangs on every motion;
Calmer the silence follows every call;
Now all is quiet save the roosting pheasant,
The bell-wether's tinkle, and the watch-dog's bark.

'Softly shine the lights from the silent kindling homestead,
Stars of the hearth to the shepherd in the fold;
Springs of desire to the traveller on the roadway;
Ever breathing incense to the ever-blessing sky.'

To read this, and to know that it was written on 'an eminence surrounded by pines on the St. George's Hill Estate,' is to know something of Meredith's habits as man and writer in his early thirties. His letters often have at least a window open to earth and sky. One day 'the smell of the earth is Elysian'; then he and every one is 'in suspense to know whether we are to get a daily ducking or live the life of non-purgatorial beings through the months'; but he has walked over to Box Hill in sunshine in the interval. In 1862, in the month of May, he was walking with Hardman, reading some of the aphorisms afterwards known through 'Richard Feverel.' Their route was by Mickleham (avoiding Leatherhead), Burford Bridge, Dorking, and Shere, and along Merrow Down to Newlands Corner, by Albury (Martin Tupper's Albury), Guildford, and Godalming, to Milford, where they had tea, bed, and breakfast (with chops), for three shillings and sixpence; then over Hindhead to Haslemere. The weather had been magnificent, the nightingales at their best, the landscape extending to the Crystal Palace and the Hog's Back.

John Morley and Cotter Morison were among his visitors

and companions. But he could do without company, and at night, too. For, as he told Miss Vulliamy, reassuring her that walking back at night from Mickleham was no hardship, he was 'an associate with owls and nightjars, tramps and tinkers,' who taught him Nature and talked human nature to him. He was then writing of Harry Richmond, a hero for whom 'stars and tramps seemed to go together.'

Meredith had a regular day every week 'on press duty' in London, and in 1862 and afterwards tried the plan of sharing 16, Cheyne Walk at intervals with Rossetti, Swinburne, and Morris. But he did not give up Copsham Cottage, and was repeatedly ('running twice a day between Mickleham and Copsham') at Mickleham, 'at the sign of The Angel,' with Miss Vulliamy, until he married her in 1864. He was on Mickleham Downs a week before Christmas, 1864, 'where the great herded yews stand on a pure snowfield. I thought to have fallen on the very throne of Silence. In a few paces I became a Druid. . . .' He seems to have lived alternately in 1865–6–7 at Mickleham and Kingston Lodge, Kingston-on-Thames. As early as 1868 he wrote from Box Hill, where his visitors included Robert Louis Stevenson, who stayed at the Burford Arms with his mother in 1878. It was nine years later that the châlet was ready for Meredith, and that he was inviting John Morley to see it and the view that was 'without a match in Surrey':

'I work and sleep up in my cottage at present, and anything grander than the days and nights at my porch you will not find away from the Alps; for the dark line of my hill runs up to the stars, the valley below is a soundless gulf. There I pace like a shipman before turning in. In the day, with the south-west blowing, I have a brilliant universe rolling up to me. . . .'

Here he was to write for thirty years.

Two years later the order of 'Sunday Tramps' — 'that noble body of scholarly and cheerful pedestrians,' Meredith calls it — was founded by Leslie Stephen. F. W. Maitland, Sir Frederick Pollock, J. Cotter Morison, Douglas Freshfield, R. G. Marsden, and A. J. Butler, were of the order. Stephen's was an 'unlimited paternal despotism,' and at the station, collecting his flock, he had 'the solicitous look of a school-master.' Ten was a good assembly. Meredith just mentions them in 1880. Writing to R. L. Stevenson, he tells how he and his son, W. M. Meredith, with a sack of cold sausages, Apollinaris and hock, met them at old Dorking station; how they walked to Leith Hill, 'consumed the soul of the sack,' talked and smoked, and then by Friday Street 'into the sloping meadows each side the Tillingbourne, leaping through Eve-lyn's Wotton, along under Ranmore to our cottage and dinner.' Stephen was leader or 'Pied Piper.' That whole net-work of paths were to him 'the scene of personally conducted expeditions, in which,' he says, 'I displayed the skill on which I most pride myself — skill, I mean, in devising judicious geographical combinations, and especially of contriving admir-able short-cuts.' He was, says Meredith himself, the original of Vernon Whitford in 'The Egoist.' For a short time — 'when I was in health,' he says in 1882 — Meredith himself was of the party; later he used to meet them on their way, when they dined with him and started for London at ten. 'Tramping with them one has the world under review, as well as pretty scenery.' Meredith was a talking walker. He declared that a shorthand writer in attendance on the Tramps would have been a benefactor to the country, but F. W. Maitland's view was that 'the occasions on which the presence of a shorthand writer was desirable coincided somewhat exactly with those on which Mr. Meredith honoured us with his company.' Mr.

Comyns Carr records that Meredith would occupy the whole of a walk with 'a purely inventive biography of some one of our common friends, passing in rather burlesque rhapsody from incident to incident of a purely hypothetical career, but always preserving in the most extravagant of his fancies a proper relevancy to the character he was seeking to exhibit.'

Tramping or not, he did not cease to love the earth and the sea, the south-west wind and the rain. When he was sixty he was walking, bathing, getting drenched with rain, and learning some Welsh, in visits that extended from Tenby through Llanelly, Llandilo, and Llandrindod, to Brecon. When he was sixty-three he held the opinion that February with a south-west wind blowing is 'as good as any spring,' and looked forward to a south-westerly April and May. At seventy-nine he was answering an inquiry as to the meaning of 'the dark-winged planet' in the 'Hymn to Colour':

'If you observe the planet Venus at the hour when the dawn does no more than give an intimation, she is full of silver, and darkness surrounds her. So she seems to me to fly on dark wings. . . .'

A year later, in 1908, appeared 'Youth in Age':

'Once I was part of the music I heard
    On the boughs or sweet between earth and sky,
    For joy of the beating of wings on high
My heart shot into the breast of the bird.

'I hear it now and I see it fly,
    And a life in wrinkles again is stirred;
    My heart shoots into the breast of the bird,
As it will for sheer love till the last long sigh.'

He died in the year after.

49

Meredith's country is the country of many of his characters. It is summed up in two sentences of 'Diana of the
Crossways.' Diana and Emma are driving together at Copsley:

'Through an old gravel-cutting a gateway led to the turf of
the down, springy turf bordered on a long line, clear as a race-
course, by golden gorse covers, and leftward over the gorse the
dark-ridge of the fir and heath country ran companionably to
the south-west, the valley between, with undulations of wood
and meadow sunned or shaded, clumps, mounds, promon-
tories, away to broad spaces of tillage banked by wooded hills,
and dimmer beyond, and farther, the faintest shadowiness of
heights, as a veil to the illimitable. Yews, junipers, radiant
beeches, and gleams of the service-tree or the white-beam,
spotted the semicircle of swelling green Down black and
silver.'

It is always Hampshire or Surrey, or it is no place in particular; always 'the great heaths' or the Downs, or the meadows
in sight of them. And it is odd if there is not some walker
after Meredith's own heart among the characters. Mr.
Rhodes in 'Diana' wanted a walk, and started at two in the
morning out of London to Copsley. Harry Richmond felt
that houses imprisoned us, that a lost father was not to be discovered by remaining in them. 'Plunged among dark green
leaves, smelling wood-smoke, at night; at morning waking up,
and the world alight, and you standing high, and marking the
hills where you will see the next morning and the next, morning after morning'; this was 'a heavenly pleasure.' He
lodged with gipsies. And then Vernon Whitford in 'The
Egoist,' the 'lean long-walker and scholar,' a 'Phœbus Apollo
turned fasting friar,' who 'attacked the dream-giving earth
with tremendous long strides, that his blood might be lively at
the throne of understanding.' When Meredith has got Whit-

ford walking he himself walks too, and does not stick too closely to the editor of the 'Dictionary of National Biography' and author of 'The English Utilitarians':

'Rain was universal; a thick robe of it swept from hill to hill; thunder rumbled remote, and between the muffled roars the downpour pressed on the land with a great noise of eager gobbling, much like that of the swine's trough fresh filled, as though a vast assembly of the hungered had seated themselves clamorously and fallen to on meats and drinks in a silence, save of the chaps. A rapid walker poetically and humorously minded gathers multitudes of images on his way. And rain, the heaviest you can meet, is a lively companion when the resolute pacer scorns discomfort of wet clothes and squealing boots. South-western rain-clouds, too, are never long sullen: they enfold and will have the earth in a good strong glut of the kissing overflow; then, as a hawk with feathers on his beak of the bird in his claw lifts head, they rise, and take veiled feature in long climbing watery lines: at any moment they may break the veil and show soft upper cloud, show sun on it, show sky, green near the verge they spring from, of the green of grass in early dew; or, along a travelling sweep that rolls asunder overhead, heaven's laughter of purest blue among titanic white shoulders: it may mean fair smiling for awhile, or be the lightest interlude; but the watery lines, and the drifting, the chasing, the upsoaring, all in a shadowy fingering of form, and the animation of the leaves of the trees pointing them on, the bending of the tree-tops, the snapping of branches, and the hurrahings of the stubborn hedge at wrestle with the flaws, yielding but a leaf at most, and that on a fling, make a glory of contest and wildness without aid of colour to inflame the man who is at home in them from old association on road, heath, and mountain.

Let him be drenched, his heart will sing. And then, trim cockney, that jeerest, consider thyself, to whom it may occur to be out in such a scene, and with what steps of a nervous dancing-master it would be thine to play the hunted rat of the elements for the preservation of the one imagined dry spot about thee, somewhere on thy luckless person! The taking of rain and sun alike befits men of our climate, and he who would have the secret of a strengthening intoxication must court the clouds of the south-west with a lover's blood.'

A walk for him is an intellectual thing. He enjoys it, but knows also that it is good for him, body and soul. The Earth is our ancient Mother, and our nurse also, with a medicine cupboard near the bed. The south-west wind is in one bottle. 'Thus,' says he, 'does Nature restore us, by drugging the brain and making her creature confidingly animal for its new growth.' That bottle is not spared in any of his books. His beautiful women have drunken of it. They are goddesses. One is called into her lover's mind with the smell of salt — 'that other spirit of woman, of whom the controlled sea-deeps were an image, who spoke to my soul in starlight.' Another is 'a swift wild spirit' who 'gives you an idea of the Mountain Echo.'

As Mr. G. M. Trevelyan says: 'The characters in his novels put on their full grandeur only when they stand in direct contact with Nature: Vernon Whitford in his sleep under the wild white [double] cherry-tree; Diana by the mountain pool above the Italian lake; Beauchamp at sea or under the Alps at dawn; Ottilia at sea or in the thunderstorm; Emilia by Wilming Weir or in the moonlit fir-tree glade; Carinthia Jane when she goes out to "call the morning" in her mountain home; Lucy by the plunging weir, amid the bilberries, long grass, and meadowsweet.' But in his poetry you

have in its concentrated hieroglyphics the religion of which
the novels exhibit some of the characteristics as found in the
laity. Then you have walking –

> 'A pride of legs in motion kept
> Our spirits to their task meanwhile,
> And what was deepest dreaming slept'

– and the incidents of walking, as a pleasure, as a joy, as a
medicine. For the Tramps themselves, and for all other Sunday or week-day walkers who delight in one another's company, and talk as they walk, he wrote the 'Stave of Roving
Tim':

> 'You live in rows of snug abodes,
> With gold, maybe, for counting;
> And mine's the beck of the rainy roads
> Against the sun a-mounting.'

And the joy of the limbs, the senses, and the brain, during
country walks – in certain isolated days – are expressed by
Meredith once and for all, with a kind of braced hedonistic
Puritanism. But though he loved what he saw and heard and
touched, his poetry was never purely sensuous, and it became
less and less so. Like Shelley, he felt the moral qualities of
Nature. It has been said of Shelley's lark, 'Bird thou never
wert'; and of Meredith's, that it is a real lark. But this is a
mistake. Meredith was more of a naturalist, and he belonged
to a generation of amateur naturalists, but he gets at least as
far away from the bird as Shelley does, if he starts closer.
Tastes differ, but to me what is descriptive in the poem reminds me too much of the bird. I can always hear a lark, and
no man can do more than interest me by an imaged inven-
tory of what it says. The opening passage of 'The Lark

Ascending' shows observation, admiration, and delight, and they are well served by fancy; the result is an encumbrance of words and a dispersed impression, half sensuous, half intellectual. That it was done with the eye on the object is obvious, but not to the point, except that it is thus distinguished from other poems relating to larks. What gives it a great claim is that it was done, and that very clearly, by a man in whom, as in no other, says Mr. Justin McCarthy, the physical and mental forces were absolute rivals and equals. The same is true of a great portion of Meredith's poetry, and I shall not dispute whether it can be fully enjoyed by those possessing neither the same powers nor the same balance between them. Nature to him was not merely a cause of sensuous pleasure, nor, on the other hand, an inhuman enchantress; neither was she both together. When he spoke of Earth, he meant more than most mean who speak of God. He meant that power which in the open air, in poetry, in the company of noble men and women, prompted, strengthened, and could fulfil, the desire of a man to make himself, not a transitory member of a parochial species, but a citizen of the Earth. Thus, in his view, a man could smile after all things. Of Shakespeare, for example, he says:

> 'Thy greatest knew thee, Mother Earth; unsoured
> He knew thy sons. He probed from hell to hell
> Of human passions, but of love deflowered
> His wisdom was not, for he knew thee well.
> Thence came the honeyed corner at his lips. . . .'

And Byron he pronounces an infidel, as not knowing Earth, but summoning her 'with bile and bilious attitude.' He seeks a superb health. Nature has inspired him to the search. Nature alone can satisfy it. She seems to him to offer sanity, true perspective. In 'The Lark Ascending' he speaks of men 'by many a battle-dint defaced,' but yielding a substance worthy of poetry, which chooses them

> 'Because their love of Earth is deep.'

So in 'Nature and Life' he speaks of men retiring to Nature, and thence returning to men:

> 'Back to them for manful air,
> Laden with the woodland's heart.'

There are places where his personal refinement seems to have reduced him to something like a variation upon 'God made the country,' as when he addresses the thrush in February:

> 'Bird of happy breath!
> I hear, I would the city heard,
> The city of the smoky fray;
> A prodded ox, it drags and moans:
> Its Morrow no man's child; its Day
> A vulture's morsel beaked to bones.'

He is always lean and hard, an athlete among poets. Sometimes he is overtrained, too fine. He got away from the Earth and the things of the Earth to intellectual analogues of them, outran the measure (wrote, for example, a kind of shorthand instead of poetry), allowed his love to exceed too far

> 'a simple love of the things
> That glide in grasses and rubble of woody wreck,'

forsook 'the great heaths' bordering the Portsmouth Road — he always lived near the Portsmouth Road — and took to regions of the mind where blows a keener and more desolating wind than ever blew from the thirty-two points. But at best his poetry is good walking country in good walking weather.

His nightingales are 'real nightingales,' very distantly related to Philomela. There are no fumes in his brain, and thence in his poetry. His country is English — not so English as Tennyson's; it is too Meredithian for that — his planet is indubitably the Earth, of which he was one of the most loyal and distinguished inhabitants.

THE THAMES

SHELLEY
ARNOLD
MORRIS

SHELLEY

*

THAT Shelley was born at Horsham, went to school at Isleworth and Eton, and to University College, Oxford, so-
journed in North and South Wales, in Cumberland, Devon,
Berkshire, and Buckinghamshire, and in London — so much
is true; but of few poets is it less true that he has a country
and a topography distinctly his own. There are great mountains in his poems, 'eagle-baffling' mountains — Alpine, Cau-
casian, Himalayan — rivers and lakes and islands, forests and
meadows, cliffs and caves, and we know that he saw some of
the finest examples of these things which the earth has to
show. I am not about to trace or conjecture the origin of all
the heavenly mountains and ocean-seeking rivers of his poems.
I have no theory as to the original of that 'little lawny
islet,' neither have I gone in search of the shelving bank
of turf

> 'which lay
> Under a copse, and hardly dared to fling
> Its green arms round the bosom of the stream,
> But kissed it and then fled, as thou mightest in dream.'

I do not propose to show that Shelley was a thoroughly
Sussex poet because the great snake in the Field Place garden
and the legendary one of St. Leonard's Forest may have given
him the primary impulse towards creating magnificent ser-
pents in poetry. All we know is that Field Place and that
woodland country provided some of the strange meats that
must have gone to the making of so strange a man. Field
Place itself, for example, was such a house that he could, as a
boy, and for the benefit of his younger sisters, imagine a long-
bearded alchemist inhabiting the garret under its roof. But
when he was ten, and at school in Isleworth, he read Ann
Radcliffe's tales, which seem to have played almost as large a

part in the composition of Shelley as Field Place, near Horsham, did.

Two years later Shelley went to Eton College. Eton is one of the few English place-names mentioned in Shelley's verse. The passage, a piece of pure, unheightened memory, is in the fragmentary 'Boat on the Serchio,' where the men, Melchior and Lionel, are provisioning the boat:

   ' "Ay, heave the ballast overboard,
And stow the eatables in the aft locker."
"Would not this keg be best a little lowered?"
"No; now all's right." "Those bottles of warm tea —
(Give me some straw) — must be stowed tenderly;
Such as we used, in summer after six,
To cram in greatcoat pockets, and to mix
Hard eggs and radishes and rolls at Eton,
And, couched on stolen hay in those green harbours
Farmers called gaps, and we schoolboys called arbours,
Would feast till eight." '

From this it is clear that he sometimes enjoyed himself as if he were going to develop into 'a woodland fellow that loved a great fire,' instead of an angelic poet. Not often did he write in a manner permitting the direct use of what the eyes saw. When he did, he could either be literal, as in 'The Sunset,' which begins:

   'He walked along the pathway of a field
   Which to the east a hoar wood shadowed o'er,
   But to the west was open to the sky . . .'

or he could loiter luxuriously over natural details for their own sake, as in 'The Question,' which has some very English passages. These two lines,

'And in the warm hedge grew lush eglantine,
Green cowbind, and the moonlight-coloured may,'

are very English; so are these three:

'And floating water-lilies, broad and bright,
Which lit the oak that overhung the hedge
With moonlight beams of their own watery light.'

A few other references to his school days are to be found in Shelley's poetry, the chief one being that in the dedication to 'The Revolt of Islam,' where he speaks of 'the hour which burst his spirit's sleep':

'A fresh May-dawn it was,
When I walked forth upon the glittering grass,
And wept, I knew not why; until there rose
From the near schoolroom voices that, alas!
Were but one echo from a world of woes —
The harsh and grating strife of tyrants and of foes.'

Whether this was at Isleworth or Eton is unknown. Certainly it was at Eton that he met the Dr. Lind who afterwards appeared in 'The Revolt of Islam' as the Hermit, 'stately and beautiful,' and as Zonoras in 'Prince Athanase':

'An old, old man, with hair of silver white,
And lips where heavenly smiles would hang and blend
With his wise words. . . .'

Above all, we know that at Eton Shelley learned to love rivers. From the time he went to school to his last residence in England, Shelley was never long away from some part of the River Thames.

At Oxford he used to walk out with Hogg regularly in the afternoons: 'it was his delight to strike boldly into the fields, to cross the country daringly on foot, as is usual with sportmen in shooting, to perform, as it were, a pedestrian steeple-chase.' But Isis and Cherwell, Bagley Woods, and Shotover Hill, enter into his poems, if at all, under many veils or transmutations.

After 1810, the year of his entrance at University College, Oxford, Shelley was very little at Field Place again, and then usually agitated by love, romantic composition, or filial impiety. For example, a letter to Hogg reveals him in January, 1811, 'most of the night pacing a churchyard,' and apparently composing the verses 'On an Icicle.' He was then in the depths of his wretchedness over the breaking off of his engagement, or understanding, with his cousin, Harriet Grove.

Before the end of March and of the next term at the University, Shelley had quitted Oxford for ever. His wanderings had begun. He was never again to spend more than a few consecutive months in any place. From lodgings in Poland Street he used to meet Harriet Westbrook at or near her school on Clapham Common. In July and August he was in Radnorshire, at his cousin Thomas Grove's house, Cwm Elan, near Rhayader. Wales he found 'excessively grand,' the scenery 'most divine' and 'highly romantic,' but nothing to him in the agitation of his mind; for the Westbrooks were at Condowell, on their way to Aberystwith. He told Hogg he did not much regard the woods, the cloudy mountains, the waterfalls; to Miss Hitchener he wrote that he was 'not wholly uninfluenced by their magic' in his lonely walks, but longed for a thunderstorm. He had married Harriet Westbrook in Edinburgh before the end of August. The end of the year was spent at Chestnut Cottage, Keswick, in sight of Derwentwater and Bassenthwaite. Even during his trouble over Hogg's advances to Harriet, the scenery, which was

'awfully grand,' affected him. In calmer mood he wrote to
Miss Hitchener:

'I have taken a long solitary ramble to-day. These gigantic mountains piled on each other, these waterfalls, these mil-
lion-shaped clouds tinted by the varying colours of innumerable rainbows hanging between yourself and a lake as smooth
and dark as a plain of polished jet – oh, these are sights attain-
able to the contemplation. I have been much struck by the
grandeur of its imagery. Nature here sports in the awful way-
wardness of her solitude; the summits of the loftiest of these
immense piles of rock seem but to elevate Skiddaw and Helvellyn. Imagination is resistlessly compelled to look back upon
the myriad ages whose silent change placed them here; to look
back, when perhaps this retirement of peace and mountain
simplicity was the pandemonium of druidical imposture, the
scene of Roman pollution, the resting-place of the savage
denizen of these solitudes with the wolf. . . .'

He was thinking of Man and Freedom and Virtue; the
mountains provided an harmonious accompaniment to his
mistily aspiring thoughts, and their grandeur was to him already in part moral and spiritual. No man could stand the
same test as the mountains stood. He visited Southey, once
one of his lords and masters, and found him 'the paid cham-
pion of every abuse and absurdity,' who said: 'You will think
as I do when you are as old.' Some of his letters of this winter
contain poems written at Keswick, one in Wordsworth's
style:

'For seven years did this poor woman live
  In unparticipated solitude.
  Thou mightst have seen her in the forest rude
  Picking the scattered remnants of its wood. . . .'

Another, in the style of Southey and Coleridge (when on the spree):

> 'The Devil went out a-walking one day,
>   Being tired of staying in hell.
> He dressed himself in his Sunday array. . . .'

More consonant with his mountain mood were the letters which he poured forth to Miss Hitchener and the 'Address to the Irish People' then under his hands. He was to spend two months in Ireland early in 1812. By the middle of April he was once more in Radnorshire.

Shelley wrote a little later a 'Hail to thee, Cambria,' in which he said:

> 'True mountain liberty alone may heal
> The pain which custom's obduracies bring.'

He had dreamed of domesticating 'in some antique feudal castle whose mouldering turrets are fit emblems of decaying inequality and oppression; whilst the ivy shall wave its green banners above like liberty, and flourish upon the edifice that essayed to crush its root.' Observe how Nature has to bow to morality. His ideas were stronger than his surroundings. He says he would welcome ghosts, because 'they would tell tales of times of old; and it would add to the picturesqueness of the scenery to see their thin forms flitting through the vaulted charnels.' His stay was first at Nantgwillt, again near Rhayader, 'embosomed in the solitude of mountains, woods, and rivers – silent, solitary, and old, far away from any town.' He was again in exalted mood, calling Miss Hitchener, by an image taken from among the mountains, 'a thunder-riven pinnacle of rock firm amid the rushing tempest and the boiling surge.' His hope was to have made the house 'the asylum of distressed virtue, the rendezvous of the friends of liberty and

truth,' but his security was not good enough. He moved on to
Cwm Elan, thence to Lynmouth, having written his 'Letter
to Lord Ellenborough,' and a long poem in couplets called
'The Retrospect: Cwm Elan,' where he addresses the woods
and mountains that had witnessed the solitary sadnesss of his
former visit,

> 'The sunken eye, the withering
> Sad traces of the unuttered pain
> That froze my heart and burned my brain . . .'

but addresses finally his wife, who gilds the gloomiest retrospect,

> 'by the reviving ray
> Which thou hast flung upon my day.'

It is one of the few of Shelley's early poems which, being
turned to for curiosity, are read with pleasure — pleasure derived from its sincere relation to human feelings and its approach to individual style.

Probably Shelley had also brought with him to Lynmouth
some beginnings of 'Queen Mab.' At Lynmouth it made
some progress, in spite of Shelley's correspondence with Godwin, the arrival of his Sussex acquaintance, Miss Hitchener,
and the surveillance that followed on the imprisonment of his
servant for posting up the Declaration of Rights in Barnstaple.
'Queen Mab' is not a poem to reflect much of the beauty of
this earth. Nor do any of Shelley's poems obviously reflect
Lynmouth. The Valley of Rocks, however, must have contributed something to the grand composite landscape of Shelley's mind. The beauty surrounding them seemed to him to
equal that of Nantgwillt, to Harriet to excel it. 'All "shows of
sky and earth, of sea and valley," are here,' says he. According to Hogg, recollections and memorials of the Valley of

Rocks abounded among those 'points, spires, and pinnacles of rocks and crags' scrawled or sketched by Shelley on fly-leaves, backs of letters, notebooks, etc.

'Queen Mab' was carried on slowly, but to an end, at Tanyr-allt, near Tremadoc in Carnarvonshire, where Shelley alighted next after quitting Devonshire. Once more he was in mountain country, the most 'strikingly grand' he had yet seen. Once more he was considerably perplexed by affairs, this time the procuring of subscriptions towards the completion of an embankment to reclaim land on the coast of Carnarvonshire.

Having flown to Ireland – as far as Killarney – and away again, Shelley stayed some time in and about London. Here his daughter Ianthe was born in June, 1813. The family thought of going to Nantgwillt for a third time, but travelled through Stratford-on-Avon and the Lake Country to Edinburgh instead.

In the following year, when staying with friends at Bracknell in Berkshire, Shelley wrote the first poem in which he is himself, something like all himself, and nothing but himself; and it is an intensely local poem. I mean the stanzas dated April, 1814, which begin:

'Away! the moor is dark beneath the moon;
   Rapid clouds have drank the last pale beam of even:
 Away! the gathering winds will call the darkness soon,
   And profoundest midnight shroud the serene lights of
      heaven. . . .'

The poem reflects one moment of space and time in the beginning of Shelley's estrangement from Harriet. In fact, so powerfully did the circumstances of the moment impress themselves on Shelley that they were reproduced in a manner which only an intimate could understand. For example, in the last verse:

'Thou in the grave shalt rest — yet, till the phantoms flee
    Which that house and heath and garden made dear to thee
      erewhile,
 Thy remembrance, and repentance, and deep musings, are
    not free
    From the music of two voices and the light of one sweet
      smile.'

He told Hogg in a letter of the same period that the house at Bracknell was a paradise, that his heart sickened at the necessity of leaving 'the delightful tranquillity of this happy home — for it has become my home. The trees, the bridge, the minutest objects, have already a place in my affections.'

   By July Shelley had left England with Mary Godwin. It was a year before he could begin to think of settling down to rest from his tortures in London at the hands of Harriet, his creditors, and his mistress's father — a period in which he learned to know 'the dark midnight river when the moon is down.' He spent part of July, 1815, looking for a house in South Devon. In August he and Mary were settled at Bishopgate, at the edge of Windsor Forest, not far from Bracknell or from Eton. With Peacock, who lived at Marlow, he took to boating. Their water journey at the end of August was the occasion of a poem — 'A Summer Evening Churchyard' — which Shelley particularly connects with a place: Lechlade in Gloucestershire. It is if anything less local than 'Away! the moor is dark,' because the place did but ripen an old emotion; yet a man who cared for Shelley would hardly see Lechlade Church without some emotion at thought of that burning-eyed poet having stood there and noticed

   'The winds are still, or the dry church-tower grass
   Knows not their gentle motions as they pass.'

That same warm, dry summer and autumn helped Shelley to write 'Alastor.' 'He spent his days,' says Mrs. Shelley, 'under the oak shades of Windsor Great Park; and the magnificent woodland was a fitting study to inspire the various descriptions of forest scenery we find in that poem.'

The Swiss tour, commemorated by 'Mont Blanc' and the 'Hymn to Intellectual Beauty,' came between Shelley's residence at Bishopgate and his residence at Marlow. He was to and fro between London, Marlow, and Bath, in the winter of 1816–17; then in February, 1817, he took Albion House at Marlow, having with him not only Mary, but her stepsister, Claire Clairmont, and Allegra, the daughter of Claire and Byron. Shelley used to walk with Peacock the thirty-two miles to London. He wandered alone, 'sometimes rather fantastically arrayed,' with a wreath of old-man's-beard and wildflowers upon his head. He also visited the poor lace-makers in winter-time, bringing presents of food, money, or clothing. The summer was fine, and Shelley often divided his days between the river and the river-side woods. 'Laon and Cythna,' his summer task, was written 'in his boat,' says Mrs. Shelley, 'as it floated under the beech-groves of Bisham, or during wanderings in the neighbouring country.' Peacock says it was chiefly written 'on a high prominence in Bisham Wood, where he passed whole mornings with a blank book and a pencil.' Shelley himself, in the dedicatory stanzas of the poem, refers to his retreat:

'Where the woods to frame a bower
With interlacèd branches mix and meet,
Or where, with sound like many voices sweet,
Waterfalls leap among wild islands green,
Which framed for my lone boat a lone retreat
Of moss-grown trees and weeds. . . .'

And, very naturally, a poem written rapidly in such a place reflects the river and the woods of Marlow. It begins with a river and ends with one. The first canto has a boat designed for Ariel to wind 'among the lawny islands fair':

'A boat of rare device, which had no sail
But its own curvèd prow of thin moonstone,
Wrought like a web of texture fine and frail. . . .'

The last canto has another boat:

'One curved shell of hollow pearl,
Almost translucent with the light divine
Of her within; the prow and stern did curl
Hornèd on high, like the young moon supine,
When o'er dim twilight mountains dark with pine
It floats upon the sunset's sea of beams,
Whose golden waves in many a purple line
Fade fast, till borne on sunlight's ebbing streams,
Dilating, on earth's verge the sunken meteor gleams.'

At the beginning of the third canto he mentions the clambering briony:

'Methought, upon the threshold of a cave
I sate with Cythna; drooping briony, pearled
With dew from the wild streamlet's sheltered wave,
Hung, where we sate to taste the joys which Nature gave.'

I doubt if it had been mentioned before by any English poet. In any case, its name is an unexpected invasion of an English hedge plant in such a poem, though it must be remembered that at this time Shelley was subject to an 'unnatural and keen excitement,' when 'the very blades of grass and the boughs of distant trees' presented themselves with microscopical distinctness.

The fragments of 'Prince Athanase' and an unfinished version of 'Rosalind and Helen' were also written at Marlow. But these might have been written anywhere, while 'The Revolt' at least owes much of its surface colouring to the accident of Shelley's presence at Marlow. The stay lasted almost a year. The house was damp. Shelley believed that health, and even life, had to be sought in Italy. He sold the house in February. For an interval of a few days he lodged at 119, Great Russell Street, and saw Hunt, Hogg, Peacock, Keats, and Mary Lamb, who lived in the same street. He left England in March, never to return, but to write poetry where Italy is mirrored more than England, and still more a kind of not wholly unearthly paradise that he had already imagined in Wales and England, as he walked their mountains and woods, or lay on his back looking up at their clouds and firmament.

MATTHEW ARNOLD

*

MATTHEW ARNOLD's two best known poems, 'The Scholar
Gipsy' and 'Thyrsis,' have been accused of being too topo-
graphical, because they name so many places. But the accusa-
tion is needless. The mention of all those places at that time
fameless has chiefly the effect of adding to the intimacy of the
poems. In a way, it is a kind of artful naïveté, expecting all
the world either to know or to care what Eynsham or Sand-
ford signifies. But, of course, it counts also to some extent,
and safely, on the fact that this twelve-mile loop of the
Thames, between the entrances of the Windrush and the
Cherwell, and the hilly country enclosed by it, is exception-
ally well known to a good sprinkling of Arnold's most likely
readers. How Cambridge people or Newcastle people are
reached by this 'topography' I cannot say, but I doubt if it is
at all necessary to be Oxonian to enjoy it. No doubt it touches
Oxford men on a weak spot, and at times may have too much
credit for doing so. The important thing, however, is that the
intimacy implied by this naming goes well with the affection
confessed in the poem, and helps the reader to take up the
suggestions made by hills, trees, rivers and blossoms, and distant spires, and thus to compose a landscape which can exist
without use of map or previous association. That is Arnold's
country par excellence.

He was born at Laleham on the Thames, near Staines, in
1822. At eighteen he went up to Oxford as an undergraduate, and spent four years there. He returned at thirty-
four as Professor of Poetry. The river and the river-side
woods and hills were part of the scenery and the dramatis
personæ of his life at three important periods. Though he left
Laleham for Rugby at the age of five, he came back again two
years later. Between thirteen and eighteen he was at Winchester on a river and among chalk hills, while some of his

A LITERARY PILGRIM IN ENGLAND

holidays were spent at Fox How, near Grasmere, where Dr. Arnold had taken a house of refuge from the Rugby country. Still at forty-four he remembered, when he found a saxifrage on the mounds of the ruined castle at Bungay, that it used to grow 'in the field on the way to papa's bathing-place at Rugby.' The Trent country, too, round Fledborough, in Nottingham-shire, touched him on revisiting it years after he had learnt it with his mother, whose father was Vicar there. But Laleham and Oxford were the capitals of his country. Fox How was a detached portion of it. There he had Wordsworth and Har-riet Martineau for neighbours, and met Charlotte Brontë (in 1850). The mountains and the lakes were much; the garden of the house was something, and in early middle age he wrote to his mother rather particularly about it, saying that not enough was made there of arbutus, and advising as to the ever-greens, laurel and rhododendron, to be planted, 'but neither the one nor the other thick enough to be crowded.' Fox How became 'the House of Paradise' to Arnold's children. He himself often revisited and made excursions in that country, sleeping at Strands at the end of Wastwater, and going on to Crummock and Buttermere, for example.

But at one time or another, during his thirty-five years as Inspector of Schools, he saw many sections of England, and had hardly a fixed abode till he took a London house – in Chester Square – in 1858, six years after his marriage. When he was in Cambridge at forty, he was so pleased that he made up his mind he would like the post of Master of Trinity; but strolling back by moonlight from Grantchester made him melancholy 'to think how at one time he was in the fields every summer evening of his life, and now it is such a rare event to find himself there.' He remained something of a sportsman. Though he once said that he expected not to shoot again, and that 'this will be no great blessing for the

72

brute creation, as I never used to hit them,' he continued at intervals to shoot at pheasants and to hit partridges. Fishing also kept him out of doors. Thus, he boated on the Wye from Goodrich Castle to Chepstow, and fished in places. Fishing helped to make him acquainted with the chalk downs about Dorking. Stopping at West Humble, Dorking, he says he almost agrees with Herman Merivale that between Box Hill and Leith Hill is the most enchanting country in England. Box Hill, he says, 'comes down upon us like the side of Loughrigg.' For fishing he had the run of Wotton, Evelyn's Wotton, and caught two-pound trout there. The fishing was 'a little too preserved and tame' for his taste, but he was delighted by the heath, pine, and whortleberries, of Leith Hill, and the immense view, and Wotton's Elizabethan quadrangle, 'with two griffins keeping guard over the entrance, dogs lying on the grass-plot, and a charming medieval-sounding clock from the clock-tower,' which made him feel in a dream. Off and on he knew that country for twenty years, and was never so much struck by it as when he saw it again on a visit from Cobham:

'The parallel foldings, of which the Wotton folding is one, running up into the greensand knot of Leith Hill, are inexhaustible in beauty, and opposite to them is the sharp slope of the chalk hills. . . . They are the best chalk hills I know anywhere, the best wooded, and the most abounding in exquisite combs and bottoms. It has been a bad year for the bee orchis there, but the *Pyramidalis* we found covering the ground.'

M. E. Grant Duff had made him a bit of a botanist late in life, and he had gathered *Œnothera* about Oxwich Bay in Gower, and pellitory and *Ruta muraria* on walls at Coleridge's Ottery. His letters from Pain's Hill, Cobham, where he moved when

73

he was fifty, abound in references to flowers and trees, chiefly in gardens.

In fact, it is only at Cobham that Arnold can really be seen at home. He had spent some years at Harrow while his sons were at school, and we have glimpses of him looking on a wonderfully clear February day far off to 'the clump of Botleys and the misty line of the Thames,' driving to Belmount, walking with Rover in December in the fields beyond Northolt, 'which are quiet and solemn in this grey weather beyond belief,' finding violets with the children, and discussing whether the pigs shall really be fattened and killed for home use. But we see almost as much of him at Aston Clinton under the Chilterns, where he often stayed with the Rothschilds, shooting, and admiring the beechwoods, and finding white violets in masses in the lanes of the Chilterns.

At Cobham the letters and the late poems really serve to fix him in one recognizable spot. 'We lay thee,' he says to Geist, the dog —

'We lay thee, close within our reach,
Here, where the grass is smooth and warm,
Between the holly and the beech,
Where oft we watch'd thy couchant form,

'Asleep, yet lending half an ear
To travellers on the Portsmouth Road. . . .'

Cobham lies on the Portsmouth road, and across it, causing it to twist sharply. When Kaiser, the dog, dies,

'the heavy news
Post-haste to Cobham calls the Muse.'

Soon after moving there, he thought this country more beautiful than the Chilterns. The heather and pines pleased him, and especially the open land of St. George's Hill. And they began at once planting and improving, as if the cottage were their own, and they had a hundred years to live there; 'its great merit,' he says, 'is that it must have had nearly one hundred years of life already, and is surrounded by great old trees.' The rhododendrons and roses and pampas grass, the strawberries and potatoes also, are his concern. He is uneasy in the dry weather for the hollies and laurels which have been moved. In short, after twelve years this country was pleasanter to him than Devonshire, near Exminster, and returning from there he remarks complacently to his son: 'I think we are going to have a really great crop of pears and plums; you know we have not had any to speak of hitherto. . . . The treatment consists in administering guano while they are flowering; this enables them to resist cold, and gives them strength to set their fruit.' He had always leant towards gardens: now lilac and laburnum made 'a heavenly moment of the year in England.' The dogs fitted in perfectly. He tells Lucy, his daughter, how he came back from London at four and found the dogs dejected, not having had their walk. So he took them 'the Burwood round,' and at one place 'the cuckoo was so loud and so close that Max was fairly puzzled and stood still. At that moment a squirrel seemed to rise out of the ground at our feet, and ran up one of the trees. Kai strained and tugged, but I had him in the chain; Max was so absorbed by the cuckoo that he never perceived the squirrel.' He says that re-reading Wordsworth for the selection made him (in 1879) 'feel more keenly than usual the beauty of the common incidents of the natural year.' Driving home from dinner at Effingham he hears nightingales in 'a thicket just before entering upon Effingham Common'; 'they were almost maddeningly beautiful.' Again he hears them 'along one of the old grass roads of this country, some thirty yards wide, leading from Bookham Common to Effingham Common, with woods on one side, and a great bowering hedge on the other.' The weather could put him 'in tearing spirits,' he says, at sixty-four:

'The east wind is gone, the south-west wind is come, and the thermometer is now (noon) 62 in shade to the north. The colour has come at last, and the horse-chestnuts and poplars are a sight. Yellows we can manage to perfection; it is the reds in which the States beat us. . . . I go about the garden – I cannot come into work – examine the acorns on the Turkey oak, with their curly-haired cups, which I never noticed before; they are very effective. Then I give Flu [his wife], who is driving to Lady Ellesmere's, a Duchesse pear to take to Lady Ellesmere, who says she shall carry it to her gardener to show him how much finer pears are grown at the Cottage than at Burwood. . . .'

He watches the abeles' 'exquisitely light yellow' on an island in the Mole opposite, and walks along the Walton Road, where the plantations of chestnut and the fern 'made a feast of brown and yellow.' 'I do enjoy this Surrey country and climate,' he says in an April-like December thaw. When he was sixty-three he was skating on Pain's Hill Lake, which was 'beautiful as ever' in snow and ice. At sixty-five he died.

But all this has little to do with Arnold's poetry, except that it tells something of the experiences, tastes, and affections, that nourished his poetry. They did not always enter very directly into his poetry. The letters show that he enjoyed looking back and revisiting, as when he writes to his mother in 1848 about going along 'that shelving gravelly road up towards Laleham' – walking up to Pentonhook after morning church, and finding 'the stream with the old volume, width, shine, rapid fullness, "kempshott," and swans, unchanged and unequalled, to my partial and remembering eyes at least'; and again in 1849, about bathing with Tom Hughes in the Thames, 'having a header off the "kempshott" where the lane from the village comes down on the river.' But he allowed this sentiment to culminate in poetry rather seldom, and chiefly in 'The Scholar Gipsy' and 'Thyrsis.' The Oxford country, in those poems, gathers to itself all of Arnold's feeling for country and garden. When he wrote 'The Scholar Gipsy' he had already had a year or two of 'an employment which I certainly do *not* like'; the Oxford life was ten years clear behind him; and in fact or in memory he had probably got up alone, as he did in October, 1854 (the year after 'The Scholar Gipsy'), 'into one of the little coombs that papa was so fond of, and which I had in my mind in "The Gipsy Scholar."' He 'felt the peculiar *sentiment* of this country and neighbourhood as deeply as ever.' Seventeen years passed, and in another October he was telling his mother how the beautiful weather had been lighting up 'the wood and stone of Oxfordshire — I say "and stone" because, to my mind, the yellows and browns of that oolite stone, which you may remember about Adderbury on the road to Oxford, make it one of the most beautiful things in the world.' That was in 1860. In May, 1863, he speaks of fine weather at Oxford 'with a detestable cold wind.' He had enjoyed it in spite of the wind, and sent his sister a fritillary; but the cold wind prevented him from beginning 'a new poem about the Cumner hillside, and Clough in connexion with it,' which he meant to have begun at Oxford—i.e. 'Thyrsis.' The poem, however, got written, and in 1866 he told J. C. Shairp and his mother something about it. It had long been in his head 'to connect Clough with that Cumner country,' and Clough had an 'idyllic side' which suited his 'desire to deal again' with that country; yet he felt strongly that, if the poem were read as a memorial poem, it would seem 'that not enough is said about Clough in it,' and he did not send it to Mrs. Clough. It is true. The poem is concerned entirely with Arnold and with what he used to love and what he has lost. He commemorates spring as much as Clough in verses like —

'So some tempestuous morn in early June,
　　When the year's primal burst of bloom is o'er,
　　　Before the roses and the longest day —
　When garden walks and all the grassy floor
　With blossoms red and white of fallen may
　　And chestnut flowers are strewn —
So have I heard the cuckoo's parting cry,
　　From the wet field, through the vext garden-trees,
　　　Come with the volleying rain and tossing breeze:
　The bloom is gone, and with the bloom go I!'

This is one of the best garden verses in English, and it happens that we know what garden suggested it. In 1864 he was at Woodford, in Epping Forest, and there he heard 'the cuckoo I have brought in in "Thyrsis."' Apparently the next two verses,

　　　'Too quick despairer, wherefore wilt thou go?'
and

　　　'He hearkens not! light comer, he is flown!'

were also 'reminiscences of Woodford.' But all was to be concentrated on Oxford, for which his feeling was abiding, and no doubt the two poems helped to preserve it and give it form. As late as 1884 he speaks of going out to Hinksey in October — again in October — and 'up the hill to within sight of the Cumner firs,' and of the indescribable effect which this landscape always has on him — 'the hillside with its valleys, and Oxford in the great Thames valley below.'

In 'Thyrsis,' the later poem, the garden and the sense of garden and cultivated land are very strong. Neither here nor in 'The Scholar Gipsy' is there more than a graceful wildness and the idea of escape; the pastoral convention in 'Thyrsis' forbade it, and in any case the most real things are those

> 'Groups under the dreaming garden-trees,
> And the full moon, and the white evening star.'

Such a line as

> 'I know these slopes; who knows them, if not I?'

has the effect of reducing the landscape to garden scale, while the feeling of

> 'A fugitive and gracious light he seeks,
> Shy to illumine; and I seek it too.
> This does not come with houses or with gold . . .'

helps to give the country a kind of allegorical thinness, as if it were chiefly a symbol of escape from the world of 'men and towns.'

But how often it is a garden in Arnold's poetry! His nightingale sings from a 'moonlit cedar.' The typical young man and woman in 'The Youth of Man' are standing

> 'where this grey balustrade
> Crowns the still valley; behind
> Is the castled house, with its woods,
> Which shelter'd their childhood – the sun
> On its ivied windows; a scent
> From the grey-wall'd gardens, a breath
> Of the fragrant stock and the pink,
> Perfumes the evening air.
> Their children play on the lawns. . . .'

A certain smooth dignity of lawn and tree transferred him to classic ground. In Hyde Park, for example, while

> 'The grass had still the green of May,
> And still the unblacken'd elms were gay . . .'

the 'soft couched cattle,' he says, were as fair

> 'As those which pastured by the sea,
> That old-world morn, in Sicily,
> When on the beach the Cyclops lay,
> And Galatea from the bay
> Mock'd her poor lovelorn giant's lay.'

'Scarce fresher,' he says, 'is the mountain sod' than the grass of Kensington Gardens; and though he was 'breathed on by the rural Pan' in his cradle, he could find peace there 'for ever new.' Longing himself to be such an islet as the gardens, he prays:

> 'Calm soul of all things! make it mine
> To feel, amid the city's jar,
> That there abides a peace of thine
> Man did not make, and cannot mar.'

So, to make an exit from this world into a scene for his 'Bacchanalia; or, The New Age,' he describes a typical rustic evening:

> 'The tinkle of the thirsty rill,
> Unheard all day, ascends again. . . .'

He observed detail beautifully, whether in wild or in cultivated country. Yet see how gentle he makes the wild in 'Iseult of Brittany,' all unconsciously, by introducing Iseult and her children there as if on a seaside holiday, the three in

fur mantles, the children with 'feathered hats,' the mother
telling them a story. It might have been 'Iseult in Kensington Gardens,' for all that the details are obviously taken from
somewhere else:

> 'The pale grass
> Is strewn with rocks, and many a shiver'd mass
> Of vein'd white-gleaming quartz, and here and there
> Dotted with holly-trees and juniper.
> In the smooth centre of the opening stood
> Three hollies side by side, and made a screen,
> Warm with the winter sun, of burnish'd green,
> With scarlet berries gemm'd, the fell-fare's food.
> Under the glittering hollies Iseult stands,
> Watching her children play; their little hands
> Are busy gathering spars of quartz and streams
> Of stagshorn for their hats; anon, with screams
> Of mad delight they drop their spoils, and bound
> Among the holly clumps and broken ground. . . .'

Probably he remembered seeing his own or a friend's children
and such a stony ground, and remembered so well that the
passage suggests a living Victorian lady more than an Arthurian ghostess. Finally, there is 'Parting' in 'Switzerland.' He
wishes to praise a clear buoyant voice, and asks:

> 'Say, has some wet bird-haunted English lawn
> Lent it the music of its trees at dawn?'

Clearly this is one of the two or three things most loved by
Arnold. In attempting to describe very different scenes, he
gets the details true and close enough, as in 'Resignation,'
where he has a note saying that 'those who have been long
familiar with the English Lake-Country will find no diffi-

culty in recalling, from the description in the text, the road-side inn at Wythburn on the descent from Dunmail Raise towards Keswick; its sedentary landlord . . . and the passage over the Wythburn Fells to Watendlath.' But anybody who did not know would not find much help in these details towards reconstructing the scene. He is more effective when he uses a few strokes only, as in the beginning of 'Rugby Chapel,' where the field, the dank yellow drifts of leaves, the elms, the few shouts of boys playing, the lights coming out in the street, the chapel unlighted, suffice for any human being as such to call up something very like it, and for Rugbeians to call up Rugby. Nothing of its kind could be more effective than the simple scene with a few plain symbols at the opening of 'The Youth of Nature':

> 'Raised are the dripping oars,
> Silent the boat! the lake,
> Lovely and soft as a dream,
> Swims in the sheen of the moon.
> The mountains stand at its head,
> Clear in the pure June night,
> But the valleys are flooded with haze.
> Rydal and Fairfield are there;
> In the shadow Wordsworth lies dead.
> So it is, so it will be for aye.
> Nature is fresh as of old,
> Is lovely; a mortal is dead.'

Though not a native of that country, he had looked at lake and mountain time after time since childhood, and they had a kind of moral or spiritual grandeur for him. Yet it was not only to Nature that he looked for calm after seeing in the country, for example, Cruikshank's picture of 'The Bottle'; not only to

'Breathless glades, cheer'd by shy Dian's horn,
    Cold-bubbling springs, or caves,'

but equally to Wordsworth, or to some other human mind,
who heard their voices 'right,' and interpreted the calm and
the majesty and gave them moral or spiritual significance.

*

It is perhaps absurd to speak of William Morris's country if one means more than that he spent great tracts of his life, working and seeing friends, at Kelmscott House in Hammersmith, and Kelmscott Manor House on the Upper Thames. He was born in Essex, at Elm House, Walthamstow, from which the family moved when he was six to Woodford Hall in the same county. When he was fourteen they moved back to Walthamstow, to Water House. These houses were on the edge of Epping Forest. Marlborough, at the edge of Savernake Forest, was his school; Oxford his University, where he met Burne-Jones, Swinburne, Rossetti, and wrote his early poems. Then he lived in London for a time, first at 17, Red Lion Square with Burne-Jones, and, then, for a time after his marriage, at 41, Great Ormond Street. Five years, from 1860 to 1865, he spent at the house built for him by Philip Webb, the Red House at Bexley Heath in Kent. He took to London again to be nearer his business, and Bloomsbury was again his choice; but now he had a home in Queen Square instead of lodgings. There he wrote 'The Life and Death of Jason' and much of 'The Earthly Paradise.' After six years in London he moved, in 1871, to Kelmscott Manor House. He did most of his work there or in the house which he called Kelmscott House, facing the Thames at Hammersmith, or in his factory at Merton Abbey on the Wandle, a few miles away across the river. He died at Kelmscott House in 1896, when he was sixty-two.

Miss May Morris's notes to the Collected Edition, coupled with Mr. Mackail's Life, show us the man very plainly — his poetry 'dropping off the end of his pen,' his dyeing stuffs, his printing, his illuminating, his public meetings against the unspeakable Turk, his letters against the unspeakable Sir Gilbert Scott, and then, in August, a letter to his wife saying that he is coming down to Kelmscott: 'Please tell May to have many worms ready for me: proper brandlings I must have; they are striped and don't smell nice – this is their sign . . .' and there is a reminder, 'Don't forget *the worms*.' This was in 1877, while Morris was at work on 'Sigurd the Volsung.' Miss Morris adds that she also understood gentles, and remembers her pride in not refusing to manipulate this interesting bait when desired by the fisherman, her father.

Morris did not use his experience directly: 'Sigurd' contains no allusion to coarse fishing. In fact, a man undertaking to reconstruct the poet and his environment from his poems would have need of a long life. The prose tells us a little more. 'News from Nowhere' is saved, if at all, by what comes straight from Morris's experience of the Thames and of Thames-side houses at Kelmscott and Hammersmith The water is real water, whereas the people and that decorated tobacco pipe are not real at all. The elms on the bank, the cuckoo's song, the blackbird's 'sweet strong whistle,' the corncrake's craking, the 'waves of fragrance from the flowering clover amidst the ripe grass' – these also are real, and so is the outside of the house (he had too little skill, perhaps, in drawing people to do the inside):

'The garden between the wall and the house was redolent of the June flowers, and the roses were rolling over one another with that delicious superabundance of small well-tended gardens which at first sight takes away all thought from the beholder save that of beauty. The blackbirds were singing their loudest, the doves were cooing on the roof-ridge, the rooks in the high elm-trees beyond were garrulous among the young leaves, and the swifts wheeled whining about the gables. And the house itself was a fit guardian for all the beauty of this heart of summer.'

At Kelmscott he was often and for long happy. He could work there. He had his wife and daughters and friends there. The river held fish. The dung bred brandlings, and Miss Morris gathered them. The sun shone frequently, and if the wind blew east it would change in the end to south-west. Moreover, he delighted very much in 'the works of the Thames-side country bumpkins,' the farmhouses with flowers in the parlour, and the village churches around, 'every one a beautiful work of art.' Oxford was not far off, and he knew the country lying between. Miss Morris tells us that the palace of 'The Well at the World's End' was their own Kelmscott, that Wilstead was Faringdon, and so on. Miss Morris's notes include extracts from diaries which show us Morris dividing his time among friends, fishing, and romance. She thus enables us to taste the same mixture as her father did in 1892. If only this were possible from beginning to end of the romances, more would read them, all would love them.

It is a pleasure to see Morris in the country, and to see more of that love of the earth which his poetry reveals less directly. He, too, loved the chalk hills which he had trodden when he walked about Marlborough and Avebury, and round Oxford. So that in 1879, August 19, when he was driving over Salisbury Plain, and had stopped at the George at Amesbury, he said he wished that he could live on the Plain, since he could not live in Iceland. He loved gardens also. For most of his life he had about him beautiful gardens, as at Walthamstow, Oxford, Bexley Heath, and Kelmscott. Water House, Walthamstow – and Woodford Hall was similar, but larger – had a square hall with a marble pavement, and a broad staircase of Spanish chestnut leading up out of it to an upper hall or gallery; and Morris read in the window-seats when he was home from Marlborough and Oxford:

'Behind the house was a broad lawn, and beyond it the feature which gave the house its name — a moat of some forty feet in breadth, surrounding an island planted with a grove of aspens. The moat was stocked with pike and perch; there the boys fished, bathed, and boated, in summer, and skated in winter. The island, rough and thickly wooded and fringed with a growth of hollies, hawthorns, and chestnuts, was a sort of fairyland for all the children, who almost lived in it.'

House, moat, and garden, I suppose, helped to give what reality there is to 'Golden Wings':

> 'Midways of a walled garden,
>   In the happy poplar land,
>   Did an ancient castle stand,
> With an old knight for a warden.
>
> 'Many scarlet bricks there were
>   In its walls, and old grey stone,
>   Over which red apples shone
> At the right time of the year.
>
> 'On the bricks the green moss grew,
>   Yellow lichen on the stone,
>   Over which red apples shone;
> Little war that castle knew.
>
> 'Deep green water fill'd the moat. . . .'

These things he had seen at Walthamstow and Woodford, and 'the red-bill'd moorhen,' and

> 'White swans on the green moat,
> Small feathers left afloat
> By the blue-painted boat;
> Swift running of the stoat. . . .'

That same moat was good enough to girdle Troy, and through the long war

> 'the carp and tench,
> In spite of arblasts and petrariæ,
> Suck at the floating lilies all day long.'

And there is very little of English country in his poems which could not have come from those Essex gardens, Epping Forest, and the downs and forest near Marlborough.

Yet Mr. Stopford Brooke has said that 'No tongue can tell how Morris loved the Earth; she was his delight, his joy, his refuge, his home; the companion of his uncompanionable thoughts; his mother from whose breasts he drank life, energy, food for his work, joy for his imagination, and incessant beauty. No one has praised her better; and his poetry of Nature reveals how close, how passionate, he was in his worship.' There is a humanity of this world in Morris's feeling for Nature, with which Wordsworth's cannot be compared. Except a few of the greatest things by Whitman, literature in the English tongue hardly shows another earth-feeling so majestic and yet so tender as in 'The Message of the March Wind.' Elsewhere Morris showed himself aware that troubling about arts and crafts might seem 'petty and unheroic' to those who were brought face to face with 'the reckless hideousness and squalor of a great manufacturing district.' He cared for the arts and for the 'shabby hell' of the city, and did not think or find the two cases incompatible, but rather that they were one, though his crowded life — busy, never hurried, and of no unusual length — was too small for his purpose. A division between the two cases is apparent in 'The Message of the March Wind,' where the lover at evening asks his mistress:

'Shall we be glad always? Come closer and hearken:
　　Three fields farther on, as they told me down there,
When the young moon has set, if the March sky should
　　　　darken,
　　We might see from the hill-top the great city's glare.'

But the division is healed in a union between love of one
woman and of the world, and the lover ends:

'But lo, the old inn, and the lights, and the fire,
　　And the fiddler's old tune and the shuffling of feet;
Soon for us shall be quiet and rest and desire,
　　And to-morrow's uprising to deeds shall be sweet.'

The scene is a kind of symbol of the union in Morris of
love for country and love for town. In Mr. Mackail's Life he
is sometimes revealed as a hearty countryman and as a conscious and satisfied Cockney. A Cockney was what he tended
to prefer calling himself, as a citizen working in the town
which was once 'London small and white and clean.' As an
artist he preferred to think of such a London, and he achieved
it by looking back in 'The Earthly Paradise,' and forward in
'News from Nowhere.' But the union was an imperfect one.
For most of his life he was a somewhat dismayed countryman,
but an imperfect Londoner. Probably he was one of those
survivors who cannot accept the distinction and division
between town and country which has been sharpening ever
since

　　　　'London was a grey-walled town,
　　　　And slow the pack-horse made his way
　　　　Across the curlew-haunted down.'

He passed from one to the other easily. In both he worked
and met his friends, artists and Socialists.

No man yet has made a perfect harmony of the two, town and country, and we know nothing about the angels. A man at least has done very well who, either on the Oxfordshire or the Middlesex shore, wrote two or three kinds of poetry and prose, lectured, organized societies and movements, designed wallpaper and chintz, wove tapestry and got others to weave it, dyed and experimented in dyeing, managed a business and kept a shop, was a public examiner and an adviser to a museum, refused the laureateship, caught perch and jack, cooked admirably, and had times when he was 'too happy to think that there could be much amiss anywhere.'

THE DOWNS AND THE SOUTH COAST

AUBREY   WHITE

COBBETT   HAZLITT

JEFFERIES   HARDY

BELLOC

JOHN AUBREY was a gossip whose odds and ends about men, things, and places, are now better than most full-dress literature. Those about men were set down at first merely as material for a biographer whom he thought his better, Anthony à Wood, and, as he was inquisitive and precise, there were some strange things amongst them, so that he said they were 'not fit to let fly abroad till about thirty years hence, for the author and the persons (like medlars) ought to be first rotten.' They were 'put in writing tumultuarily,' and he fancied himself 'all along discoursing' with Wood. The 'Brief Lives' will now survive whatever is made out of them. So with his observations of antiquities and natural history. Who but Aubrey would have noticed and entered in a book that in the spring after the Fire of London 'all the ruins were overgrown with an herb or two, but especially with a yellow flower, *Ericolevis Neapolitana*' ? Who but he would have included this in a sketched life of Thomas Hobbes? – 'Though he left his native county [Wiltshire] at fourteen, and lived so long, yet sometimes one might find a little touch of our pronunciation – old Sir Thomas Malette, one of the judges of the King's Bench, knew Sir Walter Ralegh, and sayd that, notwithstanding his great travells, conversation, learning, etc., yet he spake broad Devonshire to his dying day.'

He began early in Wiltshire, as a boy at Easton Pierse, in the parish of Kington St. Michael, at Leigh Delamere, where the Vicar taught him, and at Blandford Grammar School in Dorset. For example, he remembered that 'our old Vicar of Kington St. Michael, Mr. Hynd, did sing his sermons rather than read them,' and how 'when I was a boy, before the late civil wars, the tabor and pipe were commonly used, especially Sundays and Holydays, and at Christenings and Feasts, in the Marches of Wales, Hereford, Gloucestershire, and in all

Wales,' and 'how the water in the ditches below Devizes looks bluish' at the fall of the leaf. When a boy, too, he heard from the old men how 'in one of the great fields at War-minster in Wiltshire, in the harvest, at the very time of the fight at Bosworth field, between King Richard III and Henry VII, there was one of the parish took two sheaves, crying (with some intervals) now for Richard, now for Henry; at last lett fall the sheaf that did represent Richard and cried now for King Henry, Richard is slain.' Coming to write of Sir Philip Sidney, he recalled: 'When I was a boy nine years old, I was with my father at one Mr. Singleton's, an alderman and woollen-draper in Gloucester, who had in his parlour, over the chimney, the whole description of the funeral, engraved and printed on papers pasted together, and which, at length, was, I believe, the length of the room at least; but he had contrived it to be turned upon two pins, that turning one of them made the figures march all in order. It did make such a strong impression on my young phantasy, that I remember it as if it were but yesterday. I could never see it elsewhere. The house is in the great long street, over against the high steeple; and 'tis likely it remains there still. 'Tis pity it is not redone.' At Blandford he had Walter and Tom Raleigh, grand-nephews of Sir Walter, for schoolfellows — clever boys, proud and quarrelsome, with 'excellent tunable voices, and played their parts well on the viol.'

Perhaps the memento of Sidney's funeral and the talk of the Raleighs at Blandford turned him to a sense of the living past and dying present. But an old family, with a strong Welsh element, that had already been some generations in North Wiltshire, would of itself have provided much for the taste which we must suppose him born with. His mother's father had been born also at Easton Pierse, his mother in the neighbouring parish of Yatton Keynell. Thomas Danvers, one of his uncles, was at Bemerton when George Herbert was buried there '(according to his own desire) with the singing service for the burial of the dead, by the singing men of Sarum.' Thomas Browne, his great-uncle, remembered Sir Philip Sidney, 'and said that he was often wont, as he was hunting on our pleasant plains, to take his table book out of his pocket, and write down his notions as they came into his head, when he was writing his Arcadia.' When a boy, he says, 'he did ever love to converse with old men as living histories,' and began to draw, yet never became a painter. Thus he grew up a lover of the old days, when lords of manors kept good houses and ate at the high tables in the oriels of their 'great Gothic halls,' such as Draycot, when the halls of justices of the peace were 'dreadful to behold, the screens were garnished with corslets and helmets, gaping with open mouth, with coats of mail, lances, pikes, halberts, brown bills, batter-dashers, bucklers,' and 'the meeting of the gentry was not at tippling-houses, but in the fields or forest, with their hawks and hounds, with their bugle horns in silken baldrics.' All about him were old men to furnish him from the past. John Power, for example, an undergraduate of Gloucester Hall in the early seventeenth century, told Aubrey what an old college servant had told him about Thomas Allen the astrologer, that sometimes he met the spirits coming up his stairs 'like bees.' There was a great-nephew of this Allen, too, at Broad Hinton, on the other side of Wootton Bassett from Easton Pierse. One Jack Sydenham, who used to carry Aubrey in his arms and 'sang rarely,' had formerly served Thomas Bushell, of Enston in Oxfordshire, and remembered a workman dis-covering a rock there, 'with pendants like icicles as at Wookey Hole (Somerset), which was the occasion of making that delicate grotto and those fine walks.' Moreover, this same Jack Sydenham had served a neighbour of the Aubreys, Sir

Charles Snell, of Kington St. Michael, who had built a ship, the *Angel Gabriel*, for Sir Walter Raleigh's Guiana design, and had paid for it with his manor of Yatton Keynell, the farm at Easton Pierse, Thornhill, and the church lease of Bishop's Cannings. Aubrey had met, too, a Worcestershire man from whom Raleigh permanently borrowed a gown at Oxford. Then, at Draycot Cerne the Longs lived, and Sir Walter Long had first brought tobacco into 'our part of North Wilts, e.g. Malmesbury Hundred.' The old yeomen of the neighbourhood told him how, when they went to market at Malmesbury or Chippenham, having to pay for tobacco its weight in silver, 'they called out their biggest shillings to lay in the scales against the tobacco.' History and tradition flowed naturally to Aubrey. The country tradition that Cardinal Morton was a shoemaker's son from Bere in Dorset came to him while he was a schoolboy at Blandford. He was only eight when he first saw Stonehenge. How many thousands had seen it at that age and forgotten it, or never said so, just as they must have known once, as well as Aubrey, that 'in North Wilts the milkmaids sing as shrill and clear as any swallow sitting on a barn.' He quotes Chaucer. The wonders of the living world also were very great. He had seen with his own eyes, or some Jack or Jill had made him see, a whirlwind carry a child, with half the haycock where he had been lying, up over the elm-trees and down safe 'in the next ground.'

He was soon to know South Wiltshire almost as well as North. Perhaps his road to the school at Blandford took him past Stonehenge; for he cannot have been much above eight when lessons at Leigh Delamere, 'a mile's fine walk' or pony-ride from home, were exchanged for an ordinary school, the good-natured Rector who had taught Hobbes for an ill-natured schoolmaster. To reach Blandford he must at any rate have crossed Salisbury Plain, the whole breadth of it, three of its rivers, and the ranges dividing them. Then when he was only sixteen, in 1642, and was sent for from Oxford to avoid the war, it was to Broad Chalk he went instead of to Easton Pierse. His father was renting the Manor Farm there, close to the third of those three rivers, the Ebble. The father 'was not educated to learning, but to hawking,' and as the boy had been allured to reading by the 'Religio Medici' in 1643, and 'in those days fathers were not acquainted with their children,' it was in some ways a 'most sad' life. But he was made a complete Wiltshireman. Years later, when he stated that the Wiltshire greyhounds were the best in England, he added that he and his father had 'as good as any were in our times in Wiltshire,' and that they were generally fallow, or black, or black and white. Between the country about Easton Pierse and that about Broad Chalk he felt great differences. North Wiltshire, where they only milked cows and made cheese, and fed chiefly on milk meats, 'which cools the brains and hurts the invention,' made the people 'melancholy, contemplative and malicious,' loving religion and litigation; but in the South, on the Downs, where most is tillage, 'their flesh is hard, their bodies strong: being weary after hard labour, they have not leisure to read and contemplate religion, but go to bed to their rest, to rise betime the next morning to their labour.' The lesser differences were strange. For example, his books gathered more mould on their bindings in the hill country at Chalk than in the vale at Easton. Then, again, some of the high-lying places, like Pertwood, that might have been thought healthy, were not so; they were constantly in mist; people did not live long there.

Apparently Broad Chalk became Aubrey's home on his father's death early in the fifties of the century. He lived there mostly, but sometimes at Easton; his mother died there in 1685, but was taken to Kington St. Michael to be buried.

What with the family estates in Herefordshire and Breconshire, he was bound to be a traveller. Much of his time, says he, was spent journeying to South Wales and Herefordshire. In the end litigation lost him everything but his friends, yet he still loved travelling. The homeless man wished that the monasteries had not been put down; it was fit that there should be 'receptacles and provision for contemplative men.' 'What a pleasure 'twould have been,' he exclaimed, 'to have travelled from monastery to monastery!' He was crossed often in love, too. But even Joan Sumner, one of his least propitious ladies, led him to another part of Wiltshire, to Seend, near Melksham, where he discovered chalybeate springs. If it had not been for the jealousy of the Bath doctors, he thought he might have made the place another Bath. Even so, the village could not contain the company visiting the springs, and building was afoot.

Thus with all his misfortunes it was a happy life to look back on, sketching antiquities on horseback; spying 'Our Lady's Church steeple at Sarum like a fine Spanish needle' when he topped Red Horn Hill above Urchfont; seeing the distant mountains of Devon gleaming white with May snow, while where he stood at Llanrechid in Glamorganshire scarce any had fallen; and, above all, suddenly discovering the grey wethers – the grey stones scattered sheep-like over the slopes – on Marlborough Downs, and the great temple of Avebury. The grey wethers were then much thicker than now over the downs between Marlborough and Avebury, and looked like the scene 'where the giants fought with huge stones against the gods, as is described by Hesiod in his Theogonia.' Aubrey was twenty-two when he first saw that country.

'I never saw the country about Marlborough (he says) till Christmas, 1648, being then invited to Lord Francis Seymour's by the Hon. Mr. Charles Seymour. . . . The morrow after twelfth-day Mr. Charles Seymour and Sir William Button met with their packs of hounds at the Grey Wethers. These Downs look as if they were sown with great stones, very thick, and in a dusky evening they look like a flock of sheep. . . . 'Twas here that our game began, and the chase led us at length through the village of Avebury into the closes there, where I was wonderfully surprised at the sight of those vast stones, of which I had never heard before, as also at the mighty bank and graffe about it. I observed in the enclosures some segments of rude circles made with these stones, whence I concluded they had been in the old time complete. I left my company awhile, entertaining myself with a more delightful indagation, and then (cheered by the cry of the hounds) overtook the company, and went with them to Kennet, where was a good hunting dinner provided.'

Nobody before, it seems, had noticed the stones at Avebury, or had troubled to say so, and Aubrey naturally boasted that they excelled Stonehenge 'as a cathedral does a parish church.' Afterwards he showed them to Charles II, who had heard the boast. And he loved to revisit them. When he came there hawking with Long, of Draycot Cerne, he wrote in elevation:

'Our sport was very good and in a romantic country, for the prospects are noble and vast, the downs stocked with numerous flocks of sheep, the turf rich and fragrant with thyme and burnet . . . nor are the nut-brown shepherdesses without their graces. . . .'

He must have delighted in high places, like the top of Chalk Down, with its oaks 'shorn by the south and south-west winds,' reclining from the sixteen-miles-distant sea, and the top of Knoll Hill, near Kilmington and Maiden Bradley, that gave a prospect of the Fosseway between Cirencester and Gloucester, forty miles off; also the Isle of Wight, Salisbury steeple, and the Severn sea. When he has to tell the story of a practical joke at Marlborough, he cannot omit to picture his young blades 'walking on the delicate fine downs at the back-side of the town.' And what a pretty thing that is in the brief life of George Feriby, parson of Bishop's Cannings, near Devizes, 'an excellent musician and no ill poet'! – how he entertained Queen Anne at Wansdyke, on the top of the down, with a pleasant pastoral, 'his fellow songsters in shep-herds' weeds and bagpipes, he himself like an old bard,' and King James 'with carters singing with whips in their hands; and afterwards, a football play.' Bishop's Cannings, he says, 'would have challenged all England for music, [bell-]ringing, and football play.' He went everywhere. He went to Chit-terne, which is not in any of the books, and remarks that tobacco-pipe clay is 'excellent, or the best in England, at Chit-terne, of which the Gauntlet pipes at Amesbury are made by one of that name.' He heard the gossip of towns and villages, the dreams that came true at Broad Chalk and Amesbury. Everywhere to the last he had friends: his chief virtue, he said himself, was gratitude.

At Kilmington his friend Francis Potter was Rector, a Wiltshireman like himself, born at Mere under Castle Hill and, like Aubrey, a lover of clear-cut chalk hills, such as Cley Hill, near Warminster, and the Knolls. 'He took great de-light in Knoll Hill,' says Aubrey. This man became a Fellow of the Royal Society. He 'had an admirable mechanical in-vention,' and made quadrants with a graduated compass – his own invention. Above the well at the parsonage, which was very deep, was the most ingenious and useful contrivance Aubrey had ever seen, for emptying the vast bucket without a strain. He wrote an 'Interpretation of the Number 666.' It was a pity, says Aubrey, that he was 'staked to a private preferment in an obscure corner,' to contract moss 'like an old pole in an orchard.' But Aubrey had never enjoyed anywhere else 'such philosophical and hearty entertainment' as at Kilmington. He describes the old man like a monk, 'pretty long-visaged,' with 'pale clear skin' and grey eye, talking 'all new and unvulgar,' his house undecked as a monk's cell, but with a 'pretty contrived garden,' 'all fortified (as you may say) and adorned' with the finest of box hedges. On the other side of the old westward road lies Stourton, home of the Stourtons, of whom Aubrey has a story. The seventh Baron, like the other old peers, envied the upstart Herbert of Wilton, Lord Pembroke, and as he passed Wilton House on his way to or from Salisbury his retainers sounded trumpets and gave 'reproachful challenging words': which was, says Aubrey, 'a relique of knighthood errantry.' This Lord Stourton was executed for murder in 1557. Still farther away from Kilmington, at Gillingham, Edward Davenant, once Vicar, is buried. He lent Aubrey £500 for a year and a half and would take no interest. Christopher Wren said of him that he 'was the best mathematician in the world about thirty or thirty-five years ago.' For a time he was parson also at Poulshot, near Seend. Aubrey's 'most familiar learned acquaintance was Lancelot Morehouse, parson of Pertwood,' which is eight miles east of Kilmington, high up above the old west road, and near the west end of the Great Ridge Wood. He had been curate at Broad Chalk. He wrote against the Vicar of Kilmington's book on the number 666 and was answered 'with some sharpness.' Also he wrote on squaring the circle. It was apropos of Pertwood that Aubrey mentioned the mists on the downs. But Morehouse died at Little Langford on the Wylye whither he was preferred. He left 'his many excellent mathematical notes to his ingenious friend, John Grant, of Hindon,' two miles south of Pertwood. Two miles from Hindon, Christopher Wren was born, in the parsonage at East Knoyle.

These people shared some of Aubrey's tastes, but the greater and better part of his material related to more outstanding men and women, like Philip Sidney and his sister Mary, Countess of Pembroke, at Wilton. There were the Raleighs at Downton, and a portrait of the great Sir Walter 'in a white satin doublet, all embroidered with rich pearls, and a mighty rich chain of pearls about his neck, and the old servants have told me that the pearls were near as big as the painted ones.' At Becket Park, Shrivenham, just over the Berkshire border, in the Vale of White Horse, lived Henry Martin, of whom Aubrey says that he was 'as far from a Puritan as light from darkness'; and that when he had been caught asleep in the House of Commons, and a motion brought that such scandalous members be put out, he said: 'Mr. Speaker, a motion has been to turn out the *Nodders*; I desire the *Noddees* may also be turned out.'

West Lavington was the home of Sir John Danvers, who married Donne's Magdalen Herbert, mother of George Herbert and Lord Herbert of Cherbury. At West Lavington, too, Aubrey 'enjoyed the contentment of solitude' in the Earl of Abingdon's walks and gardens, while he arranged his 'Miscellanies.' The Buttons, with whom he went hunting to Avebury, lived at Tockenham. With their neighbours, the Longs of Draycot Cerne, he stayed frequently when he was homeless. Sir James had been swordsman, horseman, falconer, extemporaneous orator, and naturalist, a Cavalier, but suspected by 'strict' Cavaliers because Cromwell 'fell in love with his company and commanded him to wear his sword, and to meet him a-hawking.' Dorothy, his wife, was 'a most elegant beauty and wit.' From Doll, their daughter, afterwards Lady

Heron, Aubrey quotes the saying that 'Poets and bravos have punks to their mothers,' when he speaks of a love affair of Raleigh's.

Gratitude, hero-worship, curiosity, love-making, and litigation, left Aubrey no time to make more than notes: he could not finish nearly all his sentences. 'While hiding from the bailiffs in 1671 at Broad Chalk,' says his editor, Mr. Andrew Clark, Aubrey began a rustic comedy, the characters ladies and gentlemen, courtly and old-fashioned, drunken and insolent, and sow-gelders, carters, dairymaids, and gipsies, and a clergyman whom James Long had hunted 'dryfoot to the alehouse with his pack of hounds, to the great grief of the revered divine' — 'one of the old red-nosed clergy, orthodox and canonical.' 'In several cases, over the initials of his dramatis personæ, Aubrey has jotted the names or initials of the real persons he was copying.' The scene was to be Christian Malford green, a little east of Draycot Cerne and Kington St. Michael.

But either the bailiffs found him, or he went fishing in the pond where the Chalk Bourn rises. The play was not finished. There were 'no better trouts in the kingdom of England,' said Aubrey, than in his pond at Naule. And off he went to Draycot or Easton. He hoped that some 'public-spirited young Wiltshire man' would polish and complete his 'natural remarques.' Yet he lived to reach seventy-one, having just published his 'Miscellanies,' and dedicated them to the Earl of Abingdon. He died at Oxford on his travels in 1697, and was buried there, in St. Mary Magdalene's Church, undistinguished by tablet or inscription.

*

THE Whites were an Oxfordshire and Hampshire family. Gilbert White's country was the country of his birth, his life, his book, and of his death. He travelled much about Southern England, but always to or from Selborne in Hampshire. Charles II knighted a Sampson White, who was Mayor of Oxford, a mercer and a fool. This Sampson's son, Gilbert, became a Fellow of Magdalen College, Oxford, and, in 1681, Vicar of Selborne, and he left money for the purchase of land of which the rents were partly to supply the Selborne children with instruction in reading, writing, saying prayers, knitting, and sewing, partly to provide for the improvement of Honey Lane, the rocky, hollow lane from Oakhanger to the village. John White, son of this Gilbert, a barrister-at-law and justice of the peace, married a Sussex woman, Anne Holt, and their eldest son, our Gilbert White, was born in his grandfather's house, the Vicarage at Selborne, in 1720. As a child he lived at Compton, near Guildford, and at East Harting in Sussex, and was at Basingstoke Grammar School, and probably also at Farnham Grammar School; but he was only ten when his father settled finally in Selborne at 'The Wakes.' Before he was twelve, he planted an oak and an ash in his father's garden. When he was sixteen he noticed the northward flying of wild-geese on March 31, and the coming of the cuckoo on April 6. As a schoolboy he took to Basingstoke, together with 'The Whole Duty of Man,' Cicero's Letters, Virgil, Homer, Isocrates, Tacitus, Sallust, and other books, a copy of Thomson's 'Seasons.' We, who know what he became, have only these things upon which to feed our fancy about his childhood in remote Selborne, cut off from the world by obscurity and difficult and ill-kept roads.

In 1740 he entered Oriel College. At Oxford he shot, he rode, he listened to music, how much is not known, and he

made a friendship with one John Mulso, an Oriel contempor-
ary, which lasted until 1791. In 1743 he took his bachelor's
degree, but he went up to Oxford again with his dog and his
gun, and in the next year was elected a Fellow of his college.
Mulso writes to him and asks after 'Jenny' and 'the Stam-
fordian,' advises him not to play so much with 'the tangles of
Neæra's hair,' and wants confirmation of the report that he is
to marry. He was frequently going to and fro between Selborne and Oxford. His love of the South Country is clear in
his correspondence. Mulso tells him of the partridges he has
seen when afield, and wishes that White had been there; he
speaks of White's love for 'cool brown days'; and he thinks,
from White's letters describing his travels, that his friend is 'a
great and masterly hand' at landscape-painting in words. 'I
never,' wrote Mulso in one letter – 'I never see a spot which
lies much out of the level but I think of you, and say, "Now
this would please White." ' From the letters of Mulso it is
easy to see that White was a man of original character, with a
humour and a turn of speaking all his own. He was much out
of doors in many parts of England, on visits of business or
friendship and sport in Devon, Northampton, Bedfordshire,
Essex, Kent, Surrey, Sussex, Wiltshire, and Oxfordshire. He
travelled and noticed so much that his friend begged him to
make a useful book out of his observations, and so 'enable
young men to travel with taste and improve at home.' White's
character, as it appeared in his letters and in her brother's talk,
seems to have delighted Hester Mulso, afterwards Mrs.
Chapone, who was seven years younger than he; and Mulso
often mentions her in his letters, playfully and very likely with
a feeling that she might one day marry his friend. The naturalist enjoyed her society, wrote to her, sent his 'Invitation to
Selborne,' but from her playful signature of 'Yes Papa,' and
the tone of Mulso's letter at the time of her marriage with

Chapone, it is almost certain that White had not been deeply moved. His nature, genial, self-centred, slow, perhaps phlegmatic, was not disturbed. His one show of passion came when he said that Pennant did not behave 'like a gentleman.' While still in his youth he was methodical, calm, with a temperament already quite precipitated, it appears. He was minute and business-like, for example, in looking over some family estates in Essex in 1764, just as many years later he was shrewd and hard in writing of a debatable will, by which it was uncertain whether he or a hospital would profit. There is, indeed, a hint of dissatisfaction in Mulso's letter to him saying: 'I sincerely wish you had a living like Deane, and the thorough good sort of *damoiselle* that you mention, that your wishes might be completed'; but certainly he was living within his income, saving and investing.

In 1747 he received deacon's orders and became curate to an uncle at Swanaton, but he was still often at Oriel, where he had small-pox in the same year, and perhaps gave only Sundays to his curacy. In 1751 he was curate to Dr. Bristow, Vicar of Selborne, and the next year Proctor of Oxford University and Dean of Oriel. But a letter from Mulso in 1750 suggests that he was getting tired of Oxford ways, though he was still shooting and sociable.

It was in 1747 that he bought Philip Miller's 'Gardener's Dictionary,' his first purchase of the kind, and in 1751 that he began the 'Garden Kalendar,' a diary of seed-sowing, weather, planting, etc., which he kept going until his death, in this style:

'1759, *May* 1. – Pulled away the hedge round the fir-quincunx, and hoed the ground clean.

'2. – The Hanger out in full leaf; but much banged about by the continual strong east wind that has blown for many days. The buds and blossoms of all trees much injured by the winds. The ground parched and bound very hard. The cold air keeps the nightingale very silent. No vegetation seems to stir at present. Disbudded some of the vines. The buds are about an inch long.

'3. — Made second annual bed with six barrows of grass and weeds only; no dung. Planted out the five hand-glasses with the great white Dutch cucumbers, four plants in a hill. The plants are pretty much drawn. This evening the vehement east wind seems to be abated; and the air is soft and cloudy. Ground bound like a stone.

'4. — Sowed — first, four rows of small dwarf white kidney beans in the lower field garden. Earthed the Cantaleupes [melons sent him by Philip Miller, author of 'The Gardener's Dictionary'] the third time: found all the plants in a very flourishing way, and the fibres extended to the very outsides of the hills. Cut away the plants to one in some of the hills; and left two in some, stopping down the worst plant very short towards the bottom of the runners, for experiment's sake, to see what the small wood about the stems will do. Some of the plants offer for male bloom. Saw first Redstart and Cherry-sucker (Spotted Fly Catcher). Sowed about two dozen of the large white Dutch cucumber seeds for the latter hand-glasses; the first sowing got full tall and big. Delicate soft rain all afternoon and night, which soaked the ground well to the root of all vegetables.'

In 1753 he bought a new edition of Miller, and the 'Methodus Plantarum Nova' of John Ray, and he subscribed towards the making of a zigzag path up Selborne Hanger, and placed the rude stone or obelisk at the upper end. In that year, too, he became curate of Durley, near Bishop's Waltham and Cobbett's Botley, riding for the Sunday service from Selborne; and for a time he was also curate at West Deane, near Salisbury, accepting it, writes Mulso, 'because it was your sentiment that a clergyman should not be idle and unemployed.' He often rode from Deane to Selborne — a fine ride to one with an eye for the downs. At one time he combined the duty at Deane with that of Newton Valence. In 1757 he accepted the living of Moreton Binkey, Hampshire, where he never lived, and, after putting a curate in, derived £30 a year from it; and he exchanged Durley for Faringdon at about the same time. He was still in Oxford now and then, and was in 1757 unsuccessful candidate for the provostship at Oriel.

On the death of his father at this time he was thought a rich man, but his private income did not exceed the sum due from his Fellowship, which he therefore retained: he kept a maid and a man, and now and then employed another hand for gardening. For six months in 1759 – 60 he was away at Lyndon in Rutland with his naturalist brother-in-law, Barker. That was his last long absence from Selborne, where he was now apparently well content to be settled for ever, the only one of his family living there after 1761; and we have a right to assume that he was in a condition to smile cheerfully at Mulso's letter on Hester's marriage in 1761.

'You will give your good wishes that, as they have long wished for this happy state (I don't know whether I speak to be understood by you who continue an old bachelor), they may continue happy in it.'

He seems to have thought of marriage, but without any temptation; his faithful and admirable biographer, Mr. Rashleigh Holt-White, says that the obstacle was the fact that he could not have supported a family without seeking preferment elsewhere and giving up 'The Wakes.' In this present year, 1915, at least, it is hard to find a flaw in the life he led, which we may be excused for looking back upon dotingly as upon some past inaccessible and imperturbable tract of our own life. What satisfaction we must suppose to have been his, in buying now and then small plots of land with which to round off his estate; building a ha-ha, an arbour, a fruit wall, buying a sundial, post and slab and dial, to record the hours of serenity; planting trees against the walls! The names of some of his wall trees survive, as, for example, Sweet-water vine, Mr. Snooke's black-cluster vine, Nobless peach, white Muscadine vine; and of his pears, as, for example, Chaumontelle, Virgoleuse, Brown Bury, St. Germain, Swan's Egg. Year by year he went to Ringmer to stay with his aunt, Mrs. Snooke, always noticing her tortoise. In 1763 'The Wakes' became his own house. It was often full and seldom empty of guests whom he loved, and there is at least one record of a party there which cannot soon be forgotten. A Miss Catherine Battie, a beautiful girl of twenty, who was staying at Selborne in 1763, left a diary of some of her pleasures at 'The Wakes' and in the neighbouring fields. Thus she writes of a dance at White's house:

'The morn was spent at the Harpsichord, a Ball at night, began minuets at half an hour after 7, then danced country dances till near 11, went to supper, after supper sat some time, sung, laught, talked, and then went to dancing again, danced till 3 in the morning, at half an hour after 4 the company all went away; we danced 30.   Never had I such a dance in my life, nor ever shall I have such a one again I believe. . . . [Next day] got up at 10 in very good spirits (who can be otherwise in this dear place?)'

Mr. White, she records, read an acrostic 'made upon Nanny' – i.e. Miss Anna Battie. Again:

'In the evening walked to Noar Hill. Oh sweet evening, sure there never was anything equal to the romantickness of that dear dear hill; never never shall I forget Empshott and the gloomy woods, the distant hills, the South Down, the woody hills on the right hand, the forest, the valleys, oh all are heavenly, almost too much for me to bear, the sight of this beauteous prospect gives one a pleasing melancholy.'

White suggested that the young women should dress as shepherdesses for a dance, and wrote:

> 'Gilbert, a meddling, luckless swain,
>   Must alter ladies' dresses
> To dapper hats and tuck'd up train
>   And flower-enwoven tresses.
> But now the Lout, with loss of heart,
>   Must for his rashness pay;
> He rues for tamp'ring with a dart
>   Too prompt before to slay!'

Reading this diary of a hundred and fifty years ago, and looking at Catherine's portrait, it is hard to believe that she is dead.

In 1769 White bought Hudson's 'Flora Anglica,' and, says his biographer, began the serious study of botany.

In 1767 his 'Garden Kalendar' developed into the elaborate 'Naturalists' Journal,' and he began his correspondence with Thomas Pennant, to whom he was perhaps introduced by his brother, Benjamin White, Pennant's publisher. Two years later he met with Daines Barrington, and began the letters which, with those to Pennant, formed his 'Natural History.' He was writing also to his brother, John White, a naturalist, at Gibraltar, giving him this excellent advice:

'Learn as much as possible *the manners of animals*; they are worth reams of descriptions. Frequent your markets and see what birds are exposed for sale.' Birds, animals, and drawings, came frequently from Gibraltar to Selborne.

As early as 1770 his sight was decaying, but on November

13, 1771, he could yet count sixteen fork-tailed kites together on the downs. Mulso, still writing to him, calls him 'the richest man that I know, for you are the only man of my acquaintance that does not want money.'

Now he is reading 'Tristram Shandy' and now Johnson's 'Hebrides,' and again Boswell. Dryden is for him 'the greatest master of numbers of any of our English bards.' He reads Thomson, who 'falls into fustian sometimes . . . though he thinks like a poet, is often faulty in his diction.' His nephew, the young John White, stays with him, and they read Horace together, finding the Epistles 'a fine body of ethics and very entertaining and sensible.' They never fell out about anything except the quantity of a Latin syllable. Apparently Jack learned from him how to write, for his letters are absurdly like his uncle's in style. He understood the schoolmaster, if he could not have been one himself. 'Unless,' he writes, 'a schoolmaster is somewhat of a pedant, and a little sufficient in his way, he must expect to be soon faded with his drudgery.' With the two friendly families at the vicarages of Selborne and Newton Valence life went very well. As to the world, he says in 1775 that America 'is at present the subject of conversation,' and finds a quotation from Seneca 'prophetic of the discovery of that vast continent,' and he sees soldiers on their way to the war through the Hampshire lanes; but as the journal says in 1776: 'Brother Harry's strong beer which was brewed last Easter Monday with the *hordeum nudum* is now tapped and incomparably good.' And he knew his happiness. 'When the children are buzzing at the spinet,' he writes, 'and we grave folks sit round the chimney, I am put in mind of the following couplet which you will remember:

"All the distant din that world can keep
    Rolls o'er my grotto and improves my sleep." '

He notes the coming of the ring-ousels in September, and he praises the snuff-pincers for extinguishing his candles 'in a very neat manner.' He builds a new Hermitage on the hill. He adds a new parlour to his house and buys 'long annuities.' He rejoices, in 1777, that he can at last purchase 'the field behind his house, that *angulus iste* which the family have so long desired.' He weighs the tortoise at Ringmer, and notices the increase of an ounce in its weight. Even in London he keeps up his journal, noticing, in 1785, two martins and a swift in Fleet Street, and hearing owls and a green woodpecker at Vauxhall. In 1780 his aunt, Mrs. Snooke, died, and he received from her a farm and the old tortoise, Timothy. That year he reached 'with only one infirmity,' deafness. His income was about £100 from inherited property, and sometimes as much as £150 from his Fellowship. He puts Timothy into a tub of water, and finds him 'quite out of his element and much dismayed'; he addresses him through a speaking-tube without effect. He makes a gentle sloping path up the Hanger called the Bostal, instead of the steep zigzag; but there is 'a junto of Zigzaggians' among the neighbours. Though deaf, he can still enjoy hearing his nieces play jigs and minuets that run importunately in his head of a morning. He still goes to Oxford for an election now and then. He sends out verses about crocuses and about wasps in treacle. He plants mullein and foxgloves from the Hanger in his garden, and sows beech-mast in the hedges and bare parts of the down. He writes how his hepaticas do and his Persian iris, and what he adds to his borders, and when the first blackcap came, and how late the swifts have young. He is careful about the state of the roads — roads which in Cobbett's day were the worst in the world — and it is a legend that when children saw him coming they began to put stones in the ruts and got pennies for their diligence. As late as 1786 he is 'in a sad fright, having no silk breeches and stockings to make a wedding visit in.' In 1788 he is proud that his nephews and nieces number fifty-one.

At last, in 1789, his book was published. As early as 1776 Mulso had written with remarkable foresight:

'Your work upon the whole will immortalize your place of abode as well as yourself. . . . No man communicates the pleasure of his excursions, or makes the world partake of them, in a more useful manner than you do.'

He had, in fact, made a book which had three extraordinary merits. It contained valuable and new observations; it over-flowed with evidence of a new spirit – a spirit of minute and even loving inquiry into the life and personality of animals in their native surroundings – that was coming into natural history; and, thirdly, it had style or whatever we like to call the breath of life in written words, and it was delightfully and easily full of the man himself and of the delicate eighteenth-century southern countryside which he knew. But the observations are no longer new; the new spirit has been renovated by the gunless naturalists from Thoreau to Mr. W. H. Hudson of our own day. The man himself is still fresh to succeeding generations, and thousands, who care not at all how many willow-wrens there be, delight to read these letters from a man so happy and remote from our time that he thought the dying fall of the true willow-wren 'a joyous easy laughing note.' We are always pleasantly conscious of the man in his style, which strikes us as the lines and motions of a person's face strike us for good or for bad, and, even so, in a manner that defies analysis. His quack who ate a toad, his boys twisting the nests out of rabbit-holes with a forked stick, his love of the 'shapely-figured aspect of the chalk hills' above that of the 'abrupt and shapeless' mountains, his swallows feeding their young and treading on the wing, his friendly horse and fowl, his prodigious many-littered half-bred bantam sow that proved, 'when fat, good bacon, juicy and tender,' his honey-loving idiot, his crickets ('a good Christmas fire is to them like the heats of the dog-days') — these things have in his pages a value which can only be attributed to his literary genius, by which his book survives.

In 1790 he records how the trees which he planted have grown: the oak of 1731 is 4 feet 5 inches in circumference; the ash of the same year is 4 feet 6½ inches; the spruce of 1751 is 5 feet, the beech 4 feet; the elm of 1750 is 5 feet 3 inches; the lime of 1756 is 5 feet 5 inches. In 1793 he 'made rhubard tarts and a rhubard pudding which was very good'; but a bad nervous cough and a wandering gout made him languid and indolent; he suffered much pain; and on June 26, after his bed had been moved into the old family parlour at the back of his house, so that the Hanger was in sight, he died.

WILLIAM COBBETT

*

THERE is no doubt about Cobbett's country. His grandfather, George Cobbett, a labourer all his days in that neighbourhood, lies in the churchyard at Farnham in Surrey, near the Hampshire border. His father, also George Cobbett, was farmer and innkeeper, and at the inn, 'The Jolly Farmer,' beside the Wey in Farnham, William Cobbett was born in 1763, and lived for twenty years. To-day his name is as conspicuous outside the inn as if he were a brewer.

Soon after he could walk he began to work for his father in the fields. He scared birds, weeded the wheat, led a single horse harrowing barley, hoed peas, and finally reaped and drove the plough, so that when he was twelve, and his eldest brother fifteen, his father said that the three boys 'did as much work as any three men in the parish of Farnham.' Those, he said afterwards, were happy days. Other kinds of happy days he had also. For example, he and his brothers used to roll down the sand-hills at the Bourn, to the south of Farnham, and this he considered a better education than he could have got at Winchester or Westminster. He used to steal magpies' eggs on Crooksbury Hill. At Waverley Abbey, too, he used to eat fruit as he pleased out of the kitchen-garden where he was supposed to work. The hounds after a hare near Waverley, when he was eight, made one of his immortal memories. But bird-scaring was the thing, and when he saw the pale-faced children in school in Ireland, with not so much red in all their faces as a little round-faced bird-scarer he knew, he exclaimed that 'that little chap, with his satchel full of bread and cheese or bacon, he was at the *proper school.*' He began to travel early. While he was weeding at Farnham Castle, he got such an idea of Kew Gardens from the gardener, his master, that next day he walked to Kew, and for a time worked there. Also, when he was thirteen, he accompanied his father

115

to the hop-fair at Weyhill, which lies a couple of days distant westward, along one of the old roads of England, the Harrow way. At nineteen he first saw the sea, from the top of Ports-down, and the sight of the fleet riding at anchor at Spithead, though it did not make him a sailor, spoilt him, so he said, for a farmer. Next year he enlisted, and did not see England again till 1800.

He remained a lover of Surrey and Hampshire, and of what he saw there as a child. His own education there was the best education. He professed to believe that the *facilities of moving human bodies from place to place,*' which had improved so much since he walked to Kew, were 'among the *curses* of the coun-try, the destroyers of industry, of morals, and, of course, of happiness.' The labourers' cottage gardens delighted him; he called them an honour to England, 'which distinguishes it from all the rest of the world.' He admired those who could neither read nor write, but could bake and brew. And he laid it down that, 'when people are uncorrupted, they always like home best, be it in itself what it may.'

His next country home was Botley, between Bishop's Wal-tham and Southampton, and at that time, in 1805, 'through Farnham, Alton, and Bishop's Waltham, a short day's jour-ney, being barely sixty-eight miles,' from London. There he had four farms; the principal one being Fairthorn, and, since the soil was good and the neighbourhood lacked workhouse, barber, attorney, justices of the peace, and volunteers, he thought it the most delightful in the world. He began at once to plant trees, and to work, so far as a journalist could, at those country labours which he considered innocent, 'instructive in their very nature,' and healthful, while reading about them took the place in his home of 'the card-table, the dice-box, the chess-board, and the lounging bottle.' In the River Hamble he caught fish. For the benefit of the nation he promoted singlestick matches. His children 'learned to ride, and hunt, and shoot, and fish, and look after cattle and sheep, and to work in the garden, and to feed his dogs, and to go from village to village in the dark.' The one who was first downstairs in the morning 'was called the Lark for the day, and had, amongst other indulgences, the pretty privilege of making his mother's nosegay and that of any lady visitors.' Once at Alton, with twenty-three miles to go, he insisted on getting home, though it was eleven o'clock and he had dined. In spite of his companion, he knew that Mrs. Cobbett would be up expecting him, and she was, 'and had a nice fire for us to sit down at.' They lived well. 'Everything was in accordance with the largest idea of a great English yeoman of the old time. Everything was excellent, everything abundant – all served with the greatest nicety by trim waiting-damsels.' The estate increased, and one of his excuses for a new purchase was that to buy standing trees at a shilling or half a crown apiece, which will be worth three pounds in twenty years, 'is the best way of insuring a fortune for children.' But his imprisonment in 1810 for the article on the Local Militia and German Legion ruined the farm. The children sent letters and bluebells to the King's Bench, and kept a 'journal of labours' at Botley; one or two of them were always with him in the prison, and by means of their letters and drawings their education was advanced. But the farm suffered. He was imprisoned for debt in 1816. In 1820 he was bankrupt, and Botley was sold. His next holding was but four acres at Kensington for a seed-farm – 'quite enough,' wrote his daughter, 'for papa's amusement, though not sufficient to drag him into any great expenses.'

Kensington was the starting-point of his Rural Rides during the next ten years. The narratives were written down wherever he might be at the day's end. For he had, in spite of himself, become a traveller. His 'Cottage Economy' was written at Worth Lodge in Sussex; 'Cobbett's Poor Man's Friend,' at Uphusband, in his friend Blount's house, and at the inn at Everley, between Ludgershall and Upavon.

Politics gave him the excuse for his rides. He never could travel without an object. 'I never,' said he, *went a-walking in the whole course of my life, never went to walk without having some object in view other than the walk.*' That he loved travel is clear. At Everley, for example, on his way from Burghclere to Petersfield, he remarks: 'There is no pleasure in travelling, except on horseback or on foot. Carriages take your body from place to place, and if you merely want to be *conveyed* they are very good; but they enable you to see and to know nothing at all of the country.' On the other hand, he liked to feel that the rides brought him substantial advantages. It was not enough to see a great deal of the country, to have a great deal of sport, and to lay in 'a stock of health for the winter, sufficient to enable us to withstand the suffocation of this smoking and stinking Wen.' So he must teach his son Richard arithmetic as they journeyed.

Luckily, Cobbett had learnt to regard sport as a serious thing. When he praised Long Island, he began: 'Think of it – a hundred brace of woodcocks a day! Think of *that*! And never to see the hang-dog face of a tax-gatherer. Think of that! . . .' And not only shooting the edible. He liked coursing. It was an element in that 'real down-country' at Everley, 'from two to three miles for the hare to run to cover, and not a stone nor a bush nor a hillock.' Remember also the day's hare-hunting which he writes of at Old Hall, in Herefordshire, or, if you do not remember, read it here. It was on the first of his rides, in November, 1821:

'A whole day most delightfully passed a-hare-hunting, with a pretty pack of hounds kept here by Messrs. Palmer. They

put me upon a horse that seemed to have been made on purpose for me, strong, tall, gentle, and bold, and that carried me
either over or through everything. I, who am just the weight
of a four-bushel sack of good wheat, actually sat on his back
from daylight in the morning to dusk (about nine hours), without once setting my foot on the ground. Our ground was at
Orcop, a place about four miles' distance from this place. We
found a hare in a few minutes after throwing off; and in the
course of the day we had to find four, and were never more than
ten minutes in the finding. A steep and naked ridge, lying
between two flat valleys, having a mixture of pretty large
fields and small woods, formed our ground. The hares crossed
the ridge forward and backward, and gave us numerous views
and very fine sport. I never rode on such steep ground before;
and, really, in going up and down some of the craggy places,
where the rains had washed the earth from the rocks, I did
think once or twice of my neck, and how Sidmouth would
like to see me. As to the *cruelty*, as some pretend, of this sport,
that point I have, I think, settled, in one of the chapters of my
"Year's Residence in America." As to the expense, a pack,
even a full pack of harriers like this, costs less than two bottles
of wine a day, with their inseparable concomitants. And as to
the *time* thus spent, hunting is inseparable from *early rising*;
and, with habits of early rising, whoever wanted time for any
business?'

Sport probably did much to preserve and cherish the happier, freer side of his hard practical nature. Without sport he
would have said that the veal and lamb was 'so exceedingly
beautiful' he could hardly believe his eyes, but would have
been less likely to say, when he saw those borders by the
ploughed fields in Hertfordshire left to bear grass: 'This is
most beautiful! The hedges are now full of the shepherd's-

rose, honeysuckles, and all sorts of wild-flowers; so that you are upon a grass walk, with this most beautiful of all flower-gardens and shrubberies on your one hand, and with the corn on the other.' That was on the way to Chesham. He had started at four on June 24, and how sweet those flowers are, woven into a style that has flowers of no other kind! His landscapes make most others look sentimental or fanciful, or taken from pictures or books. Not for nothing had he that ancestry. You seem to feel the two old Georges, father and grandfather, as he looks from Birdlip Hill to 'the Morvan Hills in Wales,' and over that dish with Gloucester in the centre – 'All here is fine: fine farms, fine pastures; all enclosed fields, all divided by hedges; orchards a plenty.' And how you taste the November morning when he begins: 'Started at daybreak in a hazy frost for Reading. The horses' manes and ears covered with the hoar before we got across Windsor Park.'

The downs, above all, were Cobbett's country, the downs of Hampshire and Wiltshire. This is the classic passage written on November 11, 1822, at Uphusband or Hurstbourn Tarrant:

'Uphusband *once more*, and, for the sixth time this year, over the North Hampshire hills, which, notwithstanding their everlasting flints, I like very much. As you ride along, even in a *green lane*, the horses' feet make a noise like *hammering*. It seems as if you were riding on a mass of iron. Yet the soil is good, and bears some of the best wheat in England. All these high, and, indeed, all chalky lands, are excellent for sheep. But on the top of some of these hills there are as fine meadows as I ever saw. Pasture richer, perhaps, than that about Swindon, in the North of Wiltshire. . . .'

Better still he liked coming down from the chalk hills to one of the little rivers – the Itchen, the Bourn, the

Test, the Avon. His enthusiasm was great when he first caught sight of the upper valley of the Wiltshire Avon. He sat on his horse to look over Milton and Easton and Pewsey for half an hour, though he had not breakfasted. That was in late August. But the 'brightest and most beautiful' spot of all was between Heytesbury and Warminster in Wiltshire:

'For there is, as appertaining to rural objects, *everything* that *I delight* in. Smooth and verdant downs in hills and valleys of endless variety as to height, depth, and shape; rich cornland, unencumbered by fences; meadows in due proportion, and those watered at pleasure; and, lastly, the homesteads and villages, sheltered in winter, and shaded in summer by lofty and beautiful trees; to which may be added roads never dirty and a stream never dry.'

Nor is his sense of beauty always based, either consciously or unconsciously, on what he feels or knows, and his ancestors before him, to be useful and habitable. As he looked over the rich land near Sittingbourne which lacked trees he admired it, and declared at the same time: 'That I, a million times to one, prefer, as a spot to *live on*, the heaths, the miry coppices, the wild woods and the forests, of Sussex and Hampshire.' Between Farnham, Weyhill, and Botley, was the best of his England. You see it when he comes upon those contemptible bean-fed pigs going to Highworth Market in Wiltshire. Whey and beans, says he, make 'excellent pork for the Londoners, but which must meet with a pretty hungry stomach to swallow it in Hampshire,' and he proceeds to speak of a hog belonging to Mr. Blount at Uphusband, 'which now weighs about thirty score, and will possibly weigh forty, for she moves about very easily yet.'

When at last Cobbett moved out again on to a farm in the

country, it was to Ash in Surrey. He held Normandy Farm there from 1831 to his death in 1835. Thus he had but a few miles to be carried to lie in Farnham Churchyard, beside his father and grandfather, opposite the church door.

*

THE history of William Hazlitt, who wrote 'On Going a Journey,' resembles at certain points that of Borrow. Borrow's father was a Cornishman who married a Norfolk lady. Hazlitt's father came from near Tipperary, and married Grace Loftus, daughter of an ironmonger at Wisbech, Cambridge-shire. Borrow's father was a soldier, continually moving from camp to camp across England, Scotland, and Ireland. Hazlitt's father was a Unitarian minister, who moved much over the face of the globe and over both hemispheres. William Hazlitt, the essayist, was born at Maidstone in 1778. In 1780 the family were in Ireland again, at Bandon. In 1783 they emigrated to America, and spent four years at Philadelphia, and at Weymouth and Upper Dorchester, both in the neigh-bourhood of Boston. Returning to England in 1787, they stopped for several months in London before going to Wem in Shropshire. There Hazlitt dwelt fourteen years, with an in-terlude of a year at Hackney Theological College in 1793, when his elder brother John had a studio at Long-acre. At Wem he read, and in the surrounding country he both walked and read. Some of his journeys are famous. There were four in 1798 alone. In January he walked over to hear Coleridge preaching at Shrewsbury to a Unitarian congregation; a few days later he walked back along the same road with Coleridge, who had come over to Wem to see the elder Hazlitt. 'If I had the quaint muse of Sir Philip Sidney to assist me, I would write a "Sonnet to the Road between Wem and Shrewsbury," and immortalize every step of it by some fond enigmatical con-ceit.' Then Coleridge invited him to Nether Stowey. *I was to visit Coleridge in the spring.* This circumstance was never absent from my thoughts, and mingled with all my feelings.' He prepared himself by a walk to the Vale of Llangollen and back again, thus initiating himself 'in the mysteries of natural scenery,' and he was enchanted; 'that valley was to me (in a manner) the cradle of a new existence: in the river that winds through it, my spirit was baptized in the waters of Helicon.' Finally he walked down through Worcester, Gloucester, Upton ('where I thought of Tom Jones and the adventure of the muff'), and Tewkesbury (where he arrived wet, and 'sat up all night to read "Paul and Virginia." Sweet were the showers in early youth that drenched my body, and sweet the drops of pity that fell upon the books I read'), and Bridgwater (where he stopped two days and, growing tired of the river, read 'Camilla'). Coleridge and he made an excursion through Minehead to Lynton, and on Hazlitt's homeward journey shared the road from Bridgwater to Bristol. At another time Hazlitt walked across England to Wisbech to see his mother's birthplace. He walked also to see picture-galleries. Probably he had a real need to walk as a relief from seclusion among books at Wem, and the reading of Rousseau's 'Confessions' (he gave two years to the 'Confessions' and 'La Nouvelle Héloïse,' and called them the happiest years of his life), and walking as Rousseau walked, might well have turned the need into a semi-heroic delight, he being then eighteen.

Hazlitt's youth at Wem was terminated by a stay of four months in Paris in 1802, where he copied Titian's pictures at the Louvre. Then in 1803–1805 he went about England painting portraits – Coleridge's, Wordsworth's, Hartley Coleridge's, among others.

Before this Hazlitt had really become in a sense a Londoner. Through his brother John and Coleridge he met the men who wrote, from Charles Lamb down to William Godwin. Books and bookish company, and writing, especially for a living, can turn any man into a Londoner, and Hazlitt visited London very often for a poor man living in Shropshire.

In 1808 he gained a new country connexion, by marrying

Sarah Stoddart, who owned some cottages in Hampshire.
There, at Winterslow, the Hazlitts had their abode until
1812. There two children were born, the second alone sur-
viving. There they were visited by Charles and Mary Lamb.
In 1812 Hazlitt and his wife and son went to live at 19, York
Street, Westminster, which Milton had inhabited from 1652
to 1658. Hazlitt worked as dramatic critic, Parliamentary
reporter, lecturer, and contributor to newspapers and magazines. He is said never to have read a book through after he
was thirty. To make up for the lack of opportunity and excuse for walking, he played racquets. But he had intervals in
his work. Thus, in 1823 he ran up to Edinburgh to be
divorced, life with Mrs. Hazlitt having been uncomfortable
for some time, even before the love affair with Sarah Walker
which he embalmed in 'Liber Amoris.' Also, in the following
year, he married a second wife and took the journey through
France and Italy, of which he made a book. The lady preferred to remain behind in Switzerland. They never met again.

Hazlitt, however, was attached to Winterslow by other ties
than marriage. His son has told us that he was attracted by
the woods of Tytherleigh and the friendship of Mr. Baring
Wall, owner of Norman Court – by Clarendon Wood – by
Stonehenge – and by 'the thorough quiet of the place, the sole
interruption of which was the passage, to and fro, of the London mails.' His lodging was at Winterslow Hut, an old inn,
now called 'The Pheasant,' standing seven miles out of Salisbury, on the road to Andover, or about a mile before the road
to Stockbridge and Winchester branches out. 'It was there,'
says the son, 'that most of his thinking was done.' He wrote
there, I believe, the 'Life of Napoleon.' One of the best collec-
tions of his essays, posthumously made, was named after the
place, so that 'Winterslow' has come to seem a romantic
invention, and by association appropriate to Hazlitt.

'I have never had a watch,' says he in the essay 'On a Sun-dial,' 'nor any other mode of keeping time, in my possession, nor ever wish to learn how time goes. It is a sign I have had little to do, few avocations, few engagements. When I am in town, I can hear the clock; and when I am in the country, I can listen to the silence. What I like best is to lie whole mornings on a sunny bank on Salisbury Plain, without any object before me, neither knowing nor caring how time passes, and thus "with light-winged toys of feathered idleness" to melt down hours to moments. Perhaps some such thoughts as I have here set down float before me like motes before my half-shut eyes, or some vivid image of the past by forcible contrast rushes by me – "Diana and her fawn, and all the glories of the antique world"; then I start away to prevent the iron from entering my soul, and let fall some tears into that stream of time which separates me farther and farther from all I once loved! At length I rouse myself from my reverie, and home to dinner, proud of killing time with thought – nay, even without thought.'

Hazlitt makes a very great deal, when he is writing about the country, out of books and out of himself seen far off in time and space, rather like a character in fiction. He does not de-scribe much or distinguish nicely between places. Nor does he communicate a sense of happy travel or travel at all, but of a man looking back at it. He loved looking back. In the essay just quoted, church bells bring Rousseau's 'Confessions' into his mind, and the curfew, 'a great favourite with me,' reminds him of his boyhood: 'I used to hear it when a boy. It tells a tale of other times. The days that are past, the generations that are gone, the tangled forest glades and hamlets brown of my native country, the woodman's art, the Norman warrior armed for the battle or in his festive hall, the Conqueror's iron rule and peasant's lamp extinguished, all start up at the clamorous peal, and fill my mind with fear and wonder. I confess, nothing at present interests me but what has been – the recollection of the impressions of my early life, or events long past. . . .' His England is compounded chiefly out of books and early memories. You see in his essay called 'Merry England' what a part literature and art and history have played in making Hazlitt's England. And he has said himself, in an essay 'On the Love of the Country,' that association accounts chiefly for our pleasure – for his pleasure – in the country. 'It is not,' he says, 'the beautiful and magnificent alone that we admire in Nature; the most insignificant and the rudest objects are often found connected with the strongest emotions; we become attached to the most common and familiar images, as to the face of a friend whom we have long known, and from whom we have received many benefits. It is because natural objects have been associated with the sports of our childhood, with air and exercise, with our feelings in solitude, when the mind takes the strongest hold of things, and clings with the fondest interest to whatever strikes its attention; with change of place, the pursuit of new scenes, and thoughts of distant friends. . . .' 'To be young,' he says in the essay 'On the Feeling of Immortality in Youth' – 'to be young is to be as one of the immortals,' and that great and long sentence about the pageant of 'brave sublunary things' opens with: 'To see the golden sun, the azure sky, the outstretched ocean; to walk upon the green earth, and be lord of a thousand creatures; to look down yawning precipices or over distant sunny vales . . .'

And nevertheless it is a glorious idea of the earth rather than the earth itself, Wem, or Llangollen, or the Quantocks, or Salisbury Plain, that seems to inspire Hazlitt. The earth has perhaps passed into the face of his writing, but we cannot

say how or where. And he certainly has no country to be
associated with him for any other reason than that he lived in
it, walked to and fro in it, and occasionally wrote about it with
gusto.

In the essay 'On Going a Journey,' Hazlitt says: 'I go out
of town in order to forget the town and all that is in it.' The
country was a temporary delight and a luxury. London was
the fixed necessity, and inside it the epicurean cried out: 'Give
me the clear blue sky over my head, and the green turf beneath my feet, a winding road before me, and a three hours'
march to dinner — and then to thinking!' In the country he
was often thinking his best. 'It is hard,' he says, 'if I cannot
start some game on these lone heaths,' or 'there was no question in metaphysics I could not bandy to and fro for twenty,
thirty, forty miles of the Great North Road, and at it again
the next day as fresh as ever.' His towns are more particularly described and suggested than his country. He understood
what he was looking at in London, whereas in the country
perhaps he saw chiefly landscape and the mysterious mutipli-
cation of mutton and turnips. For example, the garden of the
Tuileries suggested to him perversely this passage of local
patriotism: 'For a real West End, for a substantial *cut* into the
heart of a metropolis, commend me to the streets and squares
on each side of the top of Oxford Street, with Grosvenor and
Portman Squares at one end, and Cavendish and Hanover at
the other, linked together by Bruton, South Audley, and a
hundred other fine old streets, with a broad, airy pavement, a
display of comfort, of wealth, of taste and rank, all about you,
each house seeming to have been the residence of some
respectable old English family for half a century past, and
with Portland Place looking out towards Hampstead and
Highgate, with their hanging gardens and lofty terraces, and
Primrose Hill nestling beneath them, in green, pastoral

luxury, the delight of the Cockneys, the aversion of Sir Walter and his merry men.' He himself lived as a bachelor in Down Street and in Half-Moon Street, but later, when he was less prosperous, in Bouverie Street, and finally at 6, Frith Street, Soho, whence in 1830 he was borne to St. Anne's Church, hard by, to be buried.

*

THE author of 'The Amateur Poacher,' 'The Story of my Heart,' 'The Dewy Morn,' and 'Amaryllis at the Fair,' has his domain in a very special sense. He was born and bred and lived the greater part of his life in the country where his ancestors for generations had been born, bred, and buried; and when he wrote most of his books, he either made this country his subject-matter or his setting. In 'The Gamekeeper at Home,' 'The Amateur Poacher,' 'Round about a Great Estate,' 'Toilers of the Field,' 'Hodge and his Masters,' 'The Dewy Morn,' 'The Story of my Heart,' and in passages and essays in most of his other books, he described this country intimately, either for its own sake or because he could not uncover his soul without it. He knew it so well from childish rambles, long walks as sportsman, naturalist, and reporter, and loiterings as lover and philosopher, that it became a portion of himself, as if he had partly created it, as in fact he did. If we walk from Swindon to Marlborough, Devizes, Calne, or Wootton Bassett, after reading Jefferies, we do not see the same country as if we were ignorant of him. So well did he know it that he practically never mentions any part of it by name, and then usually by a fictitious name. He was creating, not referring to places well known, or which people might visit for verification; and to understand his best books it is by no means necessary to go and look at Coate Farm, where he was born in 1848, and Coate Reservoir, where he fished and boated, and Liddington Castle on Liddington Hill, where he used to go to be alone with the sun and his own soul, and all the downland southward to Savernake Forest and westward to Avebury and Devizes. 'The Amateur Poacher' is complete in itself, and lives without aid from gossip and topography. There is no need to know that Jefferies was drawing upon his youth and boy-

hood at Coate. When towards his thirtieth year Jefferies had
to leave Wiltshire for the neighbourhood of London, he began
at once to use his enormous material freely, easily, and happily, in making 'The Amateur Poacher' and the other early
books. Then he turned his attention to the Surrey country
round about his home at Tolworth, Surbiton, and afterwards
to the neighbourhoods of Eltham, West Brighton, and Crowborough, where he spent parts of his invalid life. He now used
place-names freely, for he was writing as a journalist for a
London newspaper public, and he was writing about places to
which he was mainly but a visitor, so that his work was description pure and simple, not creation. Some excellent essays
he did of a creative kind founded on those later lands of
sojourn, as well as written there. Such, for example, are
'Hours of Spring' and 'The Winds of Heaven' in 'Field and
Hedgerow.' But although all his best work was written away
from Wiltshire, when he had left it for ever, most of it was
somehow connected with Wiltshire.

Jefferies is a great Wiltshire name, and the parish registers
of Chisledon and of Holyrood, old Swindon, are full of them.
They were farmers and labourers who intermarried with the
other Wiltshire families of similar estate – the Reeveses, Har-
veys, Garlicks, Jeroms, Chowleses, Nashes, and so on.
Richard's great-grandfather was born about 1734 at Draycot
Foliat, where the road from Swindon to Marlborough pierces
the downs, married Fanny Luckett of Lechlade, and lived for
some time at Rodbourne Cheney, before he purchased Coate
Farm and a mill and bakery at Swindon in 1800. Richard's
grandfather, John Jefferies, worked for a time with a Fleet
Street printer before he came to the bakery at Swindon; and
in London he married a wife, Fanny Ridger, and his eldest
son, James Luckett Jefferies, was born. This was Richard's
father, who spent some time in America before settling at

Coate Farm, with a town-bred wife, Elizabeth Gyde. The Gydes were from Painswick, near Stroud in Gloucestershire. Father and mother appear, fictitiously handled, in 'Amaryllis at the Fair.' Jefferies of an earlier day are alluded to in 'Saint Guido'and 'The Amateur Poacher'; they lie buried at Chisledon, where Richard Jefferies was married.

Coate Farm – forty acres of rich meadow-land and a little house at the beginning of the village street, looking south towards the line of naked downs, north to Swindon and the low dairy lands of North Wiltshire – was all of old Richard's property that came to young Richard's father. Born in this little house in 1848, Jefferies dwelt there for the most part until his marriage. Gradually he extended his curiosity and pleasure over more and more of the surrounding country. His first childish games in the garden and home fields are imaginatively recorded in 'Wood Magic.' Later he had the use of a gun in the fields and a rod on the reservoir; his adventures are treated with different degrees of heightening in 'The Amateur Poacher,' 'Bevis,' and 'After London.' As sportsman and naturalist he wandered through Burderop Woods, on the downs, and to Savernake Forest. As journalist he travelled to the towns within a radius of fifteen miles from Swindon – to Hungerford, Marlborough, Devizes, Calne, Wootton Bassett, Malmesbury, Highworth, Wantage, and Lambourn. He became antiquarian, and made the acquaintance of farmers, parsons, and country gentlemen. At police-courts, inns, and markets, and in the woods, he met characters of all sorts, picked up information about country crafts and the history and legend of the district. He kept notebooks and stored his memory. He wrote a history of the principal family, the Goddards. He contributed archæological and descriptive articles on the towns, famous houses, and churches, that he knew. Though he was never a practical farmer, he knew the men, the occupations, and the movements, of the district. The Great Western Railway works at Swindon were the subject of a masterly informative sketch. Besides being an observer, he was a dreamer and a thinker, and had his places for rapture and meditation in the fields and on the downs. His wife came to him from a neighbouring farm, one of the fields of which gave its title to his fiction 'Green Ferne Farm.'

The family lived at Coate with difficulties and dissensions: they were poor and they were dissatisfied. The house itself appears again and again, clad in thatch, now long since supplanted by slates, in 'Wild Life in a Southern County,' with the village of Coate, the reservoir, Burderop Woods, and Marlborough Forest, and the villages of Broad Hinton, Bishopston, Aldbourne, etc.; it reappears more vividly in 'The Amateur Poacher,' so that no one who has read that book as a boy forgets the stuffed fox grinning up in the garret; the garret itself, the old pistols, Cromwellian cannon-ball, and legendary skeleton; the perch-fishing in the reservoir; the gun, the gun! and Jefferies and the innkeeper's son, Dickon, coursing on the downs:

'Just at the foot of the hill the grass is tall and grey; there, too, are the dead dry stalks of many plants that cultivation has driven from the ploughed fields, and that find a refuge at the edge. A hare starts from the verge and makes up the downs. Dickon slips the hounds, and a faint halloo comes from the shepherds and ploughmen. It is a beautiful sight to see the hounds bound over the sward; the sinewy back bends like a bow, but a bow that, instead of an arrow, shoots itself; the deep chests drink the air. Is there any moment as joyful in life as the second when the chase begins? . . .'

'Round about a Great Estate' is a half-idyllic handling of some of the same material, with much that came from the

133

memories of older people, his father and grandfather, the farmers and keepers of the countryside. Hilary Luckett is a character founded probably on his father and his wife's father, Andrew Baden of Day House Farm. The others are more or less certainly to be identified if you wish. The local lore, the works and days of Hilary, the beauty of Cicely, the dairy, the meadows, and the woods, make up one of the most delicious rustic books in the world.

Here Jefferies was beginning to be freer and more masterly with his material. 'The Poacher' and 'Round about a Great Estate' are very good of their kind. In future he was to make little use of Wiltshire notebooks, but great use of imaginative memories of Wiltshire. The reservoir reappears in the fiction of 'Bevis' and, as a great inland sea, in 'After London.' The grand armies of the rooks and wood-pigeons in 'Wood Magic' were bred in Burderop Woods, the 'Okebourne Chace' of 'Round about a Great Estate.' Had he lost his sight after leaving Wiltshire, his best books would have been very much as they are now. As a naturalist, he wrote in 'The Life of the Fields': 'There have been few things I have read of or studied which in some manner or other I have not seen illustrated in this county while out in the fields.' And so, as an autobiographical artist, he tells us that his native downs and a clear spring of water somewhere amongst them helped him to his illumination: 'So many times I came to it [the spring], toiling up the long and shadowless hill in the burning sunshine, often carrying a vessel to take some of it home with me. There was a brook, indeed; but this was different, it was the spring; it was taken home as a beautiful flower might be brought. It is not the physical water; it is the sense of feeling that it conveys. Nor is it the physical sunshine; it is the sense of inexpressible beauty which it brings with it. Of such I still drink, and hope to do so still deeper.' The best things in his poor novels are when he depends on his knowledge of North Wiltshire and his personal experiences out of doors. The beautiful girl in 'Restless Human Hearts,' who fancied that as she lay on the sward she could hear the world's heart beating, foretells Amaryllis and the Felise of 'The Dewy Morn.' In 'World's End,' the hero, like Jefferies, wires ground game, and by selling it to the carrier is enabled to buy the works of poets, philosophers, historians, and scientists.

Jefferies' residence at Tolworth, Surbiton, from 1877 to 1882, introduced him to Hook, Chessington, Claygate, the Hogsmill river, and all the country of 'Nature near London.' He was astonished and delighted by the richness of the bird-life. He made pilgrimages daily to the same place as he did at home — 'to an aspen by a brook,' probably the Hogsmill, in Surrey, as to Liddington Castle, in Wiltshire. In 'Woodlands' he describes Woodstock Lane from Long Ditton to Claygate, and Prince's Lane and Prince's Covers; Thames Ditton in 'The Modern Thames'; the Hogsmill at Tolworth Court Farm in 'A Brook,' and 'A London Trout'; and so on. For the most part Jefferies was hastily providing information straight from notebooks. But here at Tolworth he must have written all his early country books — 'The Gamekeeper,' 'Wild Life,' 'The Poacher,' 'Round about a Great Estate,' and 'Hodge and his Masters.' Here began the series of diseases which destroyed him.

He never stayed long anywhere after he left Surbiton. The summer of 1882 was spent partly on Exmoor, whence came the material of 'Red Deer' and some of the essays in 'The Life of the Fields' and 'Field and Hedgerow.' By the end of the year he was at 'Savernake,' Lorna Road, West Brighton, at the edge of a noble down country, which he had visited as a child and later. We know, for example, that he had made some of the first notes for 'The Story of my Heart' at Pevensey in 1880.

The addition of the sea to the downs did for him all that could be done for him without restoring him to youth and Wiltshire. The last essays of 'Nature near London' show his delight at Beachy Head, in the waves coming round the promontory before a west wind, which 'give the idea of a flowing stream, as they did in Homer's day' — nay! his delight, in the railway-train, at the sight of Ditchling Beacon: 'Hope dwells there somewhere, mayhap in the breeze, on the sward, or the pale cups of the harebells.' In spite of ill-health, he got to know the whole range of the South Downs.

'The Story of my Heart' was written chiefly at Brighton, and the book is full of Sussex sea as well as of Wiltshire downs. 'The Dewy Morn' as we know it was probably also written at Brighton, rather after than before 'The Story of my Heart'; so, too, were 'Red Deer,' 'After London' probably, some of the essays of 'The Open Air' and 'The Life of the Fields.'

Jefferies was still at Brighton in June, 1884; in September of that year he wrote from 14, Victoria Road, Eltham. By June, 1885, he was lodging at 'Rehoboth Villa,' Jarvis Brook, Rotherfield, while he sought a cottage at Tunbridge Wells. He settled instead at 'The Downs,' Crowborough, for about a year, until the summer of 1886. Some of his essays — for example, the last four in 'The Open Air' — are recognizable as connected with Eltham. At Crowborough he wrote some of the ripest descriptions and meditations in 'Field and Hedgerow,' and perhaps 'Amaryllis at the Fair,' which was finished by May, 1886, and in one place seems to reflect the ill winter of 1885–86. His last work of all, including the introduction to 'The Natural History of Selborne' (Scott Library), and perhaps 'My Old Village,' was done at 'Sea View,' Goring, Sussex, where he was to die in August, 1887.

Though he never lived in London, Jefferies became no inconsiderable Londoner by right of a long series of visits, from the time when as a boy he used to go to the printing-house of his uncle, Thomas Harrild, in Shoe Lane. He could possess his thoughts in Trafalgar Square and under the portico of the British Museum, and, as he records in 'The Story of my Heart,' he had his great moments amid the throng by the Mansion House. 'Let the grandees go to the opera,' said he in 'Amaryllis'; 'for me the streets.' And he asked: 'Could Xerxes, could great Pompey, could Cæsar with all his legions, could Lucullus with all his oysters, ever have enjoyed such pleasure as this, just to spend money freely in the streets of London?' And again: 'Let the meads be never so sweet, the mountain-top never so exalted, still to Fleet Street the mind will return.' He was pleased with the red roofs of Bermondsey as he saw them on approaching London Bridge by train from Eltham. He loved the ships on the Thames, and, gazing at the great red bowsprit of an Australian clipper, ridiculed the idea that Italian painters, had they seen such vessels, 'would have been contented with crank caravels and tales twice told already.' The colour of the Horse Guards, the dresses of the women, the pictures in the National Gallery, the statues in the Museum, the lions in Trafalgar Square, were among his delights.

But Jefferies' country is the country, part of North Wilt-shire round about his native Coate, which he created in his early books, his pure country books, and used afterwards for the texture of autobiography, fiction, and meditation. To go over this country now with physical footsteps is an act of pure piety. But to explore the regions of Surrey where he roamed in his last healthy years, and of Sussex, where his five years of dying were chiefly spent, is legitimate curiosity. He himself was but a visitor there. He was within the London area, writing for a London public, helping them, offering them a very strong inducement, to see for themselves. Here new things are to be discovered. But in his home-country we are in a spirit-land; not even Mr. Alfred Williams's delightful gleanings from the same fields in the Vale of White Horse convince us to the contrary.

*

Mr. Hardy himself has said, in smaller type than his topographers, nearly all that need be said about his country of
Wessex. The series of local novels beginning with 'Far from
the Madding Crowd' 'seemed,' he says, 'to require a territorial
definition of some sort to lend unity to their scene,' and the
name Wessex first appeared in that novel. At the moment he
must have imagined that he was now, with a complete set of
fictitious names, a free man and could hurt no one. Possibly
he did not think to rouse curiosity. But as early as 1876 the
'Examiner' entitled an article on the modern peasant 'The
Wessex Labourer,' and gradually, 'the appellation which I
had thought to reserve to the horizons and landscapes of a
merely realistic dream-country has become more and more
popular as a practical provincial definition; and the dream-
country has, by degrees, solidified into a utilitarian region
which people can go to, take a house in, and write to the
papers from.' Mr. Hardy begs – or begged in 1895 – all
'good and gentle readers' to forget this, and 'to refuse steadfastly to believe that there are any inhabitants of a Victorian
Wessex outside the pages of this and the companion volumes
in which they were first discovered.' And yet in this same
preface he calls attention to the fact that Weatherbury,
or Puddletown, and its personages, really were at one time
very much like what they are in the book, though now so
different.

The discovery of Mr. Hardy and of the real places behind
the fictitious names has created a difficult problem. Apparently he has not tampered with geography, has not done anything but change a large proportion of the names. It was,
then, only a matter of time to identify, for example, the three
places here mentioned – 'on the turnpike road, between Casterbridge and Weatherbury, and about three miles from the

former place, Yalisbury Hill' – as Dorchester, Puddletown, and Yellowham Hill.

Mr. Hardy was born in 1840 near Yellowham Hill, at Higher Bockampton. At seventeen he was articled to an architect at Dorchester. The twenties he seems to have spent largely in London. Then, after his marriage in 1874, he lived some time at Sturminster Newton (or Stourcastle), in Blackmoor Vale. He went to 'Max Gate,' Dorchester, in 1885.

Without knowing that Mr. Hardy has written for the Dorset Archæological Society on the contents of some barrows opened on the downs, it is easy to guess something of his tastes and studies. It is even possible to believe that he could have made as fine a set of books had he altogether excluded fiction, had he never troubled to satisfy with a 'slightly-built' romance his wish 'to set the emotional history of two infinitesimal lives against the stupendous background of the stellar universe, and to impart to readers the sentiment that, of these contrasting magnitudes, the smaller might be the greater to them as men.' For it must be remembered that he has called his novels his 'Little Exhibition of Wessex Life.' If either of the partners, Wessex Life and Romance, has suffered, it is not Romance. Both in the prefaces and in the stories themselves, Mr. Hardy tells the public more than a story-teller need about his attitude towards things which it is his task to bring for the first time before the mind. Thus, he tells us in the preface to 'The Woodlanders' what he thinks of the scenery about Little Hintock, or Middlemarsh: that it 'cannot be regarded as inferior to any inland scenery of the sort in the West of England, or perhaps anywhere in the kingdom.' He comments on the fact that world-wide repute and absolute famelessness attach to spots of equal beauty and accessibility. 'The neighbourhood of High Stoy (I give, as elsewhere, the

real names to natural features), Bubb Down Hill, and westward to Montacute; of Bulbarrow, Hambledon Hill, and
eastward to Shaston, Windy Green, and Stourhead, teems
with landscapes which, by a mere accident of iteration, might
have been numbered among the scenic celebrities of the
century.' His home at Sturminster Newton was on the low
land in the midst of these hills. The opening of this story
presents us with a 'rambler who, for old association's sake,
should trace the forsaken coach-road running almost in a
meridional line from Bristol to the south shore of England.'
The spot, he says, is lonely, and 'when the days are darkening
the many gay charioteers now perished who have rolled along
the way, the blistered soles that have trodden it, and the tears
that have wetted it,' reappear in the rambler's mind. And
again, a little later, when he has got his first characters close to
High Stoy Hill and in sight of Middlemarsh among the woods,
he says, showing us how a scene must have set his mind working before he began to write extended fiction:

'From this self-contained place rose in stealthy silence tall
stems of smoke, which the eye in imagination could trace
downward to their root on quiet hearthstones, festooned overhead with hams and flitches. It was one of those sequestered
spots outside the gates of the world where may usually be
found more meditation than action, and more listlessness than
meditation; where reasoning proceeds on narrow premisses,
and results in inferences wildly imaginative; yet where, from
time to time, dramas of a grandeur and unity truly Sophoclean
are enacted in the real, by virtue of the concentrated passions
and closely-knit interdependence of the lives therein.'

So Mr. Hardy would have looked down on Middlemarsh, not
the people in the carrier's cart.

You see that he is, as he says, exhibiting Wessex to us,

giving the hills and rivers their true names and notably suggesting their appearances, but painting them with a brush
dipped in the 'earthquake and eclipse' of his own mind, and
still more so the towns and villages and the people themselves.
Everywhere he makes a double impression by the sound
rusticity of many characters, and by his own solitary, brood-
ing, strongly-coloured mind dominating men and landscape.

On the whole, then, the mixture of ancient with invented
or resuscitated or slightly perverted names very well symbo-
lizes Mr. Hardy's mixed attitude and treatment. Only one
wishes – I wish – that he had not conceded so much to the
inevitable curiosity. What a pleasure for a man to discover for
himself perhaps only a few of the originals! What a nuisance
to have an edition of the novels and poems with a map of
Wessex at the end of every single volume, showing the exact
position of the places bearing fictitious names.

'It may be well to state,' said Mr. Hardy in 1895, 'in
response to inquiries from readers interested in landscape, prehistoric antiquities, and especially old English architecture,
that the description of those backgrounds in this and its companion novels has been done from the real. Many features of
the first two kinds have been given under their existing names.
. . . And in planning the stories the idea was that large towns
and points tending to mark the outline of Wessex – such as
Bath, Plymouth, the Start, Portland Bill, Southampton, etc. –
should be named outright. The scheme was not greatly
elaborated, but, whatever its value, the names remain still.

'In respect of places described under fictitious or ancient
names – for reasons that seemed good at the time of writing –
discerning persons have affirmed in print that they clearly
recognize the originals – such as Shaftesbury in "Shaston,"
Bere Regis in "Kingsbere," Woodbury Hill in "Greenhill,"

and so on. I shall not be the one to contradict them; I accept their statements as at least an indication of their real and kindly interest in the scenes.'

It is a master speaking. He has probably formed his opinion as to whether the identifications may not tend to spoil the fiction — at least for the moment. That they stand in the way of perfect pleasure I have little doubt. But already twenty, thirty, forty years have passed over, say, Puddletown, and a man may say simply that here once was Weatherbury; or, again, in the Vale of Blackmoor he may recall that Mr. Hardy's Blackmoor was 'an engirdled and secluded region, for the most part untrodden as yet by tourist or landscape-painter, though within a four hours' journey from London.' At Bournemouth he must reflect that Sandbourne was a mere upstart exotic town, incomparably less real in 'Tess' than 'the enormous Egdon Waste' beginning at the edge of it. Egdon is nowhere so perfect as on Mr. Hardy's page. And as to Budmouth, not every one will say of it, or want to say, with Mr. Wilkinson Sherren, that 'the phantoms of Mr. Hardy's creations haunt the streets.' I have never been to Marnhull or Marlott, but if I went and if I happened to think of Tess there, neither the fiction nor the place would be much the worse for the irrelevancy. Has it ever helped anyone much to think of Weymouth in 'The Tumpet Major,' Stinsford in 'Under the Greenwood Tree,' Wareham in 'The Return of the Native' or 'The Hand of Ethelberta,' Cerne Abbas and Woolbridge in 'Tess,' Wimborne in 'Two on a Tower,' Sherborne in 'The Woodlanders' or 'A Group of Noble Dames,' Shaftesbury in 'Jude the Obscure,' Weyhill in 'The Mayor of Casterbridge,' Woodbury Hill in 'Far from the Madding Crowd'?

I prefer Mr. Hardy's poems to his novels, and there the place-names offer many pleasures and provoke several kinds of curiosity. Sometimes the place is given, it appears, out of pure fidelity to the fact. He writes no poetry that could suffer by names and dates. That something happened

'At this point of time, at this point in space,'

it pleases him to put on record, as when he signs 'Max Gate, 1899,' at the end of 'An August Midnight':

'A shaded lamp and a waving blind,
And the beat of a clock from a distant floor:
On this scene enter — winged, horned, and spined —
A longlegs, a moth, and a dumbledore;
While 'mid my page there idly stands
A sleepy fly, that rubs its hands. . . .

'Thus meet me five, in this still place,
At this point of time, at this point in space.
— My guests parade my new-penned ink,
Or bang at the lamp glass, whirl, and sink.
"God's humblest, they!" I muse. Yet why?
They know Earth secrets that know not I.'

Somehow the two stanzas of 'The Comet at Yalbury or Yell'ham' do as much as 'Two on a Tower' to 'set the emotional history of two infinitesimal lives against the stupendous background' of the stellar universe':

'It bends far over Yell'ham Plain,
And we, from Yell'ham Height,
Stand and regard its fiery train,
So soon to swim from sight.

'It will return long years hence, when
As now its strange swift shine
Will fall on Yell'ham; but not then
On that sweet form of thine.'

144

The rustic names, if anything, emphasize the littleness, yet save it from abstraction. Sometimes Mr. Hardy gains the same effect of reality by withholding the name, conspicuously as in 'Her Dilemma' (in – Church), tacitly as in 'At an Inn' and 'The Rejected Member's Wife,' where everything is precise but names are omitted. The general effect of using local names with no significance for the stranger, and no special private value of sound or association for the poet, as in

'From Pummery-Tout to where the Gibbet is . . .'

or

'Scene. – A sad-coloured landscape, Waddonvale,'

or

'By Mellstock Lodge and Avenue,'

or

'Not far from Mellstock – so tradition saith –'

or

'While High Stoy trees twanged to Bubb Down Hill,
And Bubb Down to High Stoy,'

the general effect is to aid reality by suggestions of gross and humble simplicity. It might become a trick or device, but in Mr. Hardy it is not either, though it succeeds in different degrees. In a recurring line like the following, the name gives even a kind of magic reality, and perhaps magnifies the wind which has no name:

'Gruffly growled the wind on Toller downland broad and
bare.'

The least effect is to make sure of keeping the poem to earth by keeping it to Dorset, so that a storm strikes freshly on jaded ears by means of

'The drone of Thorncombe trees,
    The Froom in flood upon the moor,
The mud of Mellstock Leaze.'

Yet there are some names which can have, perhaps, only a private significance, as in the title 'Autumn in King's Hintock Park' (a fictitious name to boot), and in the 'Weymouth' at the foot of 'The Dawn after the Dance.' The fictitious names – 'Great Forest' for 'New Forest,' e.g. – are awkward, too, in 'A Tramp-Woman's Tragedy,' where many of the names are real, and where the author is so particular as to add this note on 'Windwhistle' (near Cricket St. Thomas, on the road from Crewkerne to Chard):

'The highness and dryness of Windwhistle Inn was impressed upon the writer two or three years ago, when, after climbing on a hot afternoon to the beautiful spot near which it stands, and entering the inn for tea, he was informed by the landlady that none could be had, unless he would fetch water from a valley half a mile off, the house containing not a drop, owing to its situation.'

But the names here undoubtedly help, and, as the poem describes travel on foot in South-West England, the more a man knows about these roads perhaps the more he likes it.

Mr. Hardy's feeling for roads is a good thing to come across in poem or novel. In 'The Mayor of Casterbridge,' the exiled Henchard chooses to work on the 'old western highway,' the artery of Wessex, because, 'though at a distance of fifty miles, he was virtually nearer to her whose welfare was so dear than he would be at a roadless spot only half as remote,' and there presently he meets a Casterbridge carter upon the road. That is imaginative fact. It is clear that Mr. Hardy has felt somehow thus about a highway: he applies his feeling like a poet.

That Exeter road near which he was born reappears many times. 'The Alarm' (in memory of one of the writer's family, who was a volunteer during the war with Napoleon) centres round a homestead –

> 'In a ferny byway
> Near the great South-Wessex Highway.'

The Romans made a road which the Exeter road part used and part supplanted, and Mr. Hardy or his characters often travelled on what is known as the Ikling or Icen Way, 'where Legions had wayfared.' But in two poems he sees himself and his forefathers upon it. He says in 'The Roman Road':

> 'But no tall brass-helmed legionnaire
> Haunts it for me. Uprises there
> A mother's form upon my ken,
> Guiding my infant steps as when
> We walked that ancient thoroughfare,
>   The Roman Road.'

In 'A Wet Night' he describes himself, 'the rainshafts riddling' him, so that he exclaims:

> ' "This is a hardship to be calendared!"
> Yet sires of mine now perished and forgot,
> When worse beset, ere roads were shapen here,
> And night and storm were foes indeed to fear,
> Times numberless have trudged across this spot
> In sturdy muteness on their strenuous lot,
> And taking all such toils as trifles mere.'

Therefore I should be more likely to think of Mr. Hardy on this road than of Henchard, and in Dorchester, too, when –

'Midnight clears High Street of all but the ghosts
    Of its buried burghees,
From the latest far back to those old Roman hosts
    Whose remains one yet sees,
Who loved, laughed, and fought, hailed their friends, drank
    their toasts,
    At their meeting times here. . . .'

For Mr. Hardy has really done something to quicken and
stouten the sense of past times and generations. With him it
has been a passion, the feeling for the barrows on the downs,
for example:

'Where the sleek herds trampled daily the remains of flint-
    tipt arrows,
 Mid the thyme and camomiles.'

And that is partly why the name is not redundant in 'The
Dark-Eyed Gentleman,' where the girl with her baby recalls:

  'I pitched my day's leazings in Crimmercrock Lane,
   To tie up my garter and jog on again. . . .'

The old name softens the ribald flavour and deepens the tone
of 'my days are not sad.' But who would go to look for that
lane at Cattistock? It would be more natural to go to 16,
Westbourne Park Villas, where Mr. Hardy dates some of his
early love-poems of 1866 and 1867. Certainly the address is
more effective than any fancy name, and is not so far away
from Wessex as it would look on the map, were anyone to
insert it on the outskirts of Mr. Hardy's country.

*

MR. BELLOC's country is Western Europe, and in particular Sussex. He sees it as a Catholic, an historian, a French artilleryman, a walker, a rider, a yachtsman. 'Everywhere in the world,' he says – and Thoreau and Jefferies have said something like it – 'one can look in and in and never find an end to one's delight. . . . But England is especially a garden of this sort, or a storehouse. . . .' In another place he says: 'In every inch of England you can find the history of England.' His home as a boy was between the Sussex downs and the sea; he spent four or five years at Oxford; he has explored the Pilgrims' Way, the Stane Street, the Thames, half the hills and rivers of England, and much of the coast; he lives in the Sussex Weald. Thus he has a special sense of England, heightened, perhaps, beyond what it is in other Englishmen by his birth in France, and the sense which made him give a cry when he saw right above him from the Channel, 'through what was now a thick haze, the cliffs of England, perhaps two miles away, and showing very faintly indeed, a bare outline upon the white weather,' and 'a thought ran into his mind with violence, how, one behind the other, beyond known things, beyond history, the men from whom he came had greeted this sight after winds like these, and danger, and the crossing of the narrow seas.' In the essay 'On Dropping Anchor' he pictures himself coming to a last anchorage in his small boat at evening amid a 'distant echo of the surf from the high hills':

'The fair-way into that haven shall lie behind a pleasant little beach of shingle, which shall run aslant into the sea from the steep hillside, and shall be a breakwater made by God. The tide shall run up behind it smoothly, and in a silent way, filling the great hollow of the hills, brimming it all up like a cup – a cup of refreshment and of quiet, a cup of ending.'

His books are full of home and of travel in equal measure. Often enough he describes, not too much or too often, for he seldom falls below the level of such a passage as this:

'The wind was blowing splendidly through an air quite blue and clear for many miles, and growing clearer as the afternoon advanced in gladness. It was a sea-wind that had been a gale the day before, but during the night everything had changed in South England, and the principal date of the year was passed, the date which is the true beginning of the year. The mist of the morning had scudded before thick Atlantic weather; by noon it was lifted into clouds, by mid-afternoon those clouds were large, heralding clouds of Spring against an unbounded capacity of sky. There was no longer any struggle between them and the gale; they went by this in procession over the country and towards the east.'

He paints by precise small coloured touches, and by larger vaguer strokes coloured, if at all, from his own spirit, his sense of history and of home. Himself, travelling or at ease, appears more clearly than the land and sea, and dominates it. 'The Griffin' at March – 'Low rooms of my repose! Beams of comfort and great age; drowsy and inhabiting fires; inglenooks made for companionship' – might have been any other good inn which he chose to honour with his company and an essay. For a style so substantial and of so many verbs it is astonishing how philosophical and spiritual the results are. To bring the 'White Hart' at Wisbech before us, he can trust to saying that he was waiting there for steak and onions, reading a book; or he will tell a man merely that 'Down under the Combe at Duncton is a very good inn'; of The 'Sign of the Lion,' an inn 'that stands close to the Upper Arun and is very good,' he tells us nothing more literal than that the food and ale 'was of the kind which has been England ever since England began, and which perhaps good-fortune will preserve over the breakdown of our generation, until we have England back again.' He is just too much concerned with what England has been and may be again, with how it should be enjoyed, with an idea of England, to leave us quite a clear vision of England as he has known it. Tasted England he has deeply, like Cobbett and Mr. Hudson, but not preserved it for later generations as they have.

'Unless a man understands the Weald, he cannot easily write about the beginnings of England' – 'the people of Sussex have gone steadily forward, increasing in every good thing, until they are now by far the first and most noble of all the people in the world' – so he lays it down, and we know that he would have spoken as generously of Rutland had he dwelt there. Sussex is the sweet core of the world, and he is the fortunate inhabitant who has crept into it. He praises it as Gerald of Wales praises Manorbier, which is in Pembroke, which is the best county in Wales, which is the best land in the world.

Well, many a man has made less of the things he loves by not being able to make much of himself, the lover; and though I have a notion that he protests too much, with all his humour, I listen humbly and in delight when he speaks of 'our grass' – of the little winds 'who brought with them the scent of those first flowers in the North Wood, or beyond Gumber Corner, and the fragrance of our grass, the savour which the sheep know at least, however much the visitors to my dear home ignore it.' I like to see him mowing a field, and a man asking him, 'Mowing?' and him answering, 'Ar,' 'for so we speak to each other in the stenes of the downs.' When he is not Gas-

con, he is always humorous in his patriotism, no other Englishman so much so. Here and there he reveals what he might
have done had he not been a Sussex man. For example, he
feels, half an hour after he has left London in a fast express
north-eastward, that the East Anglians 'push with quants,
they sail in wherries, they inhabit flat tidal banks, they are at
peace.' What an East Anglian is lost in him!

He has not, however, given up to Sussex what was meant
for mankind. Going about in other counties, he has been glad
to step exactly in the footprints of ancient ancestors. On the
Pilgrims' Way, he says: 'I believed that, as I followed their
hesitations at the river-crossings, as I climbed where they had
climbed, whence they also had seen a wide plain, as I suffered
the fatigue they suffered, and laboriously chose, as they had
chosen, the proper soils for going, something of their much
keener life would wake again in the blood I drew from them,
and that in a sort I should forget the vileness of my own time,
and renew for some few days the better freedom of that
vigorous morning when men were already erect, articulate,
and worshipping God, but not yet broken by complexity and
the long accumulation of evil.' The 'differences of this
island' fascinate him. 'Surely,' he says, 'a nation grows great
in this way, by many provinces reacting one upon the other,
recognized by the general will, sometimes in conflict with it.'
He is considering the West Country, which no one can get
into 'without touching his youth again and putting his fingers
to earth, and getting sustenance from it'; and in the same
essay, 'On the Approach to Western England,' he alludes to
the Welsh Marches, 'and how, between a village and a village,
one changes from the common English parish, with the
Squire's house and the church and the cottages and all, into
the hard slate roofs and the inner flame of Wales.' When he
is living in the Midlands, he has sung, 'the great hills of the

South Country' come back into his mind; but as a rule he is not contentious once he is out of Sussex, and plainly he feels that love of England which, says he, somewhat mysteriously, 'has in it the love of landscape, as has the love of no other country; it has in it, as has the love of no other country, the love of friends.' He delights in the variety of England as he does in the variety of the separate things in an old town, which 'have character as men have,' which he traces to the power of individuals in England, and associates with 'ownership, and what comes from ownership — the love of home.' Again and again he reverts to the middle part of the South Downs, to Gumber and No Man's Land, the Rother and the Arun and Amberley Wildbrooks and to the Weald. But his pleasure in reciting long lists of rivers and hills, and towns on rivers, northward and westward of these is equally noticeable. If he had anything to learn from Ruskin in this kind, he learnt it. He is such a geographer as I wish many historians were, such a poet as all geographers ought to be, and hardly any other has been.

THE WEST COUNTRY

HERRICK
COLERIDGE
W. H. HUDSON

HERRICK

*

WHEN we think of Herrick, we think of Dean Prior in Devonshire, where he was Vicar from 1629 to 1647, and from 1662 until his death in 1674, when he was eighty-three. Yet the greater part of his life was passed in London. The family was from Leicester. Nicholas Herrick, the poet's father, was a goldsmith, with a house in Goldsmiths' Row. There Robert was born. When his father died from a fall out of an upper window of this house, he went to live in Wood Street with an uncle, also a goldsmith, and with him served an apprenticeship till 1614. Then he went to St. John's College, Cambridge. He ceased to be a goldsmith. On leaving Cambridge he entered literary society, and in particular 'the tribe of Ben' — that is to say, the company of poets and gentlemen who acknowledged Ben Jonson's supremacy, and met

'At those lyric feasts
Made at the Sun,
The Dog, the Triple Tun,
Where we such clusters had
As made us nobly wild, not mad;
And yet each verse of thine
Outdid the meat, outdid the frolic wine.'

Jonson lived on until 1637, but Herrick could not stay in London so long. How he lived is not known. He had well-to-do relatives, but in 1627 he accompanied the expedition to the Isle of Rhé as chaplain, and in 1629 went into his Devonshire exile. He was then thirty-eight, and must have had some good reason for dropping himself into so remote and small a place.

To all appearances he must by that time have been a complete Londoner, one who was well used to the variety and convenience of the city, and to the safe civilized beauty of the

suburban country. There is no indication that he preferred
'old simplicity, though hid in grey,' to 'foppery in plush and
scarlet clad.' If he went to 'see the wholesome country girls
make hay,' it was not from any disdain of

'The beauties of the Cheap, and wives of Lombard Street.'

A 'sweet disorder' and 'wild civility' in park and meadow was
probably as pleasant to him as in woman's dress, and he could
have all that he desired by a short journey on foot or in a
barge. When he was away at Dean Prior, he sent his tears
and 'supremest kiss'

> 'To thee, my silver-footed Thamesis.
> No more shall I reiterate thy Strand,
> Whereon so many stately structures stand:
> Nor in the summer's sweeter evenings go
> To bathe in thee as thousand others do;
> No more shall I along thy crystal glide
> In barge with boughs and rushes beautified,
> With soft, smooth virgins for our chaste disport,
> To Richmond, Kingston, and to Hampton Court.
> Never again shall I with finny oar
> Put from, or draw unto the faithful shore:
> And landing here, or safely landing there,
> Make way to my beloved Westminster,
> Or to the Golden Cheapside, where the earth
> Of Julia Herrick gave to me my birth. . . .'

M. Delattre thinks it probable that 'Corinna's Maying'
describes May Day as it was celebrated in London in those
days, when the young men fetched boughs of hawthorn and
brier to ornament the doors of Cheapside, Cornhill, Grace-
church Street, and 'every man would walk into the sweet
meadows and green woods, there to rejoice their spirits with

the beauty and savour of sweet flowers, and with the harmony of birds, praising God in their kind.' The fourth verse, for example, shows a perfectly suburban scene:

'Come, my Corinna, come; and coming, mark
How each field turns a street, each street a park,
   Made green and trimm'd with trees! See how
   Devotion gives each house a bough
   Or branch! Each porch, each door, ere this,
   An ark, a tabernacle is,
Made up of whitethorn, neatly interwove,
As if here were those cooler shades of love.
   Can such delights be in the street
   And open fields, and we not see't?
   Come, we'll abroad: and let's obey
   The proclamation made for May,
And sin no more, as we have done, by staying.
But, my Corinna, come, let's go a-Maying.'

It is not easy to imagine what more Herrick wanted than this combination or alternation of street and park, with good company.

But already in 1610 Herrick had begun to write in praise of pure country life. His brother Thomas had left London with a bride, and Herrick congratulated him on exchanging the city for

'The country's sweet simplicity:
   And it to know and practise, with intent
   To grow the sooner innocent
   By studying to know virtue, and to aim
   More at her nature than her name.'

Possibly at nineteen Herrick really believed that in the country all was 'purling springs, groves, birds, and well-weav'd bowers, with fields enamelled with flowers'; that there were none of those 'desperate cares th' industrious merchant has'; that men there ate only 'to cool, not cocker appetite,' and 'content makes all ambrosia' — 'boiled nettles' and all. But it is more likely that Herrick got it all from books. He accepted the view that the golden age was not yet over in the country, though he must have been pretending when he called his Muse a 'mad maiden' who might

> 'sit and piping please
> The poor and private cottages. . . .
> There, there, perhaps, such lines as these
> May take the simple villages.'

He said,

> 'Contempt in courts and cities dwell,
> No critic haunts the poor man's cell,'

but gives us no real reason to believe him when he goes on to say, as if he liked it, that in the poor man's cell you can hear your own lines read 'by no one tongue censured.' To make neat verses was one of his recreations, and so he wrote:

> 'To bread and water none is poor;
> And having these, what need of more?
> Though much from out the cess be spent,
> Nature with little is content.'

Sometimes he was practically translating, as when he bade his worthy friend Thomas Falconbridge

> 'Lastly, be mindful, when thou art grown great,
> That towers high rear'd dread most the lightning's threat:
> Whereas the humble cottages not fear
> The cleaving bolt of Jove the Thunderer.'

On the other hand, he wrote in the same strain after he had been some time in Devonshire; and since it is obvious that Dean Prior was in many ways rude and inconvenient, it is equally obvious that without compensations he did not sit down in his Vicarage and write about 'His Content in the Country,' with Prudence Baldwin, his maidservant:

> 'Here, here I live with what my board
> Can with the smallest cost afford.
> Though ne'er so mean the viands be,
> They well content my Prew and me.
> Or pea, or bean, or wort, or beet,
> Whatever comes, content makes sweet.
> Here we rejoice, because no rent
> We pay for our poor tenement
> Wherein we rest, and never fear
> The landlord or the usurer.
> The quarter-day does ne'er affright
> Our peaceful slumbers in the night.
> We eat our own and batten more,
> Because we feed on no man's score;
> But pity those whose flanks grow great,
> Swell'd with the lard of others' meat.
> We bless our fortunes when we see
> Our own beloved privacy;
> And like our living, where we're known
> To very few, or else to none.'

The compensation probably was a contented mind, and his later praise of country life is by this much better than his early, that it does tell us something about the country as well as exclaiming:

> 'O happy life! if that their good
> The husbandmen but understand.'

He put in the game of 'fox i' th' hole,' or distinguished between the 'cockrood' for snaring woodcocks and the 'glade' for catching pheasants, not for local colour in an otherwise conventional praise of country life, but because these things had become familiar to him; he had really in some measure become a countryman.

If he had not, need he ever have gone back in 1662 when the King enjoyed his own again? He had found the wherewithal to live in London from the year of his ejection, 1647, and he would not have gone back at the age of sixty-nine without a strong preference. Dean Prior was a very remote village lying close under the high south-eastern edge of Dartmoor. The road from Exeter to Plymouth passes Herrick's church on the left a little more than a mile out of Buckfastleigh. Anciently, I believe, the road left Dean Prior Church somewhat to the left, but not so far as to be said to leave it in the mud even in days of villainous roads. To-day the railway misses it and the hill beyond it by making a sharp détour down the valley of the Dart from Buckfastleigh.

No trace of Herrick is left in the hamlet except an epitaph, not his own, but one written by him for his neighbours, Sir Edward and Lady Giles, of Dean Court. Their effigies kneel facing one another in the costume of Charles I's reign, and underneath have been cut these words:

'No trust to metals nor to marbles, when
Those have their fate and wear away as men;
Times, titles, trophies may be lost and spent,
But virtue rears the eternal monument.
What more than these can tombs or tombstones pay?
But here's the sunset of a tedious day:
These two asleep are: I'll but be undress'd,
And so to bed: pray wish us all good rest.'

Herrick was truly himself only on the subject of flowers, domestic things, and women. For his own epitaph he had addressed the Robin Redbreast, asking it to cover him with leaves and moss-work, and sing his dirge, and write in foliage these words:

'Here, here the tomb of Robin Herrick is.'

Had the task been left to the birds, the result could not have been less to-day. Neither stone nor epitaph marks the grave of Herrick. But the church remains among beeches, and Dean Court, now a farm, and the Vicarage. Here he wrote and thanked God for it, and for his bread, his firing,

'The worts, the purslain, and the mess
Of watercress,'

and his 'beloved beet,' the spiced drink, the corn from the glebe, the hen that laid an egg a day, the ewes that bore twins every year, the kine that 'run cream for wine.' This was 'His Grange, or Private Wealth':

'Though clock,
To tell how night draws hence, I've none,
A cock
I have to sing how day draws on.
I have
A maid, my Prew, by good luck sent
To save
That little Fates me gave or lent.
A hen
I keep, which, creeking day by day,
Tells when
She goes her long white egg to lay.

163

> A goose
> I have, which with a jealous ear
> Lets loose
> Her tongue to tell that danger's near.
> A lamb
> I keep (tame) with my morsels fed,
> Whose dam
> An orphan left him (lately dead).
> A cat
> I keep that plays about my house,
> Grown fat
> With eating many a miching mouse.
> To these
> A Tracy I do keep whereby
> I please
> The more my rural privacy;
> Which are
> But toys to give my heart some ease;
> Where care
> None is, slight things do lightly please.'

Tracy was his spaniel. That hen must have been such a wonder that it can be understood how he came to compare Julia's leg to that daily 'long white egg.' The cat, too, is very real. He must have been a lover of cats, for in his earliest poem, that to his brother on country life, he speaks of the roof that maintains a fireside cricket choir,

> 'And the brisk mouse may feast herself with crumbs
> Till that the green-eyed kitten comes.'

Outside the Vicarage he does not stray far. If he 'traced the hare i' th' treacherous snow,' he gives us no idea of the sport or of the country. Perhaps he was short-sighted, for he seems to see very clearly little things which he could not have seen at all without special attention. His daffodils have not Wordsworth's wild moorland air. They are just flowers isolated, but they are as real as Wordsworth's. Real, too, is that 'savour like unto a blessed field,'

> 'when the bedabbled morn
> Washes the golden ears of corn.'

No poet ever loved perfumes more, indoors and out of doors, the breaths of flowers, of spices, of women, of bees, of amber, of burning wood, of wine, of milk and cream, of baked pear.

He confessed or professed that his eye and heart doted 'less on Nature than on Art,' and declared – in writing to an old London friend, Sir Clipseby Crew – that since coming to the country he had lost his 'former flame.' But, then, on the other hand, he wrote:

> 'More discontents I never had
>   Since I was born than here,
> Where I have been, and still am sad,
>   In this dull Devonshire;
> Yet, justly too, I must confess
>   I ne'er invented such
> Ennobled numbers for the press
>   Than where I loathed so much.'

Did he show this to Sir Clipseby? Probably not. What he said to the knight was very different:

> 'Cold and hunger never yet
> Could a noble verse beget;
> But your bowle with sack replete,
> Give me these, my knight, and try
> In a minute's space how I
> Can run mad and prophesy.'

Too much has been made of his insulting farewell 'to Dean Bourn, a rude river in Devon, by which sometimes he lived.' Perhaps he got splashed in crossing it on his way to London, and wrote these verses against the savage Devonians just to amuse the Londoners. Or he might have been badly treated at the ejection in 1647. In any case, a great measure of eagerness in looking forward to London might have been expected, and a proportionate disgust with whatever thwarted or delayed him 'in loathed Devonshire.' When he set foot in London 'from the dull confines of the drooping West,' he exclaimed:

> 'O fruitful Genius! that bestowest here
> An everlasting plenty year by year.
> O place! O people! manners! framed to please
> All nations, customs, kindreds, languages!
> I am a free-born Roman; suffer, then,
> That I amongst you live a citizen.
> London my home is, though by hard fate sent
> Into a long and irksome banishment. . . .'

This, I think, was mainly an exercise for London eyes. It is rather less than more sincere sounding than his praises of a country life.

How much he wrote at Dean Prior will never be known certainly. But the poem 'To the Little Spinners' must have been; and the one on 'Oberon's Palace,' where Oberon and Mab are 'led by the shine of snails'; and 'Oberon's Feast,' with its 'papery butterflies' and 'the unctuous dewlaps of a snail.' The rural poems were obviously written there, poems like 'The Hock-Cart, or Harvest Home,' with its picture of labourers devoutly following the waggon, while others,

166

> 'less attent
> To prayers than to merriment,
> Run after with their breeches rent . . .'

and then the great feast, the

> 'large and chief
> Foundation of your feast, fat beef:
> With upper stories, mutton, veal,
> And bacon. . . .'

The conclusion seems to prove him a thorough countryman of the landowning or employing class; for he bids the labourers work after their holiday, because

> 'Feed him ye must, whose food fills you;
> And that this pleasure is like grain,
> Not sent ye for to drown your pain,
> But for to make it spring again.'

He was not without company. Among his friends was John Weekes, Dean of St. Burian in Cornwall. He visited this man's house, and either there or at Dean Prior would sit with him regretting past times, but drinking until they were

> 'Plump as the cherry,
> Though not so fresh, yet full as merry
> As the cricket,'

until they saw

> 'the fire less shine
> From th' embers than the kitling's eyne.'

Prue Baldwin, his maidservant, never forsook him; others, mere 'summer birds' of passage, soon flew away, but not she.

He did her the honour to waste his scholarship in these lines
on her sickness:

> 'Prue, my dearest maid, is sick
> Almost to be lunatic:
> Æsculapius! come and bring
> Means for her recovering;
> And a gallant cock shall be
> Offered up by her to thee.'

It seems impossible to guess whether Julia or Anthea ever
lived in the same house with him. Or could Prue supply suggestions for those ladies as well as light the fires and cook the
dinners? For a time Elizabeth Herrick, widow of his brother
Thomas, kept house for him. Julia, at least, was a substantial
and not a transitory person, and when he bids her make the
wedding cake for a bride, it looks as if she were an inmate,
whether subordinate or not, at the Vicarage. And there is a
quite exceptional touch of reality in the protestation to Julia,
where he says:

> 'As if we should for ever part. . . .
> After a day or two or three,
> I would come back and live with thee.'

At Dean Court the Gileses had no children, but they had
nieces living with them, and doubtless other visitors coming
and going. He wrote 'The Entertainment: or Porch-Verse'
for the marriage of one niece, Lettice Yarde; and a 'Meadow-
Verse: or Anniversary' for another, Bridget Lowman. Many
times in the manor-house at Dean Court, now a farmhouse,
Herrick must have seen the holly up. He paints the holly and
the rosemary and bay, but not the hall or the house; as he
paints the flowers and a typical meadow, but not Dartmoor.
In fact, there seems no connexion between Herrick and Dean

Prior, except that he lived there over thirty years. It does not remind us of him, nor does his work remind us of it. But the association is growing up, and already it is a piquant, pleasant thing to fancy, or to try to establish, the connexion between the southern foot of Dartmoor and the author of those daintiest poems to flowers and ladies.

*

WHEN Coleridge was twenty-five and dedicating his poems to his brother, the Rev. George Coleridge, of Ottery St. Mary, Devon, he said:

> 'A blessed lot hath he, who, having past
> His youth and early manhood in the stir
> And turmoil of the world, retreats at length,
> With cares that move, not agitate the heart,
> To the same dwelling where his father dwelt;
> And haply views his tottering little ones
> Embrace those aged knees, and climb that lap,
> On which first kneeling his own infancy
> Lisped its brief prayer. Such, O my earliest friend!
> Thine and thy brothers' favourable lot.'

It was far from being his own lot. His father died in 1781, and the child, then nine years old, left Ottery St. Mary for London, and saw it again only on holidays. Thus the place appeared in his memory perfected and enshrined by the fixed school years in London and the restless years following Years afterwards, in 1803, when he was living beside the Greta, and not the Otter, a calf bellowing on a July evening reminded him of Ottery: 'Instantly came on my mind that night I slept out at Ottery, and the calf in the field across the river, whose lowing so deeply impressed me.' He was then past thirty. Ten years earlier he used to turn his fond retrospection into verses. He wrote a sonnet to the River Otter,

> 'Dear native brook! wild streamlet of the West!'

recalling the game of ducks-and-drakes on it, the plank bridge, the sandy bed, the willows which would always reappear to him if he shut his eyes in the sun, and wake a sigh:

> 'Ah! that once more I were a careless child!'

In 'An Autumnal Evening' he says that,

> 'Tost by storms along life's wild'ring way,
> Mine eye reverted views that cloudless day,
> When by my native brook I wont to rove
> While hope with kisses nurs'd the infant love,'

and again he hails the 'Dear native brook!' and 'Scenes of my hope.' The Otter's 'sleep-persuading stream' is mentioned again in 'Songs of the Pixies.'

What we know of Coleridge at Ottery is not much. He spent all his early years there, both play hours and school hours, for he attended the grammar-school, where his father was master. According to his account, he took no pleasure in boyish sports, but read incessantly. 'I used to lie by the wall and mope,' he said, 'and my spirits used to come upon me suddenly, and in a flood; and I then was accustomed to run up and down the churchyard and act over again all I had been reading, on the docks and the nettles and the rank grass.' Earlier than that, in his nurse's arms, he had heard an 'old musician, blind and grey,'

> 'His Scottish tunes and warlike marches play,'

and had listened to the church-bells ringing,

> 'From morn to evening, all the hot fair-day,
> So sweetly, that they stirred and haunted me
> With a wild pleasure, falling on mine ear
> Most like articulate sounds of things to come!'

For fear of punishment it was that he spent that night out by the Otter, and incurred weakness and ague for years after. He remembered his father's tears at his restoration — 'for I was the child of his old age.' Nothing embittered, but only intensified, his memories, but they were comparatively few, the only other one of his father and Ottery being connected with a walk from a farmhouse a mile away, when the old man told him 'the names of the stars, and how Jupiter was a thousand times larger than our world, and that the other twinkling stars were suns that had worlds rolling round them,' and these things sank into a mind 'habituated to the vast' by early reading about fairies and genii. A year afterwards he was to quit Devonshire, to begin the life that left him, as he thought,

> 'Still most a stranger, most with naked heart,
>   At mine own home and birthplace.'

For the next ten years, chiefly at Christ's Hospital, were to make him a town boy, one who was reared, as he did not wish his son Hartley to be,

> 'In the great city, pent 'mid cloisters dim,
>   And saw naught lovely but the sky and stars.'

The nine years at Ottery were cut off, a romantic islet, from the mainland. That the William Browne of Ottery who died in 1645 might have been the author of 'Britannia's Pastorals' seems to have helped him to love the poet; he also claimed that the Coleridges were 'connected' with the Brownes.

While he was at Christ's Hospital, Coleridge hardly had a home except the homes of friends like Charles Lamb and Mrs. Evans and her daughter Mary, and of a London uncle named Bowdon. Holidays only set him free to bathe in the New River, to take Mary Evans, 'of a summer morning, the pillage of the flower-gardens within six miles from town, with sonnet or love-rhymes wrapped round the nosegay,' to engage strangers in conversation, to expect in vain 'townsman, or aunt, or sister more beloved,' to walk round Newgate Market alone, to watch from the school roof

>   'the clouds
> Moving in heaven; or, of that pleasure tired,
> To shut his eyes, and by internal light
> See trees, and meadows, and his native stream,
> Far distant, thus beheld from year to year
> Of a long exile.'

He began to approach poetry, calling the school pump a Pierian spring, reading the verses of William Lisle Bowles, translating from Latin and Greek, addressing Mary Evans and 'sweet Genevieve' and the evening star. 'O it was,' he says, 'my earliest affection, the evening star! One of my first utterances in verse was an address to it as I was returning from the New River, and it looked newly bathed as well as I. I remember that the substance of the sonnet was that the woman whom I could ever love would surely have been emblemed in the pensive serene brightness of that planet; that we were both constellated to it, and would after death return thither.' It began:

> 'O meek attendant of Sol's setting blaze!'

Coleridge went to Jesus College, Cambridge, in 1791. We know that he talked there, declaimed passages from political pamphlets, and was heard with admiration. But Cambridge meant nothing to him in particular. The interval between school and college he had spent at Ottery, and again the Long Vacation of 1793. He ran away for a soldier, enlisting at Reading, in 1793, and was not discharged until four months later, in 1794. Then in the following summer he walked with a friend in Wales, and on the way, calling at Oxford, met Southey of Balliol College. He stopped at Bristol on his way back, collaborated with Southey in 'The Fall of Robespierre,' and got engaged to Sarah Fricker. The following March, Southey and Coleridge, their wives, their friends and their friends' wives, were to go to found the Pantisocracy in America. The Avon at Clifton, the nightingales of the Leigh Woods, were present to Coleridge while he wrote 'On the Death of Chatterton' and 'To the Nightingale.' He had a short freedom in London, enjoyed, partly with Charles Lamb, drink, smoke, and Welsh-rabbit at the 'Salutation and Cat' in Newgate Street, and a short return to Miss Fricker at Bristol and to the woods 'that wave o'er Avon's rocky steep.' When March came he was lodging alone in London, at 25, College Street.

Many of his 'Poems on Various Subjects' had now been finished; 'Religious Musings' was being written, and the publisher had advanced him thirty guineas. The prospect of making fourpence a line by verses was one of his excuses for marrying Sarah Fricker, which he did in October, 1794. They went to live at Clevedon, near Bristol, between the Severn sea and the end of the hills. The better part of his poetry was to be written by this sea within a few years.

Already his love-poems had taken some of their substance from this sea and these hills. Writing at Shurton Bars, near Bridgwater, in the month before his marriage, he spoke of the Flat Holm, the lighthouse island in the Channel, the 'channell'd isle'

'Where stands one solitary pile
Unslated by the blast.'

He fancied himself there alone,

'In black soul-jaundiced fit
A sad gloom-pampered man to sit,
And listen to the roar.'

'The Keepsake,' apparently written some years later, seems to recall the last summer before his marriage, 'the tedded hay and corn sheaves in one field,' the foxgloves, the woodbine bower, and the girl,

> 'early waked
> By her full bosom's joyous restlessness,'

coming out to him and promising marriage. The poem 'composed at Clevedon, Somersetshire,' shows the poet and his bride perhaps on a visit a little before the wedding, as they sit beside the cottage:

> 'Our cot o'ergrown
> With white-flowered jasmin, and the broad-leaved myrtle,
> And watch the clouds that late were rich with light,
> Slow-sadd'ning round, and mark the star of eve
> Shine opposite!'

But the poem as it stands may have been worked at before, during and after the marriage month. Their stay was brief enough to have been pure sweetness. They moved back to Bristol to be nearer books. For a year the poet made plans and changes, wrote the 'Watchman' and dropped it, became a father and had his poems at last published, revisited Ottery. He had many a restless moment in which to remember Clevedon, the 'quiet dell! dear cot! and mount sublime!'

> '*Here* the bleak mount . . .
> The Channel *there*, the islands and white sails . . .'

and all that he had seen 'while climbing the left ascent of Brockley Coomb, Somersetshire, May, 1795,' when he still longed for Sarah.

The last day of 1796, when his newly-written 'Ode to the Departing Year' was published, was Coleridge's first day in the cottage at Nether Stowey. He had stayed before at Stowey with his friend Poole. Now he was settling down to cultivate

an acre and a half of garden and devote his evenings to literature, and we have his own word for it that the spade produced
'a callum' on each hand. He already knew something of the
country between Stowey and Bristol. Henceforward he
ranged rather westward and over the Quantocks, but the
presence of Mrs. Barbauld was enough to induce him to walk
to Bristol, and he walked the forty miles home in one day.
When Hazlitt came over, Coleridge walked and talked him
to Lynton, thirty-five miles. He used to walk over to Bridgwater and Taunton to preach.

One of his most famous walks was over the Dorset border
to Wordsworth at Racedown. So eager was he that he 'leapt
over a gate and bounded down the pathless field' to cut off the
last corner. The two poets had met before, and Coleridge
had admired Wordsworth ever since his first book. By the
visit to Racedown their friendship was made sure. Wordsworth was then at work on 'The Borderers,' Coleridge on
'Osorio'; but in the year of friendship following they were to
do incomparable things. Wordsworth and his sister, having
repaid the visit, came to Alfoxden, near Stowey, to stay in
July, 1797.

It was while the Wordsworths were with Coleridge in June
that Lamb arrived at Nether Stowey. Coleridge, for the time
being disabled from walking, sat in 'this lime-tree bower my
prison,' and followed in imagination the walk which his
friends were taking, and wrote a poem on it, half 'gloom-
pampered' at his deprivation, half happy both with what he
imagined and with the trees of his prison, so that he concluded:

'Henceforth I shall know
That Nature ne'er deserts the wise and pure;
No plot so narrow, be but Nature there,

No waste so vacant, but may well employ
Each faculty of sense, and keep the heart
Awake to Love and Beauty.'

His less famous poems of the period are full of this country,
from Stowey,

'Thy church tower, and, methinks, the four huge elms
Clustering which mark the mansion of my friend'[1]

and his own cottage, to the Quantocks, 'sea, hill, and wood,'
with details of

'The fruit-like perfume of the golden furze,'

the rocks, the firs and slender oaks and birches, the whortleberries, the nightingales, the waterfall, the spring — that beautiful fountain at Upper Stowey where 'the images of the weeds
which hung down from its sides appear as plants growing up,
straight and upright, among the water-weeds that really grew
from the bottom of the well.' Even in 'Remorse' the Moresco
chieftain's wife seems to be addressing the Quantocks and the
Bristol Channel, when she says:

'Yon hanging woods, that touched by autumn seem
As they were blossoming hues of fire and gold;
The flower-like woods, most lovely in decay,
The many clouds, the sea, the rock, the sands,
Lie in the silent moonshine; and the owl,
(Strange! very strange!) the screech-owl only wakes!
Sole voice, sole eye of all this world of beauty!'

Isn't this the same country as the Ancient Mariner sees, coming in perhaps near Quantoxhead? —

[1] Thomas Poole.

'The rock shone bright, the kirk no less,
  That stands above the rock:
The moonlight steeped in silentness
  The steady weathercock.

'And the bay was white with silent light . . .'

On that coast you will find the wood 'which slopes down to the sea,' in those coombes the hermit's 'cushion plump':

'It is the moss that wholly hides
  The rotted old oak-stump';

and the oak where Christabel kneels in the moonlight when

'Naught was green upon the oak
But moss and rarest mistletoe.'

The 'jagged shadows of mossy leafless boughs' in the moonlight and the crying of the owls from cliff and tower are more likely to have come from the Quantocks than from nowhere. And so with 'The Ballad of the Dark Ladie,' where for the third time he uses that mossy seat:

'Beneath yon birch with silver bark,
  And boughs so pendulous and fair,
The brook falls scattered down the rock:
  And all is mossy there!

'And there upon the moss she sits,
  The Dark Ladie in silent pain. . . .'

That 'the one red leaf, the last of its clan,' hung on a Somerset tree is well known, because a note of it occurs in Dorothy Wordsworth's journal. Walks with Coleridge helped to fill her journal at Alfoxden. His waterfall and the weeds swaying in its winnow appear in her note for February 10, 1798. Alter sunlight to moonlight, and this scene from February 17 comes very close to that of 'Christabel':

'The sun shone bright and clear. A deep stillness in the thickest part of the wood, undisturbed except by the occasional dropping of the snow from the holly boughs; no other sound but that of the water and the slender notes of a redbreast, which sang at intervals on the outskirts of the southern side of the wood. There the bright green moss was bare at the roots of the trees, and the little birds were upon it. The whole appearance of the wood was enchanting, and each tree, taken singly, was beautiful. The branches of the hollies pendent with their white burden, but still showing their bright red berries and their glossy green leaves. The bare branches of the oaks thickened by the snow.'

On a walk with Wordsworth and Dorothy to Watchet and Lynton 'The Ancient Mariner' was begun in November, 1797. It was finished, as Dorothy's journal says, in March, 1798. The entries relating to 'the one red leaf, the last of its clan,' etc., are supposed to 'show, not only how much Coleridge was aided by her keen observation of Nature, but fix unmistakably the date of composition of Part I' of 'Christabel.' The May of 1798 was probably the month of 'Kubla Khan.' Coleridge had retired to a lonely farmhouse between Porlock and Lynton. He fell asleep under the influence of opium while reading in Purchas the sentence, 'Here the Khan Kubla commanded a palace to be built, and a stately garden thereunto, and thus ten miles of fertile ground were enclosed with a wall.' The poem was composed during the sleep, and would not, said Coleridge, have been so short and a fragment had not 'a person on business from Porlock' interrupted him. The 'deep romantic chasm which slanted down the green hill' alone connects it, and that tenuously, with Somerset. If Dorothy

Wordsworth did help Coleridge to the isthmus by which he and we pass out from this earth to that other, she performed a a great service, perhaps one he could not have done without; but it has not been proved yet.

This being a time of war as well as of poetry, the rambles of the poets brought them under suspicion as spies. How was a plain man to know that Coleridge 'liked to compose in walking over uneven ground or breaking through the straggling branches of a copsewood'? The suspicion seems to have turned Wordsworth out of his house, and he did not find another to suit him in the neighbourhood. The Stowey period was almost at an end. The Wordsworths went to Germany before the end of 1798; Coleridge went with them. Coleridge stayed on into June, 1799, and in a year's time he was at Greta Hall, Keswick; Wordsworth at Town End, Grasmere.

The spies who suspected Coleridge had not read his 'Fears in Solitude, written in April, 1798, during the Alarm of an Invasion.' It shows us that, though a bad soldier, he was a tolerably complete Englishman, aware of the follies both of peace and war, himself once probably one of those who speak from the newspapers

'As if the soldier died without a wound.'

Having humbled himself and felt his country's need of humility, he came on that April day to a most vivid sense of what his country was:

'O dear Britain! O my Mother Isle!
Needs must thou prove a name most dear and holy
To me a son, a brother, and a friend,
A husband and a father! who revere
All bonds of natural love, and find them all
Within the limits of thy rocky shores.

O native Britain! O my Mother Isle!
How shouldst thou prove aught else but dear and holy
To me, who from thy lakes and mountain-hills,
Thy clouds, thy quiet dales, thy rocks and seas,
Have drunk in all my intellectual life,
All sweet sensations, all ennobling thoughts,
All adoration of the God in nature,
All lovely and all honourable things,
Whatever makes this mortal spirit feel
The joy and greatness of its future being?
There lives nor form nor feeling in my soul
Unborrowed from my country. . . .'

He reminds us what a sense of England there was behind the
eye that delighted luxuriously in 'a green and silent spot amid
the hills,' a 'deep romantic chasm,' a wood 'that slopes down
to the sea.' He had as little as possible of the enjoyment of
historical association which a guide to Stratford or Carnarvon
Castle could satisfy, but at times 'uncalled and sudden, subject
to no bidding of my own or others,' the thoughts of such
association 'would come upon me like a storm, and fill the
place with something more than Nature.' As he could enjoy
this earth with another, so he could the human language of
patriotism with an 'eternal language' heard

'By lakes and sandy shores, beneath the crags
Of ancient mountain, and beneath the clouds.'

And he was good at both worlds. His work retains a stronger
flavour of the West Country than any other great poet's.
Wordsworth's country had little to give him, or he had
little power to receive. He went backwards and forwards from
Greta Hall to Dove Cottage. He walked, fished, and talked,
with the Wordsworths, read them 'Christabel,' and re-read it.

When the Wordsworths toured Scotland in 1803 he was with them for a time, but forsook them for the sole companionship of opium; he walked two hundred and sixty-three miles in eight days between Tyndrum and Perth. His poetry neared its decline. If it tastes of the North Country, it is through the names chiefly. The first part of 'Christabel' has no place-names in it; the second part, written in the North, has Bratha Head, Windérmere, Langdale Pike, Tryermaine, Knorren Moor, Irthing Flood, Borrowdale, names from the country which Coleridge explored with Wordsworth in 1799. 'Greta, dear domestic stream,' is mentioned in 'Recollections of Love,' but more as a symbol, and far less for itself, than 'seaward Quantock's heathy hills.' Where he is at his best again, in 'Dejection,' he is again close to reality, hearing the wind rave, and thinking of

> 'Bare craig, or mountain tairn, or blasted tree,
> Or pine-grove whither woodman never clomb,
> Or lonely house, long held the witches' home.'

His notebooks reveal how much he saw, and thought to use in writing, and never did: the crescent moon with the concave filled up by her own hazy light, 'as if it had been painted and the colours had run' — the moon behind a black cloud at sunrise, and 'a small cloud in the east, not larger than the moon and ten times brighter than she' — the moon and the sky again and again — the snow on Skiddaw and Grysdale Pike for the first time on October 20, which he believed to be his birthday — the October masses of 'shapeless vapour upon the mountains (O the perpetual forms of Borrowdale!),' while the birds sang 'in the tender rain, as if it were the rain of April, and the decaying foliage were flowers and blossoms.' As he sat writing at Greta Hall he saw magnificent things. He became 'no novice in mountain mischiefs.' Books were all about him.

The Wordsworths were usually accessible. Charles and Mary Lamb came to see him once. There were moments when at home all was 'Peace and Love.' As late as 1803 he could say: 'In simple earnestness, I never find myself alone, within the embracement of rocks and hills, a traveller up an alpine road, but my spirit careers, drives, and eddies, like a leaf in autumn; a wild activity of thoughts, imaginations, feelings, and impulses of motion, rises up within me. . . .' But Coleridge did not get on with his wife; he took opium; he had passed thirty, and not reached forty. He went to Malta. He lectured in London. He revisited Stowey. 'The Friend,' it is true, issued from Greta Hall. But by 1810 Coleridge had fallen back on London, whence he could go to Bristol to lecture, or to Calne to write 'Biographia Literaria,' and by chance to see his own 'Remorse' acted there by a travelling company. From Calne he went to Highgate, to the Gillmans, in 1816, and he stopped there till he was quite dead. With Lamb for company he could still walk twelve miles; he even wrote 'The Garden of Boccaccio,' and could taste the spring, but he was a man in exile, and had been once he decided to follow Wordsworth out of the West.

*

ONCE upon a time there was much talk about the supposed incompatibility of science with poetry. In a few years, if it was not already dead, the poetry was to die of eating from the tree of knowledge. One of the best rebukes to this talk was the case of Mr. W. H. Hudson, author of 'Idle Days in Patagonia,' 'The Naturalist in La Plata,' 'Birds and Man,' 'Nature in Downland,' 'Hampshire Days,' 'The Land's End,' 'Afoot in England'; also of 'Green Mansions: A Romance of the Tropical Forest,' and 'The Purple Land.' For Mr. Hudson is a poet and a man of science. His work on South America was described by Dr. Russel Wallace as 'a storehouse of facts and observations of the greatest value to the philosophic naturalist, while to the general reader it will rank as the most interesting and delightful of modern books on natural history'; he has also written some of the most romantic stories of this age, and a great body of books depicting English wild life with an exactness and enthusiasm both unrivalled and in combination unapproached. But although generation after generation of schoolboys know his 'British Birds,' and every one remembers 'Idle Days in Patagonia,' because it seems an odd place to be idle in, Mr. Hudson has so far concealed himself from the public almost as successfully as he conceals himself from both birds and men out of doors.

Mr. Hudson began by doing an eccentric thing for an English naturalist. He was born in South America. He opened his study of birds on the Pampas, and as a boy discovered a species which has since been named after him. When he had been twenty-six years in England, he could still see with his mind's eye two hundred birds of La Plata and Patagonia as distinctly as he could the thrush, the starling, and the robin, and could hear with his mind's ear the voices of a hundred and fifty. That was thirteen years ago. And he is still indignant at the loss of the great birds, especially the soaring birds, which he knew in South America, and can never see here. But forty years in England, and English blood on both sides – though on the mother's side it was Americanized – have not turned Mr. Hudson into the sort of Englishman that it is a pleasure to make a lion of. Himself has told us, and has oftener made us feel, that he is one of 'a dying remnant of a vanished people,' 'strangers and captives' in a world whose language and customs and thoughts are not theirs. 'The blue sky, the brown soil beneath, the grass, the trees, the animals, the wind, and rain, and sun, and stars, are never strange to me,' he says in 'Hampshire Days'; he has none of 'that "world-strangeness" which William Watson and his fellow-poets prattle in rhyme about'; he feels the strangeness where men with 'pale civilized faces,' eagerly talking about things that do not concern him, are crowded together, while he feels a kinship with 'the dead, who were not as these; the long, long dead, the men who knew not life in towns, and felt no strangeness in sun and wind and rain.' Jefferies also evoked these men from their graves upon the downs, but Mr. Hudson is perfectly original, and makes those prehistoric figures with 'pale furious faces' more alive than Jefferies did. Nor is this a whim of Mr. Hudson's. A passage in his last book, 'Adventures among Birds,' shows how ready he is to enter into prehistoric life. There it is for the sake of the various and innumerable birds of the undrained fens of Lincolnshire and Somersetshire that he travels 'by devious ways over the still water, by miles and leagues of grey rushes and sedges vivid green, and cat's-tail and flowering rush and vast dark bulrush beds, and islets covered with thickets of willow and elder and trees of larger growth.' His vision of that great sonorous nation of birds is beautiful. It is not the less wonderful that he is a man with a really potent sense of historical time, so potent that he seems to possess, and to employ most grimly at times, 'a consciousness of the transitoriness of most things human,' as when he sees without sadness or anger 'the wild ancient charm' of Salisbury Plain partially exiled. Nevertheless, his taste is for 'better, less civilized days.' He is, in fact, one of the few writers who could be called a child of Nature without offending either him or the other children, one of the few who could speak of 'earth which is our home' without rhodomontade. So much does he know of men and beasts on the earth and under the earth. He is even a little grim, as towards the 'pale civilized people,' towards the 'ordinary unobservant' man.

But he is equally impatient of the romantic who has been nourished on books alone. For example, he quotes a gipsy's words: 'You know what the books say, and we don't. But we know other things that are not in the books, and that's what we have. It's ours, our own, and you can't know it.' But he will not have it that there is anything mysterious in the gipsy's faculty: it is 'the animal's cunning, a special, a sublimated cunning, the fine flower of his whole nature,' and has 'nothing mysterious in it.' Then he laughs: 'It is not so much the wind on the heath, brother, as the fascination of lawlessness, which makes his life an everlasting joy to him; to pit himself against gamekeeper, farmer, policeman, and everybody else, and defeat them all; to flourish like the parasitic fly on the honey in the hive and escape the wrath of the bees.' What pleases him in the gipsy is his gipsyism, the very root of those differences which, superficially or romantically observed, give rise to 'the romance and poetry which the scholar-gipsy enthusiasts are fond of reading into him.' He professes himself a naturalist in these formidable terms. 'He' (the gipsy) 'is to me a wild, untameable animal of curious habits, and interests me as a naturalist accordingly.'

But there are naturalists and naturalists. In Mr. Hudson

curiosity is a passion, or, rather, it is part of the greater passion of love. He loves what things are. That is to say, he loves life, not merely portions selected and detached by past generations of writers. Take, for example, what he says of insects in 'Hampshire Days.' He has pronounced 'the society of indoor people unutterably irksome' to him on account of the 'indoor mind,' which sees most insects as pests. But, says he, without insects, without 'this innumerable company that each "deep in his day's employ" are ever moving swiftly or slowly about me, their multitudinous small voices united into one deep continuous Æolian sound, it would indeed seem as if some mysterious malady or sadness had come upon Nature. Rather would I feel them alive, teasing, stinging, and biting me; rather would I walk in all green and flowering places with a cloud of gnats and midges ever about me.' He so loves the humming-bird hawk-moth that he retains in his mind a lovely picture of the insect 'suspended on his misty wings among the tall flowers in the brilliant August sunshine.' The image came up as he was introduced to a 'lepidopterist' who proceeded to tell him that this season he had only seen three humming-bird hawk-moths, and that he had 'secured' all three. In the presence of this super-moth he calls himself 'a simple person whose interest and pleasure in insect life the entomologist would regard as quite purposeless.'

What he reverences and loves is the earth, and the earth he knows is, humanly speaking, everlasting. He is at home wherever grass grows, and he has hardly a trace of an amiable 'weakness' for particular places. In fact, at times he is detached enough to be a connoisseur, as when he says that the Wiltshire Downs may be neglected, 'since, if downs are wanted, there is the higher, nobler Sussex range within an hour of London.' Yet in Hampshire he speaks of villages on the Test and Itchen where he could spend 'long years in perfect contentment'; and in Wiltshire, among those very downs, he experienced a home feeling – the vast, undulating vacant land won him through its resemblances to his early home: 'I can note,' says he in 'A Shepherd's Life,' 'many differences, but they do not deprive me of this home feeling; it is the likenesses that hold me, the spirit of the place, one which is not a desert with the desert's melancholy or sense of desolation, but inhabited, although thinly, and by humble-minded men whose work and dwellings are unobtrusive. The final effect of this wide green space with signs of human life and labour in it, and sight of animals – sheep and cattle – at various distances, is that we are not aliens here, intruders or invaders on the earth, living in it but apart, perhaps hating and spoiling it, but with the other animals are children of Nature, like them living and seeking our subsistence under her sky, familiar with her sun and wind and rain.' And, again, in 'Afoot in England,' he mentions that the lowing of cattle, on account of early association, is more to him than any other natural sound.

Once he admits that 'the West Country has the greatest attraction' for him; but he writes of all the southern counties, and does not disdain the eastern or the midland counties. During these forty years he has seen England as few writers have since Cobbett. He has written about counties as far apart as Kent and Cornwall, Derbyshire and Dorsetshire, Norfolk and Monmouthshire. In all counties he has been at home with the wild life. He has visited places connected with his predecessors – White, Cobbett, and Jefferies. But I should not say that his 'country' embraces all the counties. Thus, Cornwall is foreign to him. His 'Land's End' is an uncomfortable, unsympathetic book, though every page is interesting, and many a one beautiful, as where he pictures the fishing fleet going out from St. Ives. The people were alien to him.

He was annoyed by what he considered their childishness or
savagery, and 'their occasional emotional outbreaks, which
when produced by religious excitement are so painful to
witness.' Unlike the gipsies, they seem not to have been
interesting to him as a naturalist. In fact, he was not at his
best with them. Thus, when he wished to find 'that rarity in
Cornwall, a man with a sense of humour,' he asked a man,
who was digging stones in a very stony field, where they got
stone for building houses, and having been told to 'use your
own eyes,' and obliged to explain that the question was in fun,
he related the incident to six people in Cornwall without
amusing them. There were too many Cornishmen in Cornwall. What he would have liked would have been an odd,
isolated one in Kent or Wiltshire.

On the whole I think Mr. Hudson is most at home in
Hampshire. True, he has experienced a home feeling among
the downs, and two of his best books, 'Nature in Downland'
and 'A Shepherd's Life,' are based on observations among the
downs of Wiltshire and Sussex. But he has been chiefly a
rambler in those counties. In Hampshire he has apparently
been at least a migrant with a temporary narrow range. Here
he may be seen at home with adders, absorbed in contemplat-
ing or thinking about them. Above all, 'Hampshire Days'
reveals him at home with insects. His corner of the New Forest
not only abounded in insect life, but there 'the kings and nobles
of the tribe' — the humming-bird hawk-moth, the White
Admiral butterfly, the fairest and mightiest of the dragon-
flies, the hornet, the great green grasshopper — were to be
met with. His intimacy with the insects of Hampshire
suggests residence. The book would have been different had
he not spent successive summers in the same district. Here,
again, there is a recollection of South America, where he
says of the hornet: 'As he comes out of the oak-tree shade

and goes swinging by in his shining gold-red armature, he is like a being from some other hotter, richer land, thousands of miles away from our cold, white cliffs and grey seas.' This book is full, like the others, of a profound love; but it is, I think, the happiest of them, partly because he was fortunate in the houses that received him. One old house, in the south of the New Forest, had more of Nature in and about it than any other human habitation 'in a land whose people are discovered dwelling in so many secret, green, out-of-the-world places.' Another was a cottage on the Itchen, between Winchester and Alresford, which he had to himself, without dog, cat, child, or chick – only the wild birds for company.

Hampshire, then, is Mr. Hudson's 'country.' I could add many codicils, but I shall be content with one, from 'Birds and Man,' from the chapter on 'Daws in the West Country,' where he says:

'Of all the old towns which the bird loves and inhabits in numbers, Wells comes first. If Wells had no birds, it would still be a city one could not but delight in. There are not more than half a dozen towns in all the country where (if I were compelled to live in towns) life would not seem something of a burden; and of these two are in Somerset – Bath and Wells. . . . Wells has the first place in my affections, and is the one town in England the sight of which in April and early May, from a neighbouring hill, has caused me to sigh with pleasure.'

Scattered over his rambling books are passages that give an intense, and even magical, but quite unfanciful, life to many of the towns and villages, as well as the rivers, woods, and hills, of England. They have the beauty of discoveries and the sufficingness of what is genuinely imagined. But whether he is a rambler or a sojourner, it is seldom as a traveller that he interests us. He lays little stress on his walking or cycling. They are means to an end, and his end is to be still, somewhere in the sun or under trees where birds are.

Primarily his search has been for birds. When, for example, he found himself at Chepstow, and was disappointed in his hope of seeing a rare species near by, he tells us that he had 'to extract what pleasure he could' out of the castle, the Wye, and Tintern Abbey. These things had already been discovered, and he knew it. He does not positively refuse to like what others are well known to have liked; for example, he likes a vast range of English poets from Swinburne to Bloomfield; but he must always be discovering. He discovered Swinburne by his own side-track, I have no doubt. So he discovered the city of Wells, which he informs us is the one city in the kingdom where you will hear that 'woodland sound,' the laughter of the green woodpecker; and also the city of Bath, 'a city that has a considerable amount of Nature in its composition, and is set down in a country of hills, woods, rocks, and streams, and is therefore, like the other, a city loved by daws and by many other wild birds.' He has gone about without dictionaries of literature, and practically without maps or guides. The scenes which he can best or most happily remember are those discovered by chance, which he had not heard of, or else had heard of and forgotten, or which he had not expected to see. His books now contain, fortunately, an almost countless number of these scenes, each one of them peopled, made alive, made (I should say) next to immortal, by the presence of some extraordinary or beautiful living thing, by a child, an adder, a vast ringing and echoing and re-echoing of bells, a cowman, a fox, a poet, a river, a memory, a legend, above all by birds, together with his own personality that withdraws itself, at times, far from vulgar error as from poetic illusion, but seldom far from profound humanity or natural magic, and, if it eludes our sympathy, never our wonder, curiosity, and admiration.

THE EAST COAST AND MIDLANDS

COWPER   FITZGERALD
CRABBE   BORROW
CLARE   TENNYSON
            SWINBURNE

COWPER

*

Cowper's country is easily mapped. That small circle of field and woodland, with Olney at its centre, the Ouse its diameter, Yardley Chase at the circumference, is Cowper's country and nothing else. What it was during the last third of the eighteenth century is made so clear by his poems and letters that it has a slight unreality to-day. Two volumes on it, 'The Rural Walks of Cowper' and 'Cowper Illustrated by a Series of Views,' are already old. 'The Town of Olney,' by Mr. Thomas Wright of Olney, is new. With their aid anyone can see most of the things that Cowper saw, except those that disappeared in his own time, such as the poplars at Lavendon, and were lamented by him.

Perhaps he might have adapted himself to a different country, and have so pervaded it that he would have been linked with it inseparably, as he is with Olney. But if a place had to be found for him, it would be hard to better Olney in Buckinghamshire. He was born in the next county, Hertfordshire, at Great Berkhamstead Rectory, in 1731. He spent his boyhood and youth at Westminster School and the Temple. Then in 1763, when he was about to take up a clerkship in the House of Lords, he had to be removed to a private asylum. Thus he escaped London, where it is possible, however, to imagine him spending his life, although the House of Lords differs from Olney in several respects. After his recovery he lived at Huntingdon, for most of the time in the house of the Mrs. Unwin who was for ever after to be his housemate. Her husband died there in 1767, and in the same year she and Cowper took the house at Olney. There they lived twenty years. Part of the time Lady Austen was near them. He loved her well enough to disturb her, but not to be disturbed. She imposed and inspired 'The Task.' Lady Hesketh, with whom the poet could not be unhappy, succeeded her. Cowper's garden communicated with the Vicarage garden, and he established her as vicar. When Cowper and Mrs. Unwin moved, it was at her suggestion, and then only to Weston Lodge, where they would be close to their friends the Throckmortons of Weston. The end began at Weston in 1794, with another return of insanity. They went the year after to Cowper's cousin, John Johnson, in Norfolk, where she died in 1796, he in 1800. Both were buried at East Dereham, as Lavengro knew and all the world through him.

Cowper had been happy in the country before he came to Olney. He used to stay at Southampton. He walked in the neighbourhood of Lymington. He bathed at Weymouth. Above all, he walked with his cousin, Lady Hesketh, when she was still Harriet Cowper; and he particularly remembered walking to Netley Abbey, and scrambling over hedges in every direction. Years later, when he was past fifty, she reminded him of some incident connected with the fragrance on a certain common near Southampton.

'My nostrils,' he wrote from Olney on December 6, 1785, 'have hardly been regaled with those wild odours from that day to the present. We have no such here. If there ever were any such in this county, the enclosures have long since destroyed them; but we have a scent in the fields about Olney that to me is equally agreeable, and which, even after attentive examination, I have never been able to account for. It proceeds, so far as I can find, neither from herb, nor tree, nor shrub: I should suppose, therefore, it is from the soil. It is exactly the scent of amber when it has been rubbed hard, only more potent. I have never observed it except in hot weather, or in places where the sun shines powerfully, and from which the air is excluded. . . .'

There were, then, no wild heaths near Olney. It was low,

cultivated land, and he walked about in it often, on fine days,
with Mrs. Unwin upon his arm, and very conscious of mud.
Once upon a time, when he was twenty, he had been some
sort of a sportsman. But even then he could steal time, while
out shooting, to sit under a hedge and write verses 'with my
pencil in hand and my gun by my side.' Now the country had
become a comfortable secluded garden to him where he could
think and write: as he said,

> 'Me poetry (or, rather, notes that aim
> Feebly and faintly at poetic fame)
> Employs, shut out from more important views,
> Fast by the banks of the slow-winding Ouse.'

He liked the country because it was quiet and because 'God
made' it. He liked it also for itself. He tells us that he enjoyed
the sound of mighty winds in woods, and not only the voices
of the singing birds,

> 'But cawing rooks, and kites that swim sublime
> In still-repeated circles, screaming loud,
> The jay, the pie, and even the boding owl
> That hails the rising moon, have charms for me.'

The country, in fact, gave him half his life. Perhaps it was the
lesser half. More likely it was not distinguished from the rest.
For just as he approved La Bruyère in the passage,

> 'I praise the Frenchman, his remark was shrewd –
> "How sweet, how passing sweet is solitude!
> But grant me still a friend in my retreat,
> Whom I may whisper, Solitude is sweet," '

so he brought out with him something of indoors. He enjoyed a picnic. A moss- or root-house in a spinney, for con-

versation or meditation, delighted him. Telling us how he set
forth alone,

> 'When winter soaks the fields, and female feet,
> Too weak to struggle with tenacious clay
> Or ford the rivulets, are best at home,'

he gives us a considerable sense of discomfort, only increased
by his longing for the pretty thatched cottage by the way,
which he named the 'Peasants' Nest.' Moreover, the end of
his musing on the cottage is —

> 'So farewell envy of the "Peasants' Nest."
> If solitude make scant the means of life,
> Society for me! Then seeming sweet,
> Be still a pleasing object in my view,
> My visit still, but never mine abode.'

He grew to like places as people like chairs. They pleased and
gave no offence, and they became his own. The poplars were
felled, and he himself suffered:

> ''Tis a sight to engage me, if anything can,
> To muse on the perishing pleasures of man;
> Though his life be a dream, his enjoyments, I see,
> Have a being less durable even than he.'

The letter of May Day, 1786, to Lady Hesketh, where he
refers to the loss of the trees, tells us almost all that we can
know about his country pleasures:

'Our walks are, as I told you, beautiful; but it is a walk to
get at them; and though, when you come, I shall take you
into training, as the jockeys say, and I doubt not that I shall
make a nimble and good walker of you in a short time, you
would find, as even I do in warm weather, that the prepara-
tory steps are rather too many in number. Weston, which is

our pleasantest retreat of all, is a mile off, and there is not in that whole mile to be found so much shade as would cover you. Mrs. Unwin and I have *for many years walked thither every day in the year, when the weather would permit*; and to speak like a poet, the limes and the elms of Weston can witness for us both how often we have sighed and said, "Oh! that our garden opened into this grove, or into this wilderness! for we are fatigued before we reach them, and when we have reached them, have not time enough to enjoy them." Thus stands the case, my dear, and the unavoidable *ergo* stares you in the face. Would *I* could do so too just at this moment! *We have three or four other walks*, which are all pleasant in their way; but, except one, they all lie at such a distance as you would find heinously incommodious. But Weston, as I said before, is our favourite: of that we are never weary; its superior beauties gained it our preference at the first, and for many years it has prevailed to win us away from all the others. There was, indeed, some time since, in a neighbouring parish called Lavendon, a field, one side of which formed a terrace, and the other was planted with poplars, at whose foot ran the Ouse, that I used to account a little paradise: but the poplars have been felled, and the scene has suffered so much by the loss, that though still in point of prospect beautiful, it has not charms sufficient to attract me now.'

Here, no doubt, there is some eighteenth-century under-statement, but the fact remains that Cowper was an epicurean in the matter of the country, as he was with fish and books. Even the Yardley Oak, now called Cowper's Oak, that made him say,

> 'It seems idolatry with some excuse
> When our forefather Druids in their oaks
> Imagined sanctity,'

was to him 'one of the wonders that I show to all who come
this way.' It may be, simply, that he seldom dared to give free
play to his solitary thoughts; that his social chit-chat was to
drown great silences. But on the whole the lines most characteristic of him are —

> 'How various his employments whom the world
> Calls idle, and who justly in return
> Esteems that busy world an idler too!
> Friends, books, a garden, and perhaps his pen,
> Delightful industry enjoyed at home,
> And Nature, in her cultivated trim
> Dressed to his taste, inviting him abroad —
> Can he want occupation who has these?'

He went even farther, pronouncing,

> 'Who loves a garden loves a greenhouse too.'

His own greenhouse, converted into a summer parlour by an
awning of mats, afforded him 'by far the pleasantest retreat in
Olney.' In fact, he had a very kindly feeling for the works of
man, however much he feared and admired God. From that
greenhouse, in summer, he wrote many of his Olney letters.
Even in a bad June, like that of 1783, it wanted only tobacco
to perfect it. Or so he told smoke-inhaling Bull, the independent minister at Newport Pagnell:

'My greenhouse, fronted with myrtles, and where I hear
nothing but the pattering of a fine shower and the sound of
distant thunder, wants only the fumes of your pipe to make it
perfectly delightful. Tobacco was not known in the golden
age. So much the worse for the golden age. This age of iron,
or lead, would be insupportable without it; and therefore we
may reasonably suppose that the happiness of those better days
would have been much improved by the use of it. . . .'

His poetry tastes as much of the garden as of the grove, and as much of the greenhouse. He was most at his ease, in fact, when he sat indoors at an open window on a fine morning. Take, for example, his letter to Lady Hesketh of September, 1788. He was then at Weston Lodge:

'MY DEAREST COZ, — Beau seems to have objections against my writing to you this morning that are not to be overruled. He will be in my lap, licking my face, and nibbling the end of my pen. Perhaps he means to say, I beg you will give my love to her, which I therefore send accordingly. There cannot be, this hindrance excepted, a situation more favourable to the business I have in hand than mine at this moment. Here is no noise, *save* (as the poets always express it) that of the birds, hopping on their perches and playing with their wires, while the sun glimmering through the elm opposite the window falls on my desk with all the softness of moonshine. There is not a cloud in the sky, nor a leaf that moves, so that, over and above the enjoyment of the purest calm, I feel a well-warranted expectation that such as the day is, it will be to its end. This is the month in which such weather is to be expected, and which is therefore welcome to me beyond all others, October excepted, which promises to bring you hither. At your coming you will probably find us, and us only, or, to speak more properly, *uzz.* . . .'

That being perfect Cowper, it is not easy to imagine the poet finding it agreeable to walk 'to Dinglederry and over the hill into Holbrook Valley' while it hailed and blew a hurricane, even though his companion was a good one who loved a high wind — 'so at least he assured me, and if he does but like hail-stones as well, he must have supposed himself in Paradise.' If the walk had a merit, perhaps it was to magnify the charm of home-coming. After such a one, perhaps, he wrote:

'Now stir the fire, and close the shutters fast,
Let fall the curtains, wheel the sofa round,
And while the bubbling and loud-hissing urn
Throws up a steamy column, and the cups,
That cheer but not inebriate, wait on each,
So let us welcome peaceful evening in. . . '

With him it is always peaceful evening. At least the sun has always 'the softness of moonshine.' Everything is tempered. During the French Revolution he was, he said, 'much better qualified to write an essay on the Siege of Troy.' It is news for him to relate that there was a lion at the fair 'seventy years of age, and as tame as a goose,' who licked his keeper's face, and received his head into his mouth and let it out unhurt. He glazes his own windows; he kills a troublesome tooth with oil of thyme. Eight pair of tame pigeons feed on his gravel walk. . . . But he has no idea that a hundred and thirty years after his letters will make even that silent age seem golden.

*

IF a man spends his first twenty years in and about his birthplace, that is his country. Crabbe was born (in 1754) at
Aldeburgh, on the coast of Suffolk. He went to school, served
his apprenticeship, courted his wife, in the same county. As
doctor, and afterwards as curate, he also lived several years of
early manhood at Aldeburgh. Outside Suffolk he had various
residences from time to time, but that was his country.

His father, and his father's father before, was the collector
of salt duties at Aldeburgh, and part-owner of a fishing-boat.
The other five sons took to the life of Slaughden Quay and
the North Sea, but George, the eldest, like Richard Jefferies,
had no taste for the occupations of his family, and he was
treated with alternating scorn and respect for his bookishness.
Nothing, however, was spared him. The family was poor, the
house small, the company of one sort only. 'He was cradled
among the rough sons of the ocean, a daily witness of un-
bridled passions, and of manners remote from the sameness
and artificial smoothness of polished society. . . . Nor,
although the family in which he was born happened to be
somewhat above the mass in point of situation, was the remove
so great as to be marked with any considerable difference in
point of refinement. Masculine and robust frames, rude manners, stormy passions, laborious days, and occasionally boister-
ous nights of merriment — among such accompaniments was
born and reared the "Poet of the Poor." ' It is a low coast of
marsh and heath. If it had not created Crabbe, Crabbe might
have created that coast. The sea was eating into the town; it
has never eaten up Crabbe's birthplace. The same hulks were
to be seen 'sticking sidelong in the mud' throughout a long
lifetime. It was a bad place if you were unable to get away
from it.

Crabbe missed none of the life, though he could not share

it. He says, or, to be literal, Richard says, in 'The Adventures of Richard':

> 'No ships were wreck'd upon that fatal beach,
> But I could give the luckless tale of each;
> Eager I look'd, till I beheld a face
> Of one disposed to paint their dismal case,
> Who gave the sad survivors' doleful tale
> From the first brushing of the mighty gale
> Until they struck; and, suffering in their fate,
> I long'd the more they should its horrors state
> While some, the fond of pity, would enjoy
> The earnest sorrows of the feeling boy.
>
> I sought the men return'd from regions cold,
> The frozen straits, where icy mountains roll'd;
> Some I could win to tell me serious tales
> Of boats uplifted by enormous whales,
> Or, when harpoon'd, how swiftly through the sea
> The wounded monsters with the cordage flee.
> Yet some uneasy thoughts assail'd me then:
> The monsters warr'd not with, nor wounded, men.
> The smaller fry we take, with scales and fins,
> Who gasp and die – this adds not to our sins;
> But so much blood, warm life, and frames so large
> To strike, to murder, seem'd an heavy charge. . . .
> There were fond girls who took me to their side
> To tell the story how their lovers died;
> They praised my tender heart, and bade me prove
> Both kind and constant when I came to love.
> In fact I lived for many an idle year
> In fond pursuit of agitations dear;
> For ever seeking, ever pleased to find,
> The food I loved, I thought not of its kind;

It gave affliction while it brought delight,
And joy and anguish could at once excite.'

What would such a boy have grown to had he lived as
delicately as Shelley? If he became 'Nature's sternest painter,'
Nature first made him stern. Of his mother we know little.
Richard in the poem says:

'With pain my mother would my tales receive,
And say, "My Richard, do not learn to grieve." '

It might be conjectured that his mother was on his side:

'Sure of my mother's kindness, and the joy
She felt in meeting her rebellious boy,
I at my pleasure our new seat forsook,
And, undirected, these excursions took:
I often rambled to the noisy quay,
Strange sounds to hear, and business strange to me;
Seamen and carmen, and I knew not who —
A lewd, amphibious, rude, contentious crew —
Confused as bees appear about their hive,
Yet all alert to keep their work alive.
Here, unobserved as weed upon the wave,
My whole attention to the scene I gave;
I saw their tasks, their toil, their care, their skill. . . .'

And then, on the other hand, he entered the solitudes where
later on he botanized:

'I loved to walk where none had walk'd before,
Above the rocks that ran along the shore;
Or far beyond the sight of men to stray,
And take my pleasure when I lost my way;
For then 'twas mine to trace the hilly heath,
And all the mossy moor that lies beneath:

Here had I favourite stations, where I stood
And heard the murmurs of the ocean-flood,
With not a sound beside, except when flew
Aloft the lapwing or the grey curlew,
Who with wild notes my fancied power defied,
And mock'd the dreams of solitary pride.

    I loved to stop at every creek and bay
Made by the river in its winding way,
And call to memory – not by marks they bare,
But by the thoughts that were created there.

    Pleasant it was to view the sea-gulls strive
Against the storm, or in the ocean dive
With eager scream, or when they dropping gave
Their closing wings to sail upon the wave:
Then, as the winds and waters raged around,
And breaking billows mix'd their deafening sound,
They on the rolling deep securely hung,
And calmly rode the restless waves among.
Nor pleased it less around me to behold,
Far up the beach, the yesty sea-foam roll'd;
Or, from the shore upborne, to see on high
The frothy flakes in wild confusion fly;
While the salt spray that clashing billows form,
Gave to the taste a feeling of the storm. . . .
When I no more my fancy could employ,
I left in haste what I could not enjoy,
And was my gentle mother's welcome boy.'

If Crabbe was this boy, and if he was able to return
just when he chose to a gentle mother's welcome home
from

    'Where the Cross-Keys and Plumbers'-Arms invite
    Laborious men to taste their coarse delight,'

it is small wonder that he wrote dismal poetry and resorted to opium.

For a time he boarded at schools in Bungay and Stowmarket. Then at fourteen, after an interval of work in his father's office, he went to work and learn with a surgeon near Bury St. Edmunds, and later on with another at Woodbridge. He stopped there until he was twenty – that is to say, for four years. At Great Parham, a village about ten miles away, he began courting the girl whom he was to marry when he was nearly thirty. But from Woodbridge he had to return to Aldeburgh, again to help his father and to 'cure the boy Howard of the itch,' and perform such other professional feats as he could. His skill not being great, he went to London to improve it. When he came back to Aldeburgh after a year's absence, he did not show he had succeeded. First as a surgeon's assistant, then independently, he earned with difficulty a poor living from the poorest of the neighbourhood. Thus he would have had an excess of leisure had he not botanized and written verses. The botany turned out to be good for his poetry, but bad for his medical practice, since his patients expected him to give almost for nothing the herbs which he never paid for in lanes, heaths, and gardens. He was thus fitting himself to write:

> 'This green-fringed cup-moss has a scarlet tip,
> That yields to nothing but my Laura's lip.'

But he was not bringing marriage nearer. In 1779, therefore, he suddenly went to London to venture all. Not until some days after he had pawned his watch and his instruments did he begin that progress under the hands of patrons, and Burke above all, which led to his ordination at the end of 1781 to the curacy of Aldeburgh. They did not like him at Aldeburgh. If he made any attempt, he soon gave it up – to live down the dislike of his amphibious fellow-townsmen. He was appointed chaplain to the Duke of Rutland at Belvoir Castle. His 'Village' appeared in 1783, and succeeded. He married Miss Elmy, of Great Parham, and the couple settled ultimately at Stathern in Leicestershire, where he held a curacy. They had the woods of Belvoir to ramble in, and Crabbe could botanize and write verses. Five years later, in 1789, they moved, but only to Muston in Leicestershire, Crabbe having been presented to the living.

But the beauty of the Lincolnshire border of Leicestershire was not as the beauty of Aldeburgh. One day Crabbe rode sixty miles to the coast in order to dip in the sea 'that washed the beach of Aldeburgh'; and it is not surprising that, when his wife's father died, and it became possible to dwell in the house at Great Parham, they should elect to do so. In this neighbourhood he held the curacies of Sweffling and Great Glemham, and occupied, after four years at Parham, Great Glemham Hall, and finally a house at Rendham. All three houses were close to the River Alde, and but ten miles inland westward from Aldeburgh. At Rendham he wrote much of 'The Parish Register' and began 'The Borough.' Then again he had to leave Suffolk. He held the living at Muston, and the Bishop compelled him to reside. Here he went on with 'The Borough,' and wrote 'The Tales.' But the borough was a magnified Aldeburgh, and at Aldeburgh, during a long visit, he finished it. In 'The Tales,' written in Leicestershire, and in 'Tales of the Hall,' written after his last move – which was to Trowbridge in 1814 – Crabbe returned to Suffolk from time to time. Thus, the road followed by Orlando in 'The Lovers' Journey' is said to be that often followed by Crabbe in walking from Aldeburgh to Beccles, when his sweetheart lived there. The port where Richard

watched seamen and seabirds in 'The Adventures of Richard'
is Aldeburgh also.

That coast of his boyhood was, in fact, the only scenery
which he could picture as large as life. When he drew upon
the inland country of Glemham or Belvoir or Trowbridge, he
painted fields or houses among trees gently enough, but they
were not Aldeburgh, and they were not Crabbe, or, rather,
they were that gentle boy revisiting the earth in happier circumstances. Then Crabbe showed that the feminine elements of beauty had not escaped him, or he could not have
written in 'The Hall':

'He chose his native village, and the hill
He climb'd a boy had its attraction still;
With that small brook beneath, where he would stand,
And stooping fill the hollow of his hand,
To quench th' impatient thirst – then stop awhile
To see the sun upon the waters smile,
In that sweet weariness when, long denied,
We drink and view the fountain that supplied
The sparkling bliss – and feel, if not express,
Our perfect ease in that sweet weariness.'

The atmosphere of reminiscence overcomes Crabbe, and puts
him into this mood again a little later, in a passage with a
sonnet effect:

'It was a fair and mild autumnal sky,
And earth's ripe treasures met th' admiring eye,
As a rich beauty, when her bloom is lost,
Appears with more magnificence and cost.
The wet and heavy grass, where feet had stray'd,
Not yet erect, the wanderer's way betray'd;
Showers of the night had swell'd the deep'ning rill;
The morning breeze had urged the quick'ning mill;

Assembled rooks had wing'd their seaward flight,
By the same passage to return at night;
While proudly o'er them hung the steady kite,
Then turn'd him back, and left the noisy throng,
Nor deign'd to know them as he sail'd along.
Long yellow leaves from oziers, strew'd around,
Choked the small stream, and hush'd the feeble sound;
While the dead foliage dropt from loftier trees,
Our squire beheld not with his wonted ease,
But to his own reflections made reply,
And said aloud, "Yes! doubtless we must die." '

The windmill, the rookery, the small stream, the neighbourhood of the sea, suggest the Upper Alde, perhaps at Rendham.
By the time this was written Crabbe had seen much of
Southern England, and it might be thought that 'The Ancient
Mansion' would taste, say, of Wiltshire; but then comes in
upon that beautiful autumnal beauty 'the distant sea's uncertain sound,' as well as

'Here and there a gun, whose loud report
   Proclaims to man that Death is but his sport.'

Nevertheless, it is certain that the more he lived inland and in
comfortable circumstances the more he saw calm beauty in
the country, and the less did he dwell upon mud and muddy
water and people to match, like that 'one poor dredger' in
'The Borough,'

'He, cold and wet, and driving with the tide,
   Beats his weak arms against his tarry side,
   Then drains the remnant of diluted gin
   To aid the warmth that languishes within,
   Renewing oft his poor attempts to beat
   His tingling fingers into gathering heat.'

He gave freer and freer play to the comparatively mysterious quality which saw beauty in the 'windows dim' of the ancient mansion, a quality that emerged in the earlier poems only occasionally, in a passage like this:

> 'The ocean, too, has winter views serene,
> When all you see through densest fog is seen;
> When you can hear the fishers near at hand
> Distinctly speak, yet see not where they stand;
> Or sometimes them and not their boat discern,
> Or half conceal'd some figure at the stern;
> The view's all bounded, and from side to side
> Your utmost prospect but a few ells wide;
> Boys who, on shore, to sea the pebble cast,
> Will hear it strike against the viewless mast;
> While the stern boatman growls his fierce disdain,
> At whom he knows not, whom he threats in vain.
>
>   'Tis pleasant then to view the nets float past,
> Net after net till all beyond you slip;
> A boat comes gliding from an anchor'd ship,
> Breaking the silence with the dipping oar
> And their own tones, as labouring for the shore –
> Those measured tones which with the scene agree,
> And give a sadness to serenity.'

This is Crabbe alone, leaning on Nature, and not frowning the frown of the just upon the imperfect world of men. Yet how resolute is its avoidance of adding to the mystery by artifice!

In one of his posthumous poems Crabbe asked his Muse if she could 'ken the science of the fist' – it seems that she could not – and addressed her as

> 'Muse of my service and mistress of my time,
> Who leav'st the gay, the grand, and the sublime –

>   Those who without an atmosphere are known,
>   And paintest creatures just as they are shown.'

And altogether he expressed himself a good many times to the same effect, though without assuming that 'atmosphere' is an inessential more or less deliberately superadded. When asked about the origin of the characters in his poems, he answered: 'There is not one of whom I had not in my mind the original, but I was obliged in most cases to take them from their real situations, and, in one or two instances, even to change their sex, and in many the circumstances.' He did not know that he could paint 'merely from his own fancy'; why should he? 'Is there not diversity enough in society?' He was, of course, conscious of being a pioneer. He was writing of common life without intending to amuse. It was his fear that

>   'Cities and towns, the various haunts of men,
>   Require the pencil; they defy the pen.
>   Could he, who sang so well the Grecian fleet,
>   So well have sung of alley, lane, or street? . . .
>   Can I the seats of wealth and want explore,
>   And lengthen out my lays from door to door?'

So far as he meant mere description his fear was just, because,

>   'Of sea or river, of a quay or street,
>   The best description must be incomplete.'

But he exaggerated a little ludicrously the impotence of art even at a more suitable task than description, when he assumed that the painter was setting up his paints in competition with the hues of Time and Nature. He pointed to an old tower, and exclaimed:

>   'And wouldst thou, artist, with thy tints and brush,
>   Form shades like these? Pretender, where thy blush?

In three short hours shall thy presuming hand
Th' effect of three slow centuries command?
Thou mayst thy various greens and greys contrive:
They are not lichens, nor like aught alive.
But yet proceed, and when thy tints are lost,
Fled in the shower, or crumbled by the frost;
When all thy work is done away as clean
As if thou never spread'st thy grey and green:
Then mayst thou see how Nature's work is done,
How slowly true she lays her colours on;
When her least speck upon the hardest flint
Has mark and form, and is a living tint,
And so embodied with the rock that few
Can the small germ upon the substance view.'

Being a botanist, and an Aldeburgh man to boot, who had
handled butter-tubs on Slaughden Quay, he was a little con-
temptuous of lily-fingered artists. At the time he was probably despairing of ever finding an artist who should see that
'all that grows has grace,' and should love even the 'grave
flora' of the marshland, which 'scarcely deigns to bloom.' In
a note he added further particulars about the flora of fen and
dike, concluding with these words: 'Such is the vegetation of
the fen when it is at a small distance from the ocean; and
in this case there arise from it effluvia strong and peculiar,
half saline, half putrid, which would be considered by most
people as offensive, and by some as dangerous; but there
are others to whom singularity of taste or association of
ideas has rendered it agreeable and pleasant.' There is no
doubt as to whether he ranks himself with 'most people'
or 'others.' If it were a taste that could be acquired easily
Crabbe would be better liked, and it would be more
commonly admitted that the dreadful and deeply-rutted track

torn by his sternly-moulded prose in couplets did lead to
Parnassus.

His practice was always asserting that

> 'Various as beauteous, Nature, is thy face;
> . . . . . all that grows has grace;
> All are appropriate — bog, and marsh, and fen,
> Are only poor to undiscerning men.'

He was constantly anxious

> 'Man as he is to place in all men's view,
> Yet none with rancour, none with scorn pursue.'

Just as he gave plants their proper names, instead of alluding to
them poetically, so he described men and women as, in his
opinion, they really were. As a matter of fact, he was very far
from being impersonal. The man who liked that half-saline,
half-putrid fen stink is a very powerful presence in his poems.
The drab, monotonous verse is at times so dismal in effect as
to approach a sort of sublimity, and, unfantastic though it is, it
has a nightmare effect. This drab, monotonous verse, only
not drab when it is fierce or rarelier soft, is a large part of
Crabbe's personality, and destroys his intention of photograph-
ing Aldeburgh, Rendham, Muston, Trowbridge. If anything, he predominates too much. He is large-hearted, he is
just, but never dramatic. He pities; perhaps he sympathizes;
he wishes to understand; but he treats his characters like a
schoolmaster or clergyman. In the 'Parish Register' we hear
him, when he is asked to baptize a child in a fantastic name:

> ' "Why Lonicera wilt thou name thy child?"
> I asked the gardener's wife in accents mild;'

and report said that he turned away a too youthful couple
from the altar once with accents perhaps not quite so mild.

Now mild, now stern, he is ever thus. What is miserable is so because that is his opinion of it; what is good is so because he approves. He is the censor of mankind. He weighs them in the balance, and seems even to award their punishment — what punishment could be greater than a dozen of his grey Rhadamanthine couplets? Well, in the end, perhaps, he had the laugh of Aldeburgh, and did just as well to keep clear of it.

*

There is no mistaking Clare's country. He was born at Helpston in Northamptonshire, which lies between Stamford and Peterborough, just outside the edge of Deeping Fen, on a Roman road and the Great Northern Railway. At seventy-one he was buried there. When he was nearly forty a patron gave him a new cottage three miles away towards the Fen, at Northborough, but he moved unwillingly. Once or twice he visited London. The last thirty years of his life he spent in Northampton Asylum; but, as the poems written there manifest, he was then more than ever at Helpston, cheerlessly enjoying over again the periods of childhood and of courtship. His biographer says that at the end he used to sit in a window recess at the asylum looking out over the River Nene and Northampton, but that when he was still not infirm 'he was allowed to go almost daily . . . to sit under the portico of All Saints' Church, watching the gambols of the children around him, and the fleeting clouds high up in the sky.' Most of the county and more than the borders of its neighbours were known to him. He tended sheep and geese on Helpston Heath in his seventh year; and there he found the gipsies, under King Boswell, with whom he sought relief from a love disappointment. He went to school at Glinton, four miles off, at the edge of Peterborough Great Fen. To Wisbech he went, by barge from Peterborough, when he thought that he was to become a lawyer's clerk. At Stamford, having paid a cowherd to take care of his horses during the journey thither, he bought Thomson's 'Seasons,' and behind the wall of Burghley Park, on the return journey, he devoured the book and began to write poetry. Having enlisted at the 'Blue Bell' in his native village, he was marched first to Peterborough, then to Oundle; and it was at Oundle that he bought the 'Paradise Lost' and 'Tempest' which he brought back with him on his discharge. He was a lime-burner near Bridge Casterton in Rutlandshire. Great Casterton Church he was married at, when the Marquis of Exeter had provided for him with fifteen guineas a year and a dinner in the servants' hall at Burghley. Market Deeping was the scene of perhaps his happiest day as author. He had gone there hawking his own book. The Rector had refused to buy a copy, telling him into the bargain that hawking was unbecoming. It rained, and the hawker took shelter in the covered yard of an inn among horse-dealers.

'One of them, a jolly-looking man with red hair and a red nose, after scanning Clare for a while, engaged him in conversation. "You have got something to sell there; what is it?" The answer was, "Books." "Whose books?" "My own." "Yes, I know they are your own, or, at least, I suppose so. But what kind of books, and by what author?" "Poems, written by myself." The horse-dealer stared. He looked fixedly at Clare, who was sitting on a stone, utterly dejected and scarcely noticing his interlocutor. The latter seemed to feel stirred by sympathy, and in a more respectful tone than before exclaimed, "May I ask your name?" "My name is John Clare," was the reply, pronounced in a faint voice. But the words were no sooner uttered when the jolly man with the red nose seized Clare by both hands. "Well, I am really glad to meet you," he cried. "I often heard of you, and many a time thought of calling at Helpston, but couldn't manage it." Then, shouting at the top of his voice to some friends at the farther end of the yard, he ejaculated, "Here's John Clare! I've got John Clare!" The appeal brought a score of horse-jobbers up in a moment. They took hold of the poet without ceremony, dragged him off his stone, and round the yard into the back entrance of the inn. "Brandy hot or cold?" inquired the eldest of Clare's friends. There was a refusal under both heads, coupled with the remark that a cup of tea would be acceptable. An order for it was given at once, and after a good breakfast, and a long conversation with his new acquaintances, Clare left the inn, delighted with the reception he had met with. He had sold all his books, and received for them more than the full price, several of his customers refusing to take change.'

Fame brought him acquainted with Charles Lamb, with authors, lords, publishers, but never with better company than this at Market Deeping in 1828.

Born in 1793, a year later than Shelley, Clare would have been lucky to die as young. His father was a labourer – the illegitimate child of a roving fiddler-schoolmaster and a parish clerk's daughter – a pauper in bad health; and he was a seven-months' child, one of twins. The home of the Clares was a fourth part of an old peasant's house in the High Street of Helpston, 'a narrow wretched hut, more like a prison than a human dwelling . . . in a dark, gloomy plain covered with stagnant pools of water, and overhung by mists during the greater part of the year.' He was goose-tending at seven, threshing and following the plough before his teens, until weakness and the tertiary ague stopped him. Nevertheless, looking backward in manhood, he saw no flaw in his childhood or in the cottage:

'The old house stooped just like a cave,
    Thatched o'er with mosses green;
Winter around the walls would rave,
    But all was calm within;
The trees are here all green again,
    Here bees the flowers still kiss,
But flowers and trees seemed sweeter then:
    My early home was this.'

No other poet has known such a cottage better or has described it as well as Clare; but even he has to paint it from the outside chiefly, and best of all in 'The Cross Roads,' where the cottage is not ostensibly his own, but one which he peered into as a child:

'The very house she liv'd in, stick and stone,
Since Goody died, has tumbled down and gone:
And where the marjoram once, and sage, and rue,
And balm, and mint, with curl'd-leaf parsley grew,
And double marygolds, and silver thyme,
And pumpkins 'neath the window us'd to climb;
And where I often when a child for hours
Tried through the pales to get the tempting flowers,
As lady's laces, everlasting peas,
True-love-lies-bleeding, with the hearts-at-ease,
And golden rods, and tansy running high,
That o'er the pale-tops smil'd on passers-by,
Flowers in my time that everyone would praise,
Tho' thrown like weeds from gardens nowadays;
Where all these grew, now henbane stinks and spreads,
And docks and thistles shake their seedy heads,
And yearly keep with nettles smothering o'er; —
The house, the dame, the garden known no more:
While, neighbouring nigh, one lonely elder-tree
Is all that's left of what had us'd to be,
Marking the place, and bringing up with tears
The recollections of one's younger years. . . .'

That elder-tree occurs with exact reality. It was a cottage like this that came into Clare's mind when he read a letter containing proposals for building a cottage, and he made a poem of it.

But though he liked to picture the outside of an old

labourer's cottage, he was happiest in the fields. He had had time for childhood's pleasures. By Swordy Well he could both tend the cattle and play at 'roly-poly' down the hill. He is the best of all poets at suggesting the nests and eggs of wild birds, and his 'November' contains a truthful picture of a boy sheltering from a winter storm and

> 'Oft spying nests where he spring eggs had ta'en,
> And wishing in his heart 'twas summer-time again.'

The mixture of farm labour and bird's-nesting did not content him, after he had loved and lost Mary Joyce over at Glinton when he was fifteen. He worked in the garden at Burghley Park for a change, and, running away, had a spell of truancy. Another interval he spent in enlisting, another with gipsies. Marriage at the age of twenty-seven, and a rapid succession of children that began a month later, might have done something towards settling him, but he published his first book, 'Poems Descriptive of Rural Life and Scenery,' in the year of his marriage, 1820.

It is hard to imagine a combination with more possibilities for wretchedness than that of poet and agricultural labourer. I mean a poet of any known breed. Of course, it is easy to invent a poet suddenly making poetry of all that dignity and beauty in the labourer's life which we are so ready to believe in. But such a one has not yet appeared. It is doubtful if he ever will, or if we ought to complain of the lack, since what we want to see in some perhaps impossible peasant poetry has always been an element in great poetry. If we knew their pedigrees, we should find more than one peasant among the ancestors of the poets. In fact, every man, poet or not, is a more or less harmonious combination of the peasant and the adventurer.

In no man have these two parts been more curiously combined than in John Clare, a real poet, however small, and actually an agricultural labourer out and out. He was far from being the kind of peasant poet who would be invented in an arm-chair. Mortal man could hardly be milder, more timid and drifting, than Clare. He heard voices from the grave, not of rustic wisdom and endurance, but

'Murmuring o'er one's weary woe,
Such as once 'twas theirs to know,
They whisper to such slaves as me
A buried tale of misery: —
"We once had life, ere life's decline,
Flesh, blood, and bones the same as thine;
We knew its pains, and shared its grief,
Till death, long-wish'd-for, brought relief;
We had our hopes, and like to thee,
Hop'd morrow's better day to see,
But like to thine, our hope the same,
To-morrow's kindness never came:
We had our tyrants, e'en as thou;
Our wants met many a scornful brow;
But death laid low their wealthy powers,
Their harmless ashes mix with ours:
And this vain world, its pride, its form,
That treads on thee as on a worm,
Its mighty heirs — the time shall be
When they as quiet sleep as thee!" '

He looked back to childhood, asking:

'When shall I see such rest again?'

Contact with the town —

'In crowded streets flowers never grew,
But many there hath died away'

—sharpened his nerves for natural beauty. The poet consumed the labourer in him, or left only the dregs of one, while the conditions of the labourer's life were as a millstone about his neck as poet. As a young man, sometimes neither labouring nor poetry could satisfy him, and he would escape to two brothers named Billings, men given to 'poaching, hard drinking, and general rowdyism,' whose ruinous cottage at Helpston was nicknamed 'Bachelors' Hall.' His biographer says that he was 'too deep a lover of all creatures that God had made' to become a poacher, but that nevertheless, for all his ordinary shyness, 'he was at these meetings the loudest of loud talkers and singers.' He seems to have taken most of the opportunities of leaving his cottage and Helpston, and most opportunities of coming back to them. Marriage meant crowding into that fourth part of a cottage with parents, wife, and children.

For a short time he was a minor celebrity, meeting some of the great men of his day, such as Coleridge and Lamb, after the publication of 'Poems Descriptive of Rural Life and Scenery' in 1820. But he was then no more fitted for the literary life than at birth he was fitted for the life of the fields. Delicate and passionate, he was early broken by under-feeding and over-drinking, so that he could love only the incidents of the country, the birds, the flowers, the young girl like a flower:

> 'Nor could I pull
> The blossoms that I thought divine
> As hurting beauty like to thine.'

Unlike Burns, he had practically no help from the poetry and music of his class. He was a peasant writing poetry, yet cannot be called a peasant poet, because he had behind him no tradition of peasant literature, but had to do what he could with the current forms of polite literature. The mastering of these forms absorbed much of his energy, so that for so singular a man he added little of his own, and the result was only thinly tinged with his personality, hardly at all with the general characteristics of his class.

His work is founded chiefly on literary models. Yet he lacked the intellect and power of study to live by the pen as he lacked the grit to live by hoe and pitchfork. A small income was subscribed for him, but he failed to found even a moderately sound productive life on it. Never, except in fancy rhyme, had he the Plenty which he desired, or the cottage of his verses, 'After reading in a letter proposals for building a cottage.' His only lasting pleasure was in remembering happier things, with the reflection:

> 'Ah! sweet is all that I'm denied to share;
> Want's painful hindrance sticks me to her stall.'

He said truly:

> 'No, not a friend on earth had I
> But mine own kin and poesy.'

He never became any more docile to the fate of agricultural labourers than he had been when a young man. After walking home for the first time with the girl who was to be his wife, and saying good-bye, he waited about, watching the lights of her house, for an hour or two. He then set out homeward, but lost his way in the dark, and sat down contentedly when the moon rose, to write a love-song. In the morning he awoke by the brink of a canal where he had slept, exhausted at the end of a long night's wandering.

But it was in his power to do for his native district something like what Jefferies did for his. He possessed a similar fresh, sweet spirituality to that of Jefferies, a similar grasp and love of detail. Some of his plain descriptions anticipate and at

223

least equal the 'Nature article' of to-day. His was a pedestrian
Muse

> 'who sits her down
> Upon the molehill's little lap,
> Who feels no fear to stain her gown,
> And pauses by the hedgerow gap.'

And he often wrote long formless pieces full of place-names
and of field-lore charmingly expressed, songs uttering his love
and his pathetic joy in retrospection, poems mingling the two
elements. A thousand things which the ordinary country
child, 'tracking wild searches through the meadow grass,' has
to forget in order to live, Clare observed and noted – as, for
example, how in July's drought

> 'E'en the dew is parched up
> From the teasel's jointed cup.'

In putting down some of these things with a lowly fidelity, he
often achieves a more rustic truth than other poets, as in –

> 'And rambling bramble-berries, pulpy and sweet,
> Arching their prickly trails
> Half o'er the narrow lane.'

Sometimes he attains almost to magic, as in –

> 'For when the world first saw the sun,
> These little flowers beheld him, too;
> And when his love for earth begun,
> They were the first his smiles to woo.
> There little lambtoe bunches springs
> In red-tinged and begolden dye,
> For ever, and like China kings
> They come, but never seem to die.'

He was something more and less than a peasant become articulate. For example, he had an unexpected love, not only of the wild, but of the waste places, the 'commons left free in the rude rags of Nature,' 'the old molehills of glad neglected pastures.' Though he did call the henbane 'stinking,' he half loved it for the places, like Cowper's Green, where he found it, with bramble, thistle, nettle, hemlock,

> 'And full many a nameless weed,
> Neglected, left to run to seed,
> Seen but with disgust by those
> Who judge a blossom by the nose.
> Wildness is my suiting scene,
> So I seek thee, Cowper Green.'

To enumerate the flowers was a pleasure to him, and he did so in a manner which preserves them still dewy, or with summer dust, perhaps, on 'an antique mullein's flannel-leaves.' Can he ever have cultivated his garden? If he did, and then wrote —

> 'Hawkweed and groundsel's fanning downs
> Unruffled keep their seeded crowns,'

he must have been a kind of saint; and, indeed, he had such a love for wild things as some saints have had, which he shows in the verses:

> 'I left the little birds
> And sweet lowing of the herds,
> And couldn't find out words,
> Do you see,
> To say to them good-bye,
> Where the yellowcups do lie;
> So heaving a deep sigh
> Took to sea.'

When he lamented leaving his old home, he did not mention the building itself, but the neighbouring heath,

> 'its yellow furze,
> Molehills and rabbit tracks that lead
> Through beesom, ling, and teasel burrs . . .'

the trees, the lanes, the stiles, the brook, the flowers, the shepherd's-purse that grew in the old as well as the new garden;

> 'The very crow
> Croaked music in my native fields.'

One of his Asylum Poems, first printed by Mr. Arthur Symons, is full of place-names that were music to him, and become so to us — 'Langley Bush,' 'Eastwell's boiling spring,' 'old Lee Close oak,' 'old Crossberry Way,' 'pleasant Swordy Well' again, 'Round Oak,' 'Sneap Green,' 'Puddock's Nook,' 'Hilly Snow' — as he mourns:

> 'And Crossberry Way and old Round Oak's narrow lane
> With its hollow trees like pulpits I shall never see again.
> Enclosure like a Buonaparte let not a thing remain,
> It levelled every bush and tree and levelled every hill
> And hung the moles for traitors, though the brook is running still
> It runs a naked stream cold and chill.'

But he had the farm life also by heart, and, along with blackbird and robin and magpie, drew the dog chasing the cat, the cows tossing the molehills in their play, the shepherd's dog daunted by the rolled-up hedgehog, the maids singing ballads at milking or hanging out linen around the elder-skirted croft, while

'The gladden'd swine bolt from the sty,
    And round the yard in freedom run,
Or stretching in their slumbers lie
    Beside the cottage in the sun.
The young horse whinneys to his mate,
    And, sickening from the thresher's door,
Rubs at the straw-yard's banded gate,
    Longing for freedom on the moor.'

No man ever came so near to putting the life of the farm, as it is lived, not as it is seen over a five-barred gate, into poetry. He gives no broad impressions – he saw the kite, but not the kite's landscape – yet his details accumulate in the end, so that a loving reader, and no one reads him but loves him, can grasp them, and see the lowlands of Northamptonshire as they were when the kite still soared over them.

By birth and almost continuous residence, Edward Fitz-Gerald was a complete East Anglian. He was born at Bred-field House, near Woodbridge, in Suffolk. His school was King Edward the Sixth's at Bury St. Edmunds, in the same county; his University, Cambridge. When the family moved from Bredfield, FitzGerald being then sixteen, it was to Wherstead, near Ipswich. From there, ten years later, they went to Boulge Hall, near Woodbridge, again. The thatched cottage by one of the gates of Boulge Hall became Fitz-Gerald's own particular den in 1837 when he was twenty-eight. His friend, the Rev. George Crabbe, son and bio-grapher of the poet, was Vicar of Bredfield, and a close neighbour; Bernard Barton lived at Woodbridge; Arch-deacon Groome at Monk Soham; the Rev. John Charles-worth, whose daughter FitzGerald admired and E. B. Cowell married, at Bramford, near Ipswich; Mrs. Kerrich, Fitz-Gerald's sister, at Geldeston, where the roses blew, he said, 'as in Persia,' and made him regret June's going with an Omar-like sorrow; and James Spedding and Frederick Tennyson were among the visitors from farther away. Fitz-Gerald wrote 'Euphranor' at the cottage, and was sufficiently contented with his life there to acquire a liking for winter's 'decided and reasonable balance of daylight and candlelight.' At the Hall Farm he spent many an evening smoking with the farmer, Job Smith. After the farmhouse was burnt down and Job Smith took Farlingay Hall, nearer Woodbridge, FitzGerald lodged with him off and on for seven years from 1853. There, he studied Persian, and translated 'Salámán and Absál' and part of the 'Rubáiyát.' There Carlyle paid him a visit, read and talked with him, and accompanied him to Framlingham, Dunwich, and Aldeburgh. His next move, in 1860, was into lodgings at Woodbridge, with a gunmaker on

Market Hill. He lived thirteen years over the shop or in the
yacht *Scandal.* For a short time after that he had rooms next
door; then, in 1875, made his home at Little Grange, not far
from Bredfield or Woodbridge. Alfred Tennyson was among
the visitors at Little Grange, and he pictured FitzGerald, in
the dedication to 'Tiresias,'

'Beneath your sheltering garden-tree,
    And while your doves about you flit,
And plant on shoulder, hand, and knee,
    Or on your head, their rosy feet,
As if they knew your diet spares
    Whatever moved in that full sheet
Let down to Peter at his prayers;
    Who live on milk and meal and grass.'

FitzGerald's excursions from Little Grange were chiefly
to other East Anglian places, such as Aldeburgh, Lowestoft,
and Merton. He would sail in the *Scandal* to Lowestoft, and
put up at 11 or 12, Marine Terrace, to be near the fisherman
'Posh' Fletcher, whom he adored. At Merton he used to stay
with the Rector, George Crabbe, son of the Rector of Bredfield; and there he died.

If FitzGerald liked any town, it was Bath, where he lodged
during April and May in 1854, to be near his sister, Mrs. de
Soyres. Landor, whom he met there, has exceeded his
praises of the city only in length. He recommended it to
Frederick Tennyson if he should ever live in England because it was 'a splendid city in a lovely, even a noble, country,'
and its streets 'as handsome and gay as London, gayer and
handsomer because cleaner and in a clearer atmosphere.' He
even talked of living there. But he never did. His affection
for 'the kind, clean air of the country' was part of his personal
delicacy and idiosyncrasy. When he was staying at 19, Char-

lotte Street, Rathbone Place, in 1844, he tried to persuade Carlyle to leave 'the accursed den,' 'his filthy Chelsea.' The radishes that he had for his breakfast in London had 'a savour of earth that brings all the delicious gardens of the world back into one's soul, and almost draws tears from one's eyes.' A cloud over Charlotte Street, as he is writing to Bernard Barton, 'seems as if it were sailing softly in the April wind to fall in a blessed shower upon the lilac buds and thirsty anemones somewhere in Essex; or, who knows? perhaps at Boulge;' and he fancies his red-armed housekeeper shutting the cottage windows at Boulge, and the parrot, Beauty Bob, casting a bird's eye out at the shower and blessing the useful wet, and the German Ocean dimpling 'with innumerable pin-points' of rain, and porpoises sneezing 'with unusual pellets of fresh water.' And when he got back to Boulge all his love of natural cleanness came out in a letter to Frederick Tennyson about the verdure, and the 'white clouds moving over the new-fledged tops of oak-trees, and acres of grass striving with buttercups,' and about Constable's effort 'to paint up to the freshness of earth and sky,' and about the sublime absurdity of trying 'to paint dew with lead.' No wonder he was a vegetarian, with his, humanly speaking, extreme physical and mental scrupulosity. Tennyson told him:

> 'None can say
> That Lenten fare makes Lenten thought,
> Who reads your golden Eastern lay. . . .'

Yet the clean, sweet verses all but give a religious tone to his 'Rubáiyát.'

Living most of his life in Suffolk, he naturally heard Suffolk slighted, and naturally defended it. For example, writing in a tremendous east wind, he recalls the frosty starlight, perfectly still, yet moaning, of three nights agone:

'What little wind there was carried to us the murmurs of the waves circulating round these coasts so far [ten miles] over a flat country. But people here think that this sound so heard is not from the waves that break, but a kind of prophetic voice from the body of the sea itself announcing great gales. Sure enough we have got them, however heralded. Now, I say that all this shows that we in this Suffolk are not so completely given over to prose and turnips as some would have us. I have always said that being near the sea, and being able to catch a glimpse of it from the tops of hills and of houses, redeemed Suffolk from dullness; and, at all events, that our turnip-fields, dull in themselves, were at least set all round with an undeniable poetic element.'

But even in his day – even in Suffolk – there was a new race of squires, who seemed to him to use the earth simply as an investment, and robbed it of trees and birds, and made the country of his youth hideous. Also that county had become in fifty years the cemetery of his friends And so, he says, 'I get to the water: where Friends are not buried nor Pathways stopt up.' With bottled porter and bread and cheese, and a chewing sailor, he sailed round to Aldeburgh and Lowestoft in the little boat that went 'like a violin.' When the *Scandal* was sold, he could still sail on the River Deben, 'looking at the crops as they grow green, yellow, russet, and are finally carried away in the red and blue waggons with the sorrel horse.' In the years when it was too late for sailing he still went to the sea. At Dunwich, 'that old Dunwich,' he read Lowell's essays out of doors, where the robin was singing and the blackberries were ripening by the old walls. He stopped at Aldeburgh – he had lodged at one time or another in 'half the houses' there – and watched the harvest moon go up, and the hunter's moon, and wrote his two 'plenilunal' letters to Mrs.

Kemble, and read Froude's 'Carlyle,' wishing he had known as much when Carlyle was alive, that he might have loved as well as admired the man. Less than a year later he was dead himself, and taken to Boulge for a grave.

Wherever it is possible in his scanty writings, FitzGerald paints in something of his surroundings. The beauty of many passages in his letters shows what a bent and gift he had for description. And yet, better than most description is that paragraph in his preface to 'Polonius' where he speaks of Northamptonshire. His father, and he himself afterwards, had estates in the county at Naseby. Castle Ashby, a house built by Inigo Jones, belonging to the Marquis of Northampton, is on a tributary of the Nene between Olney and Welling-borough, in the south-western quarter of the county. Fitz-Gerald was looking at the pictures there in 1842. Speaking in 'Polonius' of the old fashion of putting 'monitory truisms' on dials, clocks, and fronts of buildings, and after mentioning 'Go about your business,' which is on St. James's Church at Bury St. Edmunds, he says:

'The parapet balustrade round the roof of Castle Ashby, in Northamptonshire, is carved into the letters "Nisi Dominus custodiat domum, frustra vigilat qui custodit eam." This is not amiss to decipher as you come up the long avenue some summer or autumn day, and to moralize upon afterwards at the little Rose and Crown at Yardley [Cowper's Yardley], if such good home-brewed be there as used to be before I knew I was to die.'

And then 'Euphranor.' Some tastes may prefer Mr. Rupert Brooke's impassioned verses on 'Grantchester,' but for the present I think it may be said that 'Euphranor' discovers the charm of Cambridge and the Cambridge meadows, from a University man's point of view, as 'Thyrsis' and The 'Scholar

Gipsy' discovers that of Oxford. May sunshine on meadow
and water; billiards, bowls, and light ale; argument and jest;
Plato and Chaucer, alternate and mingle and contrast in such
a manner as no Cambridge man would believe possible anywhere else unless it were — just conceivably — at Oxford:

> 'All breathing of youth, good-humour, and truth, in the time
>   of the jolly spring weather,
> In the jolly spring-time, when the poplar and lime dishevel
>   their tresses together.'

The end of the day, when the company — all but the horseman Phidippus — return afoot from Chesterton, is classic:

'We walked along the fields by the Church, cross'd the
Ferry, and mingled with the crowd upon the opposite shore;
Townsmen and Gownsmen, with the tassell'd Fellow-Com-
moner sprinkled here and there — Reading men and Sporting
men, Fellows, and even Masters of Colleges, not indifferent to
the prowess of their respective Crews — all these conversing on
all sorts of topics, from the slang in *Bell's Life* to the last new
German revelation, and moving in ever-changing groups
down the shore of the river, at whose farther bend was a little
knot of Ladies gathered up on a green knoll faced and illu-
minated by the beams of the setting sun. Beyond which point
was at length heard some indistinct shouting, which gradually
increased until "They are off — they are coming!" suspended
other conversation among ourselves; and suddenly the head of
the first boat turn'd the corner; and then another close upon
it; and then a third; the crews pulling with all their might
compacted into perfect rhythm; and the crowd on shore turning round to follow along with them, waving hats and caps,
and cheering, "Bravo, St. John's!" "Go it, Trinity!" — the
high crest and blowing forelock of Phidippus's mare, and he

himself shouting encouragement to his crew, conspicuous over all — until, the boats reaching us, we also were caught up in the returning tide of spectators, and hurried back towards the goal; where we arrived just in time to see the Ensign of Trinity lowered from its pride of place, and the Eagle of St. John's soaring there instead. Then, waiting a little while to hear how the winner had won, and the loser lost, and watching Phidippus engaged in eager conversation with his defeated brethren, I took Euphranor and Lexilogus under either arm (Lycion having got into better company elsewhere), and walk'd home with them across the meadow leading to the town, whither the dusky troops of Gownsmen with all their confused voices seem'd as it were evaporating in the twilight, while a Nightingale began to be heard among the flowering Chestnuts of Jesus.'

That passage alone is enough to make some men stop a moment outside Jesus, and take another look at Trinity, and ascertain which is No. 19, King's Parade, where FitzGerald lodged as an undergraduate.

*

Borrow was born at East Dereham in Norfolk. His parents were a Cornishman married to a Norfolk woman of Huguenot descent, and sometimes he boasted of Norfolk, sometimes of Cornwall, and once of Borrowdale. Some say he was a Celt, though he was much more like his mother than his father, who seems to have been a very plain man, honouring God and George III, and capable of honouring George IV had he lived long enough. East Dereham was his mother's home, but in his earliest years he did not long dwell there. He moved with his father's regiment, as he has in part recorded in 'Lavengro.' We know through Dr. Knapp that they were stationed at Pett and at Hythe in 1806, at Canterbury in 1807. In 1812 he was attending school at Huddersfield; in 1813 and 1814 at Edinburgh; in 1815 at Clonmel. Parts of the years 1809 and 1810 were spent at Dereham, the latter part of 1810 at Norman Cross in Huntingdonshire, and wandering by Whittlesea, where he appears to have met, not only the old viper-hunter who tells the tale of the King of the Vipers, but also Jasper Petulengro, to whom he was sworn a brother. He wandered free, and while he nearly killed himself with poisonous berries, he learnt to handle vipers with love and impunity. He went to school at Dereham in 1811, but in 1814 and 1815, and again until 1819, to the grammar-school at Norwich. The school fostered his independence by attacking it. He and some others proposed to go and live in caves upon the seashore, but got no farther east than Acle before they were detained and returned.

One way and another Borrow consented to spend much time in and about Norwich. He was, roughly speaking, a Norwich man. The passage leading to his father's house in Willow Lane has become Borrow's, instead of King's, Court. His friend Thurtell, boxer, friend of boxers, murderer, was son of a Mayor of Norwich. His sworn brother, Jasper Petulengro, reappeared in 1818 at the Tombland Fair in Norwich; and on Mousehold Heath, outside the city, Borrow frequently visited the gipsy encampment, and, according to his account, learnt their language. He fished in the Yare, where it flows past Earlham Hall. At Norwich in 1819, in Tuck's Court, St. Giles's, he was articled clerk to Messrs. Simpson and Rackham, solicitors, living with Simpson in the Upper Close. His desk now, perhaps, for the first time served the purpose of a young man who was learning Welsh, Danish, Hebrew, Arabic, Gaelic, and Armenian. William Taylor – 'Godless Billy Taylor' – of 21, King Street, a German scholar, a friend of the French Revolution and of Southey, and the philosopher and literary master of Borrow's teens, was a Norwich man. In the Guildhall of Norwich, Borrow read the books which taught him what he knew of Anglo-Saxon, Early English, Welsh, and Scandinavian. Here in Norwich he began to write his translations of German, Danish, Swedish, and Dutch poetry for the magazines. Norwich was on the title-page of his first book, a translation of a German 'Faustus,' in 1825, and of his second, the 'Romantic Ballads,' in 1826.

His father died in 1824, his articles expired soon after, and next day Borrow went up to London. London is the second, if not the first, home of most writing men, and it was to be Borrow's, but not immediately. He lodged at 16, Millman Street, Bedford Row, compiled a series of 'Celebrated Trials,' wrote for the magazines, did very much what he was told – only he was not told enough – by editors and publishers. Thus he was both ill and poor when Jasper reappeared, and, according to 'Lavengro,' offered him a loan of £50. Borrow refused, but wrote 'The Life and Adventures of Joseph Sell' (we have his word for it), and with the gains in his pocket got

well out of London by the coach to Amesbury. Here followed those western and midland travels which provided some
of the foundations of 'Lavengro' and 'The Romany Rye.'
Mumper's Dingle may have been Mumber Lane, five miles
from Willenhall in Staffordshire. Shropshire is Shropshire,
and Horncastle is Horncastle, but the book is not topography.
If he had mentioned no names, nobody would have had any
idea of the route, or have had any ground for beginning to
conjecture. The books, written over twenty years later, present us with a memory of inland England, refined by dream,
modified by romance. It would be difficult for one describing
a journey to give a less realistic account of the country, the
roads, and the conditions of travel. Only the towns, London,
Norwich, Edinburgh, Horncastle, and the other stopping-
places, are more or less clearly drawn, and are mentioned by
name. The old bee-keeper's garden is real enough, but it has
no locality. The country which Borrow makes most impressive is the Irish bogland. Level, misty, uninhabited, it lends
itself perfectly to the purposes of his mystery:

'The skies darkened, and a heavy snow-storm came on; the
road then lay straight through a bog, and was bounded by a
deep trench on both sides. I was making the best of my way,
keeping as nearly as I could in the middle of the road, lest,
blinded by the snow which was frequently borne into my eyes
by the wind, I might fall into the dyke, when all at once I
heard a shout to windward, and turning my eyes I saw the
figure of a man, and what appeared to be an animal of some
kind, coming across the bog with great speed, in the direction
of myself; the nature of the ground seemed to offer but little
impediment to these beings, both clearing the holes and abysses
which lay in their way with surprising agility; the animal was,
however, some slight way in advance, and, bounding over the

237

dyke, appeared on the road just before me. It was a dog, of what species I cannot tell, never having seen the like before or since; the head was large and round, the ears so tiny as scarcely to be discernible, the eyes of a fiery red; in size it was rather small than large; and the coat, which was remarkably smooth, as white as the falling flakes. It placed itself directly in my path, and showing its teeth, and bristling its coat, appeared determined to prevent my progress. I had an ashen stick in my hand, with which I threatened it; this, however, only served to increase its fury; it rushed upon me, and I had the utmost difficulty to preserve myself from its fangs.

' "What are you doing with the dog, the fairy dog?" said a man, who at this time likewise cleared the dyke at a bound. . . .'

Now, that is Borrow's country, the country of his soul. It may be felt in his Spain, in his Wales, in his London, in his Salisbury Plain, but it is essentially an imaginative country, the product of his studies and of his temperament, with those early memories of Ireland as an airy groundwork. Perhaps it is Celtic. His principal walking tours in middle and later life were in Celtic lands – in Wales, Ireland, Scotland, Cornwall, and the Isle of Man.

After the experiences which are supposed to have been the foundations of 'Lavengro' and 'The Romany Rye,' Borrow seems to have lived alternately in Norwich and in London, doing uncongenial work, and too little of that to live by according to his liking. London became part of his country, because certain regions were afterwards to be associated with him, still more because his impressions of it in those autobiographical books have the same perfectly individual quality as his impression of Irish bogland. He lodged at 26, Bryanstone Street, Portman Square, in 1826; in 1829 and 1830 he was in

Bloomsbury, at 17, Great Russell Street, and afterwards at 7, Museum Street. His home in Norwich was still with his mother in Willow Lane. Both here and in London he was poor enough to have to develop his powers of walking. Thus, when in 1833 he had to go to London for an interview with the Bible Society, he walked up. The 112 miles took him 27½ hours, and he was careful to relate that his total expenditure by the way was fivepence halfpenny, on a roll of bread, two apples, a pint of ale, and a glass of milk.

Seven years passed before Borrow was again more than a visitor to England. Then, in 1840, he married Mrs. Clarke, and settled in her house at Oulton. Oulton Cottage is gone, but its summer-house, a little peaked octagonal building with top-lights and windows, close to the edge of the Broad, survives under a mantle of ivy. Off and on, for about forty years, Borrow's headquarters were at Oulton. In that summer-house he wrote or put together 'The Zincali' and 'The Bible in Spain,' and wrote 'Lavengro.' The preface to the second edition of 'The Zincali' paints the scene for us as it was to Borrow, as it took its place in Borrow's country. He was writing 'The Bible in Spain.' It was the year 1841:

'I proceeded slowly – sickness was in the land, and the face of Nature was overcast – heavy rain-clouds swam in the heavens – the blast howled amid the pines which nearly surround my lonely dwelling, and the waters of the lake which lies before it, so quiet in general and tranquil, were fearfully agitated. "Bring lights hither, O Hayim Ben Attar, son of the miracle!" And the Jew of Fez brought in the lights, for though it was midday I could scarcely see in the little room where I was writing.

'A dreary summer and autumn passed by, and were succeeded by as gloomy a winter. I still proceeded with "The

Bible in Spain." The winter passed and spring came with cold, dry winds and occasional sunshine; whereupon I arose, shouted, and, mounting my horse, even Sidi Hatismilk, I scoured all the surrounding district, and thought but little of "The Bible in Spain."

'So I rode about the country, over the heaths, and through the green lanes of my native land, occasionally visiting friends at a distance, and sometimes, for variety's sake, I staid at home and amused myself by catching huge pike, which lie perdue in certain deep ponds skirted with lofty reeds, upon the land, and to which there is a communication from the lagoon by a deep and narrow watercourse. I had almost forgotten "The Bible in Spain." '

The book was finished, published, sold in large numbers. Borrow became a great man. In London he met Princes, Bishops, Ambassadors, and members of Parliament. In the country he wished to be a justice of the peace, but instead quarrelled with his neighbours, and earned a bad reputation by his violence, his queerness, and his consorting with gipsies. He rode or walked about the country. He made an excursion into Hungary and Roumania in 1844. For his wife's health he moved to Yarmouth in 1853, and stayed until 1860. He now – in 1853 – made the first of his longer tours in Britain. He walked over Cornwall, from Plymouth to Land's End, and he visited his cousins at Trethinnick, his father's birthplace in the parish of St. Cleer's, near Liskeard. Wales, more especially North Wales, he walked over in a summer holiday in the following year. In 1856 he was in the Isle of Man; in the next year he walked throughout south-west and central Wales. When his mother died in 1858, he recruited his health and spirits by a walk in the Highlands of Scotland. The holiday of 1859 was spent in Ireland; his wife and stepdaughter being left in Dublin, he walked to Connemara and the Giant's Causeway.

In 1860 Borrow and his wife and stepdaughter took a house at 22, Hereford Square, West Brompton. From there he used to stroll to the gipsy encampments of the suburbs or to his friend Gordon Hake at Roehampton, and on to the 'Bald-faced Stag' in Kingston Vale or to Richmond, reciting from the Welsh or Scandinavian bards, admiring the scenery of the park with 'Ah, this is England!' and bathing in the Pen Ponds. At Hake's he met Mr. Watts-Dunton. He did not give up his longer walks. Thus, in 1866, when his step-daughter married a Belfast man, he visited the pair, and crossed to Scotland for a month's tour to Ecclefechan, Yetholm, Abbotsford, Melrose, Berwick, Edinburgh, Glasgow. Next year he deposited his wife at Bognor while he walked through Sussex and Hampshire to the New Forest. His wife died in 1869. For a few years longer he continued in London; Leland came to pay homage at Hereford Square in 1870; in or about 1872 he was seen at Ascot, in the Cup week, by Francis Hindes Groome, stopping a row between gipsies and soldiers; then in 1874 he went back again to Oulton Cottage. He still walked about the country, visited Norwich and the Norfolk Hotel; but he was getting very old, and was left much alone. He still sang as he walked. The house was equally far past its prime; man and house were neglected. Gipsies were allowed to camp on his land. He was a mysterious, impressive figure to strangers and children upon the road. Children called him 'gipsy!' or 'witch!', not 'This *is* a man!' as a child did in Cornwall twenty-five years before. 'Startled rowers on the lake' heard him chanting verses. He died in his bed, with no one else in the house in 1881, and was taken to West Brompton cemetery to be buried beside his wife.

Borrow's country may mean one of three very different

things. There is the country with which he was personally connected — that is to say, Norwich and Mousehold Heath, Oulton and Yarmouth. There is the country which he travelled with a notebook and described with a view partly to accuracy. There is the wild, weird, unsubstantial country of Ossian's poetry, of Goethe's 'Erl-King,' of Celtic legend, and of his own imagination, nourished on such food, but not born of it. He admired grandeur, which he described in 'The Bible in Spain' and 'Wild Wales'; for Byron also was among his prophets. But except when the grand was also mysterious, he produced no very remarkable effects. His business was not with forms, but with atmosphere. He knew no natural history. The outward eye was very little to him. He walked for the sun and the wind, for the joy and pride of his prowess in walking, and to get from one place to another. Therefore his country, save when he wrote as a descriptive tourist, is just English open country without motor-cars or even railways. It was what was essential to him, what had survived in his memory from childhood or youth on to middle age. It was as far as possible from poetic painting with the eye on the object. It cannot be indicated by statues, tablets, guides. 'He could,' said Mr. A. Egmont Hake, 'draw more poetry from a widespreading marsh, with its straggling rushes, than from the most beautiful scenery, and would stand and look at it with rapture.' It was what he saw *in it*, not what was there for the photographer, that mattered, and is recorded in 'Lavengro' and 'The Romany Rye.' The rest concerns the tradespeople of Norwich and topographers who have to live.

*

TENNYSON was more English, in a local sense, than any other poet except Michael Drayton, who put all the beauties and antiquities of England into his 'Polyolbion.' His wet meadows, his 'long, dark, rank wood-walks drenched with dew,' his cloudy wolds, his low sandy shores, composed a landscape such as every one sees walking or riding in England. The weather is English weather of every variety. The Tennysons were Yorkshire and Lincolnshire people, and the poet was born at Somersby Rectory in Lincolnshire. He spent all his school days within the county, either at Louth or at home; his free days and some of his nights on the wolds or by the shore of Lincolnshire; and FitzGerald said he should never have left 'old Lincolnshire, where there were not only such good seas, but also such fine hill and dale among "the wolds" which he was brought up in, as people in general scarce thought on.' His earliest poems are full of the little things and the great things of that country – from the flowers and box-edges and 'the seven elms, the poplars four,' of his father's garden, and the brook below it, to the 'ridged wolds,' the 'waste, enormous marsh,' the sand-dunes and the sea. 'The May Queen,' said FitzGerald, was 'all Lincolnshire inland,' as 'Locksley Hall' was its seaboard. The Rectory garden is seen and felt in the 'Ode to Memory,' 'The Blackbird,' and 'The Progress of Spring':

> 'The thicket stirs,
> The fountain pulses high in sunnier jets,
> The blackcap warbles, and the turtle purs,
> The starling claps his tiny castanets.'

The Somersby brook and its tributary 'runlet tinkling from the rock' at Holywell, and its 'haunts of hern and crake' and 'coot and hern,' come again and again into Tennyson's poetry. It is the hill above Somersby that he climbs when he says:

'From end to end
Of all the landscape underneath,
I find no place that does not breathe
Some gracious memory of my friend;

'No grey old grange, or lonely fold,
Or low morass and whispering reed,
Or simple stile from mead to mead,
Or sheepwalk up the windy wold;

'Nor hoary knoll of ash and haw
That hears the latest linnet trill,
Nor quarry trench'd along the hill
And haunted by the wrangling daw.'

The 'old style' Northern Farmer, who asked when dying, 'Do Godamoighty knaw what a's doing a-taäkin' o' meä?' was an old farm bailiff of eighty who said to a great-uncle of Tennyson's, 'God A'mighty little knows what He's about a-taking me. An' Squire will be so mad an' all.' The 'new style' man was one in his neighbourhood who used to say, 'When I canters my 'erse along the ramper (highway), I 'ears "Proputty, proputty, proputty."' Ruskin says somewhere that Tennyson's sea is practically always muddy North Sea. He must have a trained eye for mud who sees it in the 'slow-arching wave' of 'The Last Tournament,' which,

'Heard in dead night along that table shore,
Drops flat, and after the great waters break
Whitening for half a league, and thin themselves,
Far over sands marbled with moon and cloud,
From less and less to nothing.'

244

Tennyson, who was also something of a connoisseur, thought his native seas next after the Cornish seas.

From Lincolnshire, at the age of eighteen, Tennyson went to Trinity College, Cambridge. At first the country was to him simply 'disgustingly level,' but the town and the country must have confirmed more than ever the taste for gardens, lawns, and marshland, which is consummately expressed in 'In Memoriam' often and in Mariana's grange —

> 'About a stone-cast from the wall
>   A sluice with blacken'd waters slept,
> And o'er it many, round and small,
>   The cluster'd marish-mosses crept.
> Hard by a poplar shook alway,
>   All silver-green with gnarled bark:
> For leagues no other tree did mark
>   The level waste, the rounding grey' —

albeit, as a matter of fact, the grange was no particular one, but one that 'rose to the music of Shakespeare's words, "There, at the moated grange, resides this dejected Mariana" ': so said Tennyson himself. He also said that, if he was thinking of any particular mill in writing 'The Miller's Daughter,' it was Trumpington Mill, near Cambridge. 'The Gardener's Daughter,' again, written at Cambridge, has the atmosphere of a cathedral or University town, and the suburb fields:

> 'A league of grass, wash'd by a slow broad stream,
> That, stirr'd with languid pulses of the oar,
> Waves all its lazy lilies, and creeps on,
> Barge-laden, to three arches of a bridge
> Crown'd with the minster-towers.'

After leaving Cambridge, Tennyson lived at High Beech

in Epping Forest, at Tunbridge Wells, at Boxley near Maidstone, and after his marriage, in 1850, at Warninglid, Sussex; at Chapel House, Twickenham; Farringford, in the Isle of Wight; and Aldworth, near Haslemere. He also visited North and South Wales several times, Ireland, Cornwall, Devonshire, Dorset, Gloucestershire, Somersetshire, Yorkshire, Lincolnshire, the New Forest, Bournemouth, Torquay. At one period of his life, he has told us, he used to chronicle in 'four or five words or more' whatever struck him as picturesque in Nature, but without writing them down. Thus many were lost. He himself, however, has recorded how he made the line

'Let the great world spin for ever down the ringing grooves of
     change,'

when he was travelling by the first train from Liverpool to Manchester in 1830. A vast crowd at the station hid the wheels, which he thought 'ran in a groove.' The phrase in 'Enoch Arden,'

'And isles alight in the offing,'

was made at Brighton on a day of sun and shadow, at sight of islands of light upon the sea. The 'torrents of eddying bark,' which Robin Hood points out on the oak-trees in 'The Foresters,' were first noticed on the trunks of the Spanish chestnuts in Cowdray Park. The bark of these trees, on the left-hand side as you enter from Eastbourne, has magnificent ascending spirals.

The poet's own notes, and his son Lord Tennyson's, enable us to be certain of the origin of many descriptions which almost obviously were taken straight from a certain place at a certain time. The beeches and great hollies, the open fern and

246

heath, the grove where Pelleas lies down, and it seems to him
that

> 'the fern without
> Burnt as a living fire of emeralds,
> So that his eyes were dazzled looking at it'

– these are taken from the New Forest. But in 'Pelleas and
Ettarre' it is called the Forest of Dean. Another Hampshire
scene is this of Bosham, noted on the spot for 'Becket':

> 'Bosham, my good Herbert,
> Thy birthplace – the sea-creek – the petty rill
> That falls into it – the green field – the grey church.'

Then the town below the rocks, the quay, the bay, and the
phosphorescent harbour-buoy, of 'Audley Court,' are drawn
from Torquay as it was, and Audley Court itself partly from
Abbey Park. Apropos of the line in 'The Brook,'

> 'When all the wood stands in a mist of green,'

Tennyson remarked that he remembered this moment as 'particularly beautiful one spring' at Park House, near Maidstone,
where his sister and brother-in-law, the Lushingtons, lived.
The prologue to 'The Princess' is founded on a fête and feast
of the Maidstone Mechanics' Institute held at Park House.
A nightingale so very far north as Yorkshire, singing in an
oblivious fearless 'frenzy of passion' in a friend's garden, suggested the line in 'The Princess,'

> 'Bubbled the nightingale and heeded not.'

The song

> 'The splendour falls on castle walls'

was written after the poet had been listening to a bugle blown under the 'Eagle's Nest' at Killarney, which made eight distinct echoes. Windermere, it seems, may have suggested the Lady of the Lake

> 'sitting in the deeps
> Upon the hidden bases of the hills,'

making Excalibur. While rowing there with FitzGerald in 1835 he repeated the lines with satisfaction. From a memory of Festiniog, in North Wales, came the image in 'Geraint and Enid' of one

> 'That listens near a torrent mountain-brook,
> All thro' the crash of the near cataract hears,
> The drumming thunder of the huger fall
> At distance. . . .'

The end of the poem was written in Wales. Both 'The Marriage of Geraint' and 'Geraint and Enid' have many possibly Welsh elements in their scenery; for example, in Earl Yniol's castle,

> 'a castle in decay,
> Beyond a bridge that spann'd a dry ravine . . .'

and in the

> 'Little town with towers, upon a rock,
> And close beneath, a meadow gemlike chased
> In the brown wild, and mowers mowing in it.'

That section of 'In Memoriam' comparing the hush of his song before the 'deepest grief of all' to the hush of 'half the babbling Wye' by the sea-tide was written at Tintern; but so also was 'Tears, idle tears,' which retains no trace of its origin.

After Tennyson had a settled abode at Farringford and Aldworth as Laureate and family man, we know more than

ever about the places where he wrote or from which he took
details of his scenery. 'Enoch Arden,' e.g. was written in a
summer-house 'looking over Freshwater Bay, toward the
downs,'

> 'a grey down
> With Danish barrows.'

'The Charge of the Light Brigade,' 'Aylmer's Field,' 'Boa-
dicea,' most of 'Maud,' and of the earlier 'Idylls of the King,'
were written at Farringford. Much of the scenery of 'Maud'
comes from the Isle of Wight, and the last part of it, including

> 'No more shall commerce be all in all, and Peace
> Pipe on her pastoral hillock a languid note,'

was written within sound of the ships' cannon in the Solent
before the Crimean War. 'Crossing the Bar' came to the poet
during a crossing of the Solent after his illness in 1888–89.
Above all, the invitation of 1854 to F. D. Maurice,

> 'Come, when no graver cares employ,'

contains a sketch of Farringford, its protecting pine-groves,
the neighbouring down, and the view of sea, battleship, and
seashore.

At Aldworth 'Balan and Balin,' and many other poems
were written, and among them shorter pieces, like 'The Ring,'
which include such glimpses as this,

> 'A thousand squares of corn and meadow, far
> As the grey deep,'

of the surrounding landscape.

Had Tennyson told us nothing of the sources of his details,
much less would have been discovered. For though he was a
note-taker and a curious observer and connoisseur of land-

scape, he had as a rule, like greater poets, in his mind's eye a country, whether wild or cultivated, which was more than a mere composite of consciously collected elements. All that can be said, as a rule, is that this country was English. And it was modern English, so that King Leodegran saw cultivated land,

> 'A slope of land that ever grew,
>   Field after field, up to a height, the peak
>   Haze-hidden,'

just as Tennyson did; while Enid had, like him, 'a pool of golden carp' near her old home, and that old home was a tufted ruin of the nineteenth century. If there is one element peculiar to Tennyson, apart from the eye-seen accuracy of 'oilily bubbled up the mere,' it is that of the great house, its grove, park, and garden. The houses are clothed in vine or jasmine; they have honeysuckled porches; their gates are 'griffin-guarded,' or

> 'A lion ramps at the top,
>   He is claspt by a passion-flower';

their groves are of lime or elm or acacia; their gardens are rich in laurel, rose, lily, and lavender; their hillsides 'redder than a fox' with beech buds; and near by is a pool with water-lilies —

> 'An English home: grey twilight pour'd
>   On dewy pastures, dewy trees,
>   Softer than sleep — all things in order stored,
>   A haunt of ancient peace.'

Beyond the oaks of the park are wilder lands, mountains, wastes of gorse, cliffs and roaring seas; but these are painted with a vividness and scrupulosity somewhere short of love. The poet is happiest of all where he mingles refined figures, knightly or gentle, with soft, sunny copses or gardens, as he does perhaps most perfectly in 'The Lady of Shalott' or the fragment of 'Sir Launcelot and Queen Guinevere':

> 'Then, in the boyhood of the year,
> Sir Launcelot and Queen Guinevere
> Rode thro' the coverts of the deer,
> With blissful treble ringing clear.
> She seem'd a part of joyous Spring:
> A gown of grass-green silk she wore,
> Buckled with golden clasps before;
> A light-green tuft of plumes she bore
> Closed in a golden ring.'

There are parks and tracts of low, warm downland in Kent, Surrey, Sussex, and Hampshire, where spring or autumn often seems to translate into substance the spirit of Tennyson's typical poetry, where his Arthurian knights and ladies and his Cambridge scholars and poets would be exquisitely well placed.

SWINBURNE said that the sea and not the earth was his mother.
The earliest enjoyment he could remember was being shot
naked out of his father's arms, 'like a stone from a sling,' head
foremost into the sea. His nickname was 'Seamew' or 'Sea-
gull,' which explains why he began 'To a Seamew' with the
lines,

> 'When I had wings, my brother,
> Such wings were mine as thine,'

and why in 'On the Cliffs' he says 'we seamews.' When he
came to write 'Thalassius,' an autobiographical poem of the
same class as Shelley's 'Epipsychidion,' he depicted a poet,
born like himself in April, who was found on the seashore
and nurtured by an old warrior poet in the lore of Liberty,
Love, Hate, Hope, and Fear (i.e. 'fear to be worthless the
dear love of the wind and sea that bred him fearless'). The
whole poem shows us what Swinburne would have wished to
be, and to some extent what he thought himself. Thus the
old warrior poet blesses him, or rather Thalassius:

> 'Child of my sunlight and the sea, from birth
> A fosterling and fugitive on earth;
> Sleepless of soul as wind or wave or fire,
> A man-child with an ungrown God's desire;
> Because thou hast loved naught mortal more than me,
> Thy father, and thy mother-hearted sea;
> Because thou hast given thy flower and fire of youth
> To feed men's hearts with visions, truer than truth;
> Because thou hast kept in those world-wandering eyes
> The light that makes one music of the skies;
> Because thou hast heard with world-unwearied ears
> The music that puts light into the spheres;

Have therefore in thine heart and in thy mouth
The sound of song that mingles north and south,
The song of all the winds that sing of me,
And in thy soul the sense of all the sea.'

In his own song as in his life, north and south were mingled.
He was born in Belgravia, but spent half of his early years at
his grandfather's house at Capheaton in Northumberland,
half at East Dene, between Ventnor and Niton in the Isle of
Wight. At 'The Orchard,' near East Dene, lived other relatives whose kindness he recalled in the dedication of 'The
Sisters' to the Lady Mary Gordon, his aunt. Near by, in Bonchurch graveyard, he was buried. On the road between Newport and Shorwell in the Isle, he recited 'When the hounds of
spring are in winter's traces' before 'Atalanta' was published.
On the sands of Tynemouth three years before 'Poems and
Ballads,' he recited the 'Laus Veneris.' And he preferred to
think and call himself 'a northern child of earth and sea,' like
Balen of Northumberland, whose pleasures, remembered at
the point of death, were assuredly Swinburne's own:

'The joy that lives at heart and home,
The joy to rest, the joy to roam,
The joy of crags and scaurs he clomb,
The rapture of the encountering foam
    Embraced and breasted of the boy,
The first good steed his knees bestrode,
The first wild sound of songs that flowed
Through ears that thrilled and heart that glowed,
    Fulfilled his death with joy.'

Like his Mary Stuart, he loved better the moors of the North,
where 'the wind and sun make madder mirth,' than the South.
He became a swimmer and climber who had to find utterance

for his pride by making Tristram of Lyonesse also swimmer and climber. He climbed Culver Cliff in the Isle of Wight, ever before and ever since reputed to be inaccessible, to prove his nerve. It was a happiness, too, to place Tristram and Iseult in a Northumbrian Joyous Gard that is half Capheaton. He became the rider who put such zest into Mary Stuart's cry, 'Oh that I were now in saddle!' and into the riding together of Tristram and Iseult.

But Swinburne was more in the South than in the North. His school was Eton, his University Oxford, his regular abode for about thirty years Putney. His Northern scenes are mostly impassioned idealized memories. 'Winter in Northumberland' is not equal to 'By the North Sea.' The moors, cliffs, and sea, of the North enter again and again into his poems in the form of images, and the dialect Northumbrian pieces are exquisite exercises; but it was to the South that he turned when he took actual scenery for the subject of his poems, as he did after his youth was over.

His earlier poems, dramatic and lyric, had no place for any distinctive landscape. Their country is either poets' country or a region somewhat 'out of the eyes of worldly weather,' 'out of the sun's way, hidden apart,' for what is there of sea and downs but the names in a verse like this? —

'The low downs lean to the sea; the stream,
     One loose, thin, pulseless, tremulous vein,
Rapid and vivid and dumb as a dream,
     Works downward, sick of the sun and the rain;
No wind is rough with the rank rare flowers;
The sweet sea, mother of loves and hours,
Shudders and shines as the grey winds gleam,
     Turning her smile to a fugitive pain.'

It is, of course, very far from being pictorial in effect, or, I

SWINBURNE

suppose, in purpose. It is subsiding to a state of mind like that
verse in 'On the Downs':

'As a queen taken and stripped and bound
Sat Earth discoloured and discrowned;
As a king's palace empty and dead
The sky was, without light or sound,
And on the summer's head
Were ashes shed.'

It gives us no idea of what the poet saw, but a powerful one of
what he thought about it. Later still he addressed 'Heart's-
ease Country' to Miss Isabel Swinburne, which begins,

'The far green westward heavens are bland,
The far green Wiltshire downs are clear,'

but tells us only that heart's-ease flourished there, and that the
poet cared to rhyme and alliterate concerning them, and to
draw the moral:

'How hearts that love may find hearts' ease
At every turn on every way.'

So, too, the 'Ballad of Bath' is a compliment, with less local
habitation than name.

Where Swinburne is precise is in his coast scenes: at Tinta-
gel with Tristram; in Sark, thrilled by the sea and the memory
of Hugo's visit, which he rendered into something more like
music than painting; in Guernsey, where

'The heavenly bay, ringed round with cliffs and moors,
Storm-stained ravines, and crags that lawns inlay,
Soothes as with love the rocks whose guard secures
The heavenly bay . . .'

255

in that forsaken garden which is depicted with a niceness impossible to any less masterly versifier,

'In a coign of the cliff between lowland and highland,
    At the sea-down's edge between windward and lee,
Walled round with rocks as an inland island,
    The ghost of a garden fronts the sea.
A girdle of brushwood and thorn encloses
    The steep square slope of the blossomless bed
Where the weeds that grew green from the graves of its roses
            Now lie dead. . . .'

but above all on the coast of Norfolk and Suffolk. That coast, visited often during the years of his friendship with Mr. Watts-Dunton, is commemorated or created in many poems. His method is entirely his own, a potent alternation of bold and definite description with raptures and reveries kindled by the landscape and seascape described. Thus, 'In the Salt Marshes' opens with a general impression, a keynote to the scene and the meditation inspired by it:

'Miles, and miles, and miles of desolation!
    Leagues on leagues on leagues without a change!
Sign or token of some eldest nation
    Here would make the strange land not so strange.
Time-forgotten, yea, since time's creation,
    Seem these borders where the sea-birds range.'

Stanzas follow where 'the plumage of the rush-flower,' the 'clear grey steeples,' and 'the sharp straits' wandering —

'In and out and in the wild way strives,'

— are set down as faithfully as from a notebook, but never

without an interweaving of what further contributes to that first general impression:

> 'Streak on streak of glimmering sunshine crosses
> All the land sea-saturate as with wine.'

Thus in the end it is no mere versification of scenery, but a composite and ideal landscape painting of

> 'A land that is thirstier than ruin;
> A sea that is hungrier than death;
> Heaped hills that a tree never grew in;
> Wide sands where the wave draws breath.'

No other English poet has achieved or even attempted anything on this scale so local in subject, so universal in effect. In 'Evening on the Broads' perhaps there is too daring an attempt to make poetry of a piece of touring, but at its best this poetry is the legitimate union of an individual landscape with an individual mind, powerful enough to create for posterity a musical rather than a plastic impression inseparable from the original scene by any of Swinburne's lovers. The essence of it is very simple: one verse of the address to the Sun in 'Dunwich' expresses it:

> 'Time, haggard and changeful and hoary,
> Is master and God of the land:
> But the air is fulfilled of the glory
> That is shed from the lord's right hand.
> O father of all of us ever,
> All glory be only to thee
> From heaven, that is void of the never,
> And earth, and the sea.'

If another verse be needed, it is the one answering the question, 'Where is man?'

'Here is all the end of all his glory –
  Just grass and barren silent stones.
Dead, like him, one hollow tower and hoary
  Naked in the sea-wind stands and moans,
Filled and thrilled with its perpetual story;
  Here, where earth is dense with dead men's bones.'

He adds Dunwich to the poets' country. By observation, not naturalistic but spiritual, and by the emphasis of reverie and meditation, simple and conventional, but rapturous, he made that coast Swinburne's country par excellence.

THE NORTH

WORDSWORTH
EMILY BRONTË

*

Iт is more natural and legitimate to associate Wordsworth with certain parts of England than any other great writer. And for three reasons: he spent the greater portion of his life in one district; he drew much of his scenery and human character from that district and used its place-names very freely in his poems; and both he and his sister left considerable records of his times and places of composition. Moreover, he wrote a guide to the Lakes and a poem that is not quite so useful as a guide-book, but much better.

He was born at Cockermouth in Cumberland, his father being of old Yorkshire, his mother of old Westmorland, stock. At Cockermouth, at Penrith where dwelt his mother's parents, and at Hawkshead where he went to school, Wordsworth spent his boyhood. Then in 1787, at the age of seventeen, he went to St. John's College, Cambridge. His vacations were spent in the Lake Country, on the banks of the Emont, in the Yorkshire dales and in Dovedale, and lastly on the Continent. Having taken his degree, he stayed for some time in London, took a walking tour, as usual with a companion, in North Wales, and revisited France in 1791–92. In 1793 he was again walking in England, in the Isle of Wight, across Salisbury Plain, and on to Bath, Bristol and the Wye. With his sister, two years later, he settled in a farmhouse at Racedown, near Crewkerne in Dorset. There in 1797 Coleridge came over from Nether Stowey to see him. The visit was repaid, and within the year Wordsworth had settled at Alfoxden, three miles from Nether Stowey, and at the foot of the Quantocks. He stayed only one year at Alfoxden; then walked again to Bristol, the Severn, and the Wye, with his sister. They and Coleridge wintered in Germany. Once more Wordsworth walked in Yorkshire and the Lake Country. By the end of 1799 he and his sister had taken Dove

Cottage, at Town End, Grasmere, which he had noticed in his wanderings. Coleridge and his wife visited them there in 1800. In 1802 Wordsworth married Mary Hutchinson of Penrith and brought her to Dove Cottage. After the birth of his first child in 1803, he made a tour of Scotland with his sister and Coleridge, visiting Scott at Lasswade. In 1806 the household consisted of Wordsworth, his wife, his sister, and his three children. Dove Cottage was too small for them, and the winter of 1806 was spent at the farmhouse of Coleorton in Leicestershire, near Wordsworth's friend, Sir George Beaumont. In 1808 they finally left Dove Cottage, but not Grasmere, for Allan Bank, which they changed for the Grasmere Parsonage in 1811. Coleridge and De Quincey were their guests at Allan Bank. In 1813 the Wordsworths, again with three children, instead of the five with whom they entered the Parsonage, moved to Rydal Mount, two miles away, above Rydal Lake. Whilst they lived few of them were long away from it. There Wordsworth himself died in 1850. His chief absences from Rydal were to see the Vale of Yarrow with Hogg, the Ettrick shepherd, in 1814; to visit Switzerland and Italy in 1820, Belgium and Holland in 1823, North Wales in 1824, Belgium and the Rhine and Ireland in 1828, Abbotsford in 1831, Rome, Florence, and Venice, in 1837. At Rydal Mount he was himself visited by men as different as these scenes, while among his neighbours were De Quincey at Dove Cottage, Hartley Coleridge at Nab Cottage, Arnold of Rugby at Fox How, Southey at Keswick.

Except at Racedown and at Coleorton, Wordsworth usually dwelt and wrote in a mountainous country. The earliest poem which he was content to save and publish is the 'Extract from the conclusion of a poem composed in anticipation of leaving school.' Nearly sixty years later he dictates to Miss Fenwick this characteristic note on it:

'Written at Hawkshead. The beautiful image with which this poem concludes suggested itself to me while I was resting in a boat along with my companions under the shade of a magnificent row of sycamores, which then extended their branches from the shore of the promontory upon which stands the ancient, and at that time the more picturesque, Hall of Coniston, the seat of the Le Flemings from very early times.'

Then of 'An Evening Walk,' a long descriptive and local poem addressed to his sister, he could not refrain from quoting certain images, to explain that the shepherd directing his dog by waving his hat was seen 'while crossing the Pass of Dunmaile Raise,' and that the oak-tree 'fronting the bright west' first struck him on the way from Hawkshead and Ambleside and gave him extreme pleasure. Several of the other early poems are connected by their titles with certain localities, such as the 'Remembrance of Collins, composed upon the Thames near Richmond,' the 'Descriptive Sketches taken during a Pedestrian Tour among the Alps,' the 'Lines left upon a Seat in a Yew-tree, which stands near the Lake of Esthwaite.' Then, 'The Female Vagrant' of 1798 was part of a much longer poem called 'Guilt and Sorrow: or Incidents upon Salisbury Plain,' written after his walk of 1793, which left 'imaginative impressions' of a permanent force upon his mind. But even here some of the features 'are taken from other desolate parts of England,' while the vagrant woman was born on Derwent's side. This poem was finished at Racedown, where Wordsworth wrote also 'The Borderers,' and the story of 'The Ruined Cottage,' now a part of the first book of 'The Excursion.'

Alfoxden and the neighbourhood of Coleridge stimulated Wordsworth towards the composition of some of his best and some of his best-known poems. 'The Idiot Boy,' 'Her Eyes are Wild,' 'We are Seven,' 'The Thorn,' and others, were the outcome of the plans made by the two poets on that famous walk from Alfoxden to Lynton and the Valley of Stones, and back again, of which the chief product was 'The Ancient Mariner.' Wordsworth has told us that he met the heroine of 'We are Seven' at Goodrich Castle during his visit to the Wye in 1793; that the Liswyn Farm of the 'Anecdote for Fathers' was also on the Wye, whilst Kilve is near Alfoxden; that 'The Idiot Boy' was 'composed in the groves of Alfoxden almost extempore,' 'A Whirl-Blast from behind the Hill' in the holly grove, the 'Night-Piece' on the road between Nether Stowey and Alfoxden; that 'The Complaint of a Forsaken Indian Woman' was written after a reading of Samuel Hearne's 'North American Journey,' and 'The Last of the Flock' after seeing at Holford the incident described, both at Alfoxden. 'The Thorn,' he says, arose from his first noticing, on a stormy day, a certain thorn-tree on a ridge of the Quantocks, and thereupon resolving to invent something which should make the thorn permanently as impressive as the storm had made it for the moment. 'Peter Bell' is another poem with Welsh as well as Somersetshire connexions. Peter's appearance was stolen from a 'wild rover' with whom the poet walked from Builth almost to Hay; but the number of his wives was 'taken from the number of trespasses in this way of a lawless creature in the county of Durham.' The story of 'Ruth' came from Somersetshire; the poem was written in Germany.

But by far the greatest of Wordsworth's early poems inseparably related to a place is 'Lines written above Tintern Abbey.' Its thought culminated on the happy tour with his sister after leaving Alfoxden, and it took the final form of words during the four or five days' walking which brought the brother and sister from Tintern to Bristol, but was not written down until the last day. 'No poem of mine,' he said, 'was composed under circumstances more pleasant for me to remember than this.'

But the poems so far mentioned are not so inseparably connected with the places of their subject or origin as those belonging to the years after Wordsworth had settled at Grasmere. For a time he had Coleridge again for a neighbour — at Greta Hall — and for a companion on his lesser walks and his excursion to the Highlands, talking and sharing his poetry and his private sadness. Wordsworth could have written the earlier poems, perhaps, anywhere; the later ones must have been very different, if they had come to birth at all, in other surroundings. Wordsworth had long desired this Westmorland country. Moreover, when he came to write his 'Guide to the Lakes,' he soberly declared that, though there could be no rivalship with Switzerland in bulk and height, 'an elevation of 3,000 feet is sufficient to call forth in a most impressive degree the creative, and magnifying, and softening powers of the atmosphere.' He spoke of the clouds only to conclude that they made him think of 'the blank sky of Egypt, and of the cerulean vacancy of Italy, as an unanimated and even a sad spectacle.' In his soberest and his wildest moments this country delighted him. If with nothing else, it inspired him with gratitude; and in the same note where he says that 'It was an April morning! fresh and clear,' was suggested by the wild, beautiful brook running through Easedale, he adds that he had 'composed thousands of verses by the side of it.' 'To a Butterfly,' 'The Sparrow's Nest,' the 'Stanzas written in my Pocket Copy of Thomson's "Castle of Indolence,"' the three poems 'To the Daisy,' and the poem 'To the Cuckoo,' were written in the orchard at Dove Cottage. On the same day as 'The Cuckoo' — on March 26, 1802 — Wordsworth wrote also 'My Heart leaps up,' but late at night. The other famous pieces written there include 'The Idle Shepherd-Boys,' 'The Pet Lamb,' the 'Farewell' addressed to the cottage when Wordsworth and his sister went to fetch Mrs. Wordsworth, 'Louisa,' 'The Affliction of Margaret,' 'The Sailor's Mother,' 'Michael,' 'To the Small Celandine,' 'Yew-Trees,' 'She was a Phantom of Delight,' 'O Nightingale, thou surely art,' 'I wandered lonely as a Cloud,' parts of the 'Recluse.' And Dorothy Wordsworth's journal gives many facts relating to the origin, the composition, and the revision, of the poems, and to the poet's state of mind during the process and the invariable fatigue following his concentration. The journal describes, for example, the walk on April 15, 1802, a day of furious wind:

'A few primroses by the roadside — wood-sorrel flower, the anemone, scentless violets, strawberries, and that starry, yellow flower which Mrs. C[larkson] calls pilewort. When we were in the woods beyond Gowbarrow Park we saw a few daffodils close to the waterside. We fancied that the sea had floated the seeds ashore, and that the little colony had so sprung up. But as we went along there were more and yet more; and at last, under the boughs of the trees, we saw that there was a long belt of them along the shore, about the breadth of a country turnpike road. I never saw daffodils so beautiful. They grew among the mossy stones about and above them; some rested their heads upon these stones, as on a pillow, for weariness; and the rest tossed and reeled and danced, and seemed as if they verily laughed with the wind, that blew upon them over the lake; they looked so gay, ever glancing, ever changing.'

A more ordinary entry is that on Sunday, August 31, 1801, when the corn was cut, and the prospect, 'though not tinged with a general autumnal yellow, yet softened down into a mellowness of colouring, which seems to impart softness to the forms of hills and mountains.' At eleven Coleridge came from over Helvellyn while Dorothy was walking 'in the still clear moonshine in the garden.' Wordsworth being in bed, the two chatted till half-past three, and Coleridge read part of 'Christabel.' Next day they walked in the wood by Grasmere. Wordsworth read 'Joanna' and the 'Firgrove' to Coleridge. The men bathed. Coleridge discovered a rock-seat among brambles in the orchard. . . .

Miss Fenwick's notes from Wordsworth's dictation are even more precise, and one of them tells us that the old man in 'Resolution and Independence' was met a few hundred yards from the cottage, and the account of him taken from his own mouth; that the poet was in the state of feeling described at the beginning 'while crossing over Barton Fell from Mr. Clarkson's, at the foot of Ullswater, towards Ashham,' and the image of the hare was 'observed on the ridge of the Fell.' Then of 'Hartleap Well,' also written at Grasmere, he tells us that the first eight stanzas were composed extempore one winter evening not long after they had heard the story from a peasant as they were journeying in wild weather 'from Sockburn on the banks of the Tees to Grasmere.' And 'there was not,' says Myers, 'in all that region a hillside walk or winding valley which has not heard him murmuring out his verses as they slowly rose from his heart.' He mentions in particular the old upper road from Grasmere to Rydal as an habitual haunt, and also a green terrace on the Easedale side of Helm Crag, known as Under Lancrigg, where Wordsworth composed much of the 'Prelude,' walking to and fro, humming the verses to himself, and then repeating them to his wife and sister, who sat by at their work.

The move to Allan Bank and then to Rydal probably made no difference to Wordsworth's work, but 'The Excursion' seems more naturally the work of a resident at Allan Bank than at Dove Cottage. Wordsworth was forty-three at the time of the second move and a distributor of stamps, and his best moments were now separated by longer intervals. 'The Skylark' was written at Rydal, but the more characteristic products of middle age and of that comparatively imposing residence were poems of a stiffer or statelier or sometimes more classic nature, such as 'Laodamia,' 'Dion,' the 'Vernal Ode,' and the 'Evening Ode, composed on an evening of extraordinary splendour and beauty.' As much as ever he composed in the open air, so that one of his servants, on being asked permission to see her master's study, led him to the library 'where he keeps his books,' but added, 'His study is out of doors,' and his cottage neighbours were glad to see him home from an absence, and to 'hear him *booing* about again.' His travels themselves were fruitful in two different ways – by the stimulus of novelty, or the stimulus of absence and deprivation. His Scottish tours gave him the stir and the impulse which led to 'The Highland Reaper' and 'Yarrow Revisited.' The German visit of 1798 seems to have given the final pang of intensity which makes 'Lucy Gray,' 'Ruth,' 'Nutting,' the 'Lucy' lyrics, so beautiful and so free from all immediate local colouring. 'The White Doe of Rylstone' grew out of a tradition of Bolton Priory, which Wordsworth saw in 1807. London gave him 'Star-Gazers' by the stimulus of novelty, and 'The Reverie of Poor Susan' by the stimulus of absence. The sonnet on Westminster Bridge is not a local poem, but proves that Wordsworth on a great occasion made no distinction between God-made country and man-made town.

*

EMILY BRONTË's country is that tract of the West Riding of Yorkshire which is the scene of 'Wuthering Heights' and of Mrs. Gaskell's 'Life of Charlotte Brontë.' She was born at Thornton in 1818, but by 1820 the family had moved to Haworth Parsonage, where she was to die in 1848. Thornton was 'desolate and wild; great tracks of bleak land, enclosed by stone dykes, sweeping up Clayton Heights.'

Haworth left nothing undone that Thornton may have commenced. From their earliest years the six little children 'used to walk out, hand in hand, towards the glorious wild moors, which in after-days they loved so passionately.' Emily was seldom to leave this country, and never without learning how much she was part of it. When she was seven she was away with her sisters at school, 'the pet nursling of the school,' at Cowan's Bridge. After that home and the moors were her school. She and her sisters, Charlotte and Anne, 'used to walk upwards towards the "purple-black" moors, the sweeping surface of which was broken by here and there a stone quarry; and if they had strength and time to go far enough, they reached a waterfall, where the beck fell over some rocks into the "bottom." They seldom went downwards through the village.' She was 'a tall, long-armed girl,' 'taller than Charlotte,' 'full of power,' 'a strange figure – tall, slim, angular, with a quantity of dark brown hair, deep, beautiful hazel eyes that could flash with passion' – 'kind, kindling, liquid eyes' – 'features somewhat strong and stern, and the mouth prominent or resolute,' 'extremely reserved in manner. I distinguish reserve from shyness, because I imagine shyness would please if it knew how; whereas reserve is indifferent whether it pleases or not.' She was happy with her sisters, or with her dog, walking on the moors. Three months away from them at another school, when she was sixteen, made her wretched.

'My sister Emily,' wrote Charlotte, 'loved the moors. Flowers brighter than the rose bloomed in the blackest of the heath for her; out of a sullen hollow in a livid hillside her mind could make an Eden. She found in the bleak solitude many and dear delights; and not the least and best loved was — liberty. Liberty was the breath of Emily's nostrils; without it she perished. The change from her own home to a school, and from her own very noiseless, very secluded, but unrestricted and unartificial mode of life, to one of disciplined routine (though under the kindest auspices) was what she failed in enduring. Her nature proved here too strong for her fortitude. Every morning, when she woke, the vision of home and the moors rushed on her, and darkened and saddened the day that lay before her. Nobody knew what ailed her but me. I knew only too well. In this struggle her health was quickly broken; her white face, attenuated form, and failing strength, threatened rapid decline. I felt in my heart she would die if she did not go home, and with this conviction obtained her recall.'

She returned home to bake the bread, iron the washing, read, and walk on the moors. Yet again, when she was seventeen, she went away from home to work as a teacher near Halifax. Again she gave way and had to return home. For the last time she left home with Charlotte, at the age of twenty-four, to go to M. Héger's school at Brussels. There she had a vision of home which makes the first of her posthumous poems in Charlotte Brontë's edition:

'There is a spot, 'mid barren hills,
    Where winter howls, and driving rain;
But if the dreary tempest chills,
    There is a light that warms again.

'The house is old, the trees are bare,
　Moonless above bends twilight's dome;
But what on earth is half so dear —
　So longed for — as the hearth of home?

'The mute bird sitting on the stone,
　The dank moss dripping from the wall,
The thorn-trees gaunt, the walks o'ergrown,
　I love them — how I love them all! . . .

'A little and a lone green lane
　That opened on a common wide;
A distant, dreamy, dim blue chain
　Of mountains circling every side

'A heaven so clear, an earth so calm,
　So sweet, so soft, so hushed an air;
And, deepening still the dream-like charm,
　Wild moor-sheep feeding everywhere. . . .'

Once back at Haworth, she never left it, though for some
time she had not the company of her sisters or even her
brother. She had her bulldog and Anne's spaniel and the cats.
In distinguishing Emily's love of animals from Charlotte's,
Mrs. Gaskell reveals Emily: 'The helplessness of an animal
was its passport to Charlotte's heart; the fierce, wild intract-
ability of its nature was what often recommended it to Emily.'
Charlotte took many traits of Shirley's character from Emily,
such as her reading on the rug with her arm round her rough
bulldog's neck; her giving a mad dog a drink, being bitten by
it, and then searing the bite with a red-hot iron without telling
anyone. She loved the bulldog, as she also punished him, without fear.

She fits into the moorland — she is part of it — like the curlew and the heather, and she herself knew it. The moorland

was a necessity to her, but it was also her chief pleasure and joy. Her poems always imply it, and often express it. These stanzas are among the most explicit:

'Awaken, o'er all my dear moorland,
  West-wind, in thy glory and pride!
Oh! call me from valley and lowland
  To walk by the hill-torrent's side!

'It is swelled with the first snowy weather;
  The rocks they are icy and hoar,
And sullenly waves the long heather,
  And the fern leaves are sunny no more.

'There are no yellow stars on the mountain;
  The bluebells have long died away
From the brink of the moss-bedded fountain,
  From the side of the wintry brae.

'But lovelier than corn-fields all waving
  In emerald, and vermeil, and gold,
Are the heights where the north-wind is raving,
  And the crags where I wandered of old.'

So great was her love that the genius of the moorland says to her in one poem:

'Few hearts to mortals given,
  On earth so wildly pine;
Yet few would ask a heaven
  More like this earth than thine.'

She asked for nothing, while she was on this earth and on the moor, save her own heart and liberty. Her poems and her life, in fact, reveal her as a wild spirit, as what Byron seemed in his poetry when he had a background of mountains and

thunder. Her background is the everlasting wild itself and
'Wuthêring Heights.' She 'rides on the whirlwind' in the
country described in the first chapter of that book:

' "Wuthering" being a significant provincial adjective descriptive of the atmospheric tumult to which its station is exposed in stormy weather. Pure, bracing ventilation they must
have up there at all times, indeed: one may guess the power of
the north wind blowing over the edge by the excessive slant of
a few stunted firs at the end of the house, and by a range of
gaunt thorns all stretching their limbs one way, as if craving
alms of the sun. . . .'

For a moment sometimes she lets in the 'soft thaw winds
and warm sunshine' – 'I only see two white spots on the whole
range of moors: the sky is blue, and the larks are singing, and
the becks and brooks are all brim full' – but they chiefly
emphasize the cold, gaunt grey which they relieve. She herself would have had a heaven after this pattern, as she says
again:

> 'We would not leave our nature home
> For *any* world beyond the tomb.
> No, mother, on thy kindly breast
> Let us be laid in lasting rest,
> Or waken but to share with thee
> A mutual immortality.'

'The action,' said Rossetti, 'of "Wuthering Heights" is
laid in hell.' Charlotte Brontë, pretending that her sister
was 'Ellis Bell,' said:

'The statuary found a granite block on a solitary moor.
Gazing thereon, he saw how from the crag might be elicited
a head, savage, swart, sinister; a form moulded with at least

one element of grandeur – power. He wrought with a rude chisel, and from no model but the vision of his meditations. With time and labour the crag took human shape; and there it stands, colossal, dark, and frowning, half statue, half rock: in the former sense, terrible and goblin-like; in the latter, almost beautiful. For its colouring is of mellow grey, and moorland moss clothes it; and heath, with its blooming bells and balmy fragrance, grows faithfully close to the giant's foot.'

But not even Charlotte Brontë can have seen that not only had shapes like the hard race of men been carved out of that rock, but one like an immortal mountain nymph – Emily herself.

SCOTLAND

BURNS
SCOTT
STEVENSON

BURNS

*

BURNS'S country was the Western Lowlands of Scotland.
Burns was the Lowlands of Scotland. The poor, free peasantry culminated in him. Poetry does not sum up, but his
poetry was the flower and the essence of that country and its
peasantry. He was great because they were all at his back,
their life and their literature. To speak of his country is
merely to consider a few scatterings of the elements which he
mixed into lasting songs. A clay cottage at Alloway, near
Ayr, was his birthplace. His father held seven acres there, and
built the house. While Burns was still a small schoolboy they
took a larger farm near by, and at fifteen he began to work on
the poorest land in Ayrshire as his father's chief servant. Not
till he was eighteen did they move to Lochlie, a larger farm
still, in the parish of Tarbolton. For a year he was away at
Irvine as a flax-dresser. He and his brother Gilbert took
Mossgiel Farm, three miles from Lochlie, in 1783. Next year
his father died. He had written some of the poems we know
at Lochlie, but he wrote most at Mossgiel and at Ellisland in
Dumfriesshire, which he took in 1789.

The best account of Burns's country from a visitor is that
written by Keats in July, 1818, when he walked through it.
The 'richly meadowed, wooded, heathed, and rivuleted' land,
'with a grand sea view terminated by the black mountains of
the Isle of Arran,' outwent his expectations.

'I had,' he says, 'no conception that the native place of
Burns was so beautiful; the idea I had was more desolate.
His "rigs of barley" seemed always to me but a few strips of
green on a cold hill. O prejudice! it was as rich as Devon. . . .
We came down upon everything suddenly: there were in our
way the "bonny Doon," with the brig that Tam o' Shanter
crossed, Kirk Alloway, Burns's cottage, and the Brigs of Ayr.

First we stood upon the bridge across the Doon, surrounded by every phantasy of green in tree, meadow, and hill: the stream of the Doon, as a farmer told us, is covered with trees "from head to foot" – you know those beautiful heaths so fresh against the weather of a summer's evening – there was one stretching along behind the trees.'

Burns saw it differently. He was a peasant, and had lived on the earth. True, there were moments, after he had been to Edinburgh and toured a little, when he thought more of Ossian's country than of fishing towns and fertile carses. But he could not do without the fertile carses, and it is more characteristic of him to relate how he 'rambled over the rich, fertile carses of Falkirk and Stirling, and was delighted with their appearance: richly waving crops of wheat, barley, etc., but no harvest at all yet, except, in one or two places, an old-wife's ridge.' These were the necessities. Luxuries and necessities also were to be found near at hand in the Lowlands, in the woods about the Ayr, 'the fragrant birch and hawthorn hoar,' or where

> 'The braes ascend, like lofty wa's,
> The foaming stream deep-roaring fa's,
> O'erhung wi' fragrant spreading shaws,
> The birks of Aberfeldy.'

He was a peasant, but he was a rambler also. So little of a Presbyterian was he that he approved of 'set times and seasons of more than ordinary acts of devotion, for breaking in on that habituated routine of life and thought which is so apt to reduce our existence to a kind of instinct, or even sometimes, and with some minds, to a state very little superior to mere machinery.' So he wrote on New Year's Day morning in 1789. 'This day,' he continued, 'the first Sunday of May; a

breezy blue-skyed noon some time about the beginning, and a
hoary morning and calm sunny day about the end, of autumn
– these, time out of mind, have been with me a kind of holiday.' In autumn, he said, he wrote more verses than in all the
rest of the year, when

> 'the ev'ning's clear,
> Thick flies the skimming swallow;
> The sky is blue, the fields in view,
> All fading green and yellow. . . .'

The letter where he says so shows us the rambler, for he tells
George Thomson: 'That tune, "Cauld Kail," is such a
favourite of yours that I once more roved out yesterday for a
gloamin'-shot at the Muses.' He composed, with a tune in his
head, while he was walking or riding.

His poetry shows us the delicate wild country at the edge of
the ploughland or in the midst of it, which is the more delicate
for the contrast, and perhaps for the fact that the poet had so
long known the plough. It has the freshness of the line
common in folk-songs:

> 'As I walked forth one midsummer morning.'

Burns walks forth 'to view the corn an' snuff the caller air.'
So the Muse saw him in 'The Vision':

> 'When ripen'd fields and azure skies
> Call'd forth the reaper's rustling noise,
> I saw thee leave their evening joys,
> And lonely stalk,
> To vent thy bosom's swelling rise,
> In pensive walk.'

He loves the corn and the roses, the scent of beanfields and of
wild foliage. He muses early in the summer morning by Nith

side. The briers and woodbines budding, the partridges calling, 'inspire his Muse.' He loves the woods, and laments
their destruction as keenly, though with anger, as Cowper or
Wordsworth. He loves, too, the single tree in the field, and
praises the tree as well as the girl when he compares her with

> 'yon youthful ash
> That grows the cowslip braes between,
> And drinks the stream with vigour fresh.'

He ranges from the scene of 'Countrie Lassie' –

> 'In simmer, when the hay was mawn,
>   And corn wav'd green in ilka field,
> While claver blooms white o'er the lea,
>   And roses blaw in ilka bield . . .'

up to the burn that strays in 'gowany glens' –

> 'Where bonnie lasses bleach their claes;
> Or trots by hazelly shaws and braes,
>   Wi' hawthorns grey,
> Where blackbirds join the shepherds' lays
>   At close o' day . . .'

– and even up to the curlew's moorland.

How much he loved the Highland, 'where savage streams
tumble over savage mountains, thinly overspread with savage
flocks, which sparingly support as savage inhabitants,' is not
quite plain. I think that he as an individual inclined to love
the mountains, but that his ancestry mixed a kind of fear or
hate with his love. The 'muirs an' dizzy crags' were the playground of 'warlocks grim an' wither'd hags,' and not only of
'Caledonia, thy wild heaths among.' Without Peggy's charms,
what would he have done

> 'Where, braving angry winter's storms,
>   The lofty Ochils rise'?

What, without the other sweet lassie of parentage humble, would he have said of

> 'Yon wild mossy mountains sae lofty and wide,
>   That nurse in their bosom the youth o' the Clyde,
>   Where the grouse lead their coveys thro' the heather to feed,
>   And the shepherd tents his flock as he pipes on his reed'?

To generation after generation of his ancestors the mountains must have been indifferent when not dangerous. If he loved them apart from passing associations, it was as symbols of the eternal and unconfined.

And so with winter and wild weather. Many of his poems show the ancient agricultural man's love of spring and fine weather. In the winter night he thinks of the silly sheep on the hills, and the helpless bird, and though he can pass the time in rhyme, yet

> 'While frosty winds blaw in the drift,
>   Ben to the chimla-lug
>   I grudge a wee the great folks' gift,
>   That live sae bien an' snug.'

If he had not himself been starved with cold, there was that in him which knew what it meant. When he sings,

> 'The birds sit chittering on the thorn,
>   A' day they fare but sparely,
>   And lang's the night frae e'en to morn —
>   I'm sure it's winter fairly,'

he is looking out as a peasant whose fires have not always

281

roared. Yet in May he could write of 'Coila's haughs an' woods,'

> 'When lintwhites chant amang the buds,
>   And jinkin' hares, in amorous whids,
>   Their loves enjoy;'

and also of the joys of winter:

> 'Ev'n winter bleak has charms to me,
>   When winds rave thro' the naked tree;
>   Or frosts on hills of Ochiltree
>   Are hoary grey;
>   Or blinding drifts wild-furious flee,
>   Dark'ning the day!'

He loved winter as he did the mountains, and probably the sea in the same way, though the Muse did claim to have seen him 'seek the sounding shore, delighted with the dashing roar.' She said, too, that she had seen him struck by 'Nature's visage hoar' under the north wind, and he has told us himself that 'There is scarcely any earthly object gives me more — I don't know if I should call it pleasure, but something which exalts me, something which enraptures me — than to walk in the sheltered side of a wood or high plantation, in a cloudy winter day, and hear a stormy wind howling among the trees and raving o'er the plain.' Yet it is, as it were, against a background of such weather that his spring gentleness is so gentle, as it is against a background of winter, of mountains, and of hard labour at the plough, that his flowers and green leaves and bright waters are so sweet.

SCOTT

*

Scott's country was Scotland, as Michael Drayton's was England and Wales. Had he had a mind to, he might have emulated Drayton's 'Chorographical Description of all the Tracts, Rivers, Mountains, Forests, and other Parts of this Renowned Isle of Great Britain,' as Drayton might have emulated Scott at a story had he had a mind to.

Before he was three Scott left Edinburgh for the country of his ancestors, and came to live at Sandy-Knowe Farm in Tweeddale. It was thought that 'natural exertion, excited by free air and liberty,' might restore the use of his lame right leg; and he says himself that 'the impatience of a child soon inclined me to struggle with my infirmity, and I began by degrees to stand, to walk, and to run,' to become 'a healthy, high-spirited, and, my lameness apart, a sturdy child.' Sixty years later, when Lockhart was writing his Life, there were two old women living who had been servants at Sandy-Knowe when Scott arrived there, and could remember him.

'The young ewe-milkers delighted,' said one of the two, 'to carry him about on their backs among the crags; and he was "very gleg (quick) at the uptake, and soon learned every sheep and lamb by headmark as well as any of them." His great pleasure, however, was in the society of the "aged hind" recorded in the epistle to Erskine, "auld Sandy Ormiston," called from the most dignified part of his function "the Cow-bailie," who had the chief superintendence of the flocks that browsed upon "the velvet tufts of loveliest green." If the child saw him in the morning, he could not be satisfied unless the old man would set him astride on his shoulder, and take him to keep him company as he lay watching his charge. The Cow-bailie blew a particular note on his whistle, which signified to the maid-servants in the house below when the little boy wished to be carried home again. He told his friend, Mr. Skene of Rubislaw, when spending a summer day in his old age among those well-remembered crags, that he delighted to roll about in the grass all day long in the midst of the flock, and that "the sort of fellowship he thus formed with the sheep and lambs had impressed his mind with a degree of affectionate feeling towards them which had lasted throughout life." There is a story of his having been forgotten one day among the knolls, when a thunder-storm came on; and his aunt, suddenly recollecting his situation, and running out to bring him home, is said to have found him lying on his back, clapping his hands at the lightning, and crying out, "Bonny! bonny!" at every flash.'

In the introduction to the third canto of 'Marmion,' Scott tells Erskine that he is now aping 'the measure wild of tales that charmed him yet a child,' and that there above the Tweed

> 'was poetic impulse given,
> By the green hill and clear blue heaven.'

He learned to know men and earth and history together. The local information, he says, which had some share in forming his tastes, came from 'the old songs and tales which then formed the amusement of a retired Border family' —

> 'Of lovers' slights, of ladies' charms,
> Of witches' spells, of warriors' arms;
> Of patriot battles, won of old
> By Wallace wight and Bruce the bold;
> Of later fields of feud and fight,
> When, pouring from their Highland height,
> The Scottish clans, in headlong sway,
> Had swept the scarlet ranks away.'

For the most part there were few to talk down to him, except, of course, in school hours, and he hits on a very good simple thing when he says: 'I rather suspect that children derive impulses of a powerful and important kind in hearing things which they cannot entirely comprehend; and, therefore, that to write *down* to children's understanding is a mistake; set them on the scent, and let them puzzle it out.' He read Homer, 'a few traditionary ballads,' and the old songs collected by Allan Ramsay. He says also that Dodsley's account of Shenstone's Leasowes made him envy the poet's grounds more than his 'pipe, crook, flock, and Phillis to boot'; that he never forgot a phrase from an almanack of Charles II's time, advising the reader in June to walk for his health's sake 'a mile or two every day before breakfast, and, if he can possibly so manage, to let his exercise be taken upon his own land.' This, then, was the boy that was father to the man Walter Scott.

Then, in 1778, at seven years old, he went to the High School of Edinburgh. He grew too fast, became delicate, and was again transplanted to the country, this time to an aunt's at Kelso upon the Tweed. All his time, except four hours at the village grammar-school, was now his own. He read Shakespeare and Spenser, Percy's 'Reliques of Ancient Poetry,' and the novelists. And his feeling for natural beauty was awakened for the first time.

'The neighbourhood of Kelso,' says Scott himself, 'the most beautiful, if not the most romantic village in Scotland, is eminently calculated to awaken these ideas. It presents objects, not only grand in themselves, but venerable from their association. The meeting of two superb rivers, the Tweed and the Teviot, both renowned in song – the ruins of an ancient abbey – the more distant vestiges of Roxburgh Castle

– the modern mansion of Fleurs, which is so situated as to combine the ideas of ancient baronial grandeur with those of modern taste, are in themselves objects of the first class, yet are so mixed, united, and melted, among a thousand other beauties of a less prominent description, that they harmonize into one general picture, and please rather by unison than by concord. I believe I have written unintelligibly upon this subject, but it is fitter for the pencil than the pen. The romantic feelings which I have described as predominating in my mind naturally rested upon and associated themselves with these grand features of the landscape around me; and the historical incidents, or traditional legends connected with many of them, gave to my admiration a sort of intense impression of reverence, which at times made my heart feel too big for its bosom. From this time the love of natural beauty, more especially when combined with ancient ruins, or remains of our fathers' piety or splendour, became with me an insatiable passion, which, if circumstances had permitted, I would willingly have gratified by travelling over half the globe.'

In his youth and early manhood he visited most of his native land and of its coast, and saw mountains which were as grand as the lesser hills of Tweeddale, wild, but not unkind, had seemed to the imagination of childhood.

While still a boy he 'entered upon the dry and barren wilderness of forms and conveyances' with his father in Edinburgh, but at the same time composed romances in friendly rivalry with a friend, which were rehearsed upon their walks 'to the most solitary spots about Arthur's Seat and Salisbury Crags.' He would walk out to breakfast at Prestonpans, and return at evening. The Law formed a background for a very picturesque Freedom. He had, for example, 'a dreamy way of going much farther than he intended' when he was walking

286

or riding or fishing above Howgate, and he tells us how on one occasion the beauty and the hospitality of Pennycuik House 'drowned all recollection of home for a day or two.' When his father protested that he was meant for a pedlar, the lad was not offended. His principal object was to see romantic scenery and places of historic interest. The field of Bannock- burn and the landscape seen from Stirling Castle equally attracted him. So vividly could he people scenes with 'combat- ants in their proper costume' that he kept a fellow-traveller awake by his picture of the assassination of the Archbishop of St. Andrews, crossing Magus Moor.

Having put on the gown of an advocate, Scott was often free to put it off and take longer excursions northward or southward. On his first autumn vacation, for example, he used Kelso as a centre for travels as far afield as Flodden and Hexham. He shot wild-duck and the gulls, herons, and cor- morants, that flew past his reading nest in a tree above the Tweed. He coursed hares. This was the 'Life in the Forest' which he celebrated afterwards in the poem beginning,

> 'On Ettrick Forest's mountains dun
> 'Tis blithe to hear the sportman's gun,'

and ending,

> ''Tis blithe at eve to tell the tale,
> How we succeed and how we fail,
> Whether at Alwyn's lordly meal,
> Or lowlier board of Ashestiel;
> While the gay tapers cheerly shine,
> Bickers the fire and flows the wine –
> Days free from thought, and nights from care,
> My blessing on the forest fair!'

At this time also Scott made the first of his seven 'annual

raids' into Liddersdale, to see the ruins of Hermitage Castle, and to gather 'riding ballads' from descendants of the moss-troopers. Hence came his material for the 'Minstrelsy of the Border' and the character of Dandie Dinmont (William Elliot of Millburnholm Farm).

It was to make himself acquainted with the case of a drunken minister of Girthon, for one of his first briefs, that Scott went to Galloway. He was thus, according to Lockhart, carried into the scenery of 'Guy Mannering' for the first and only time; 'and several of the names of the minor characters of the novel (*M'Guffog*, for example), appear in the List of witnesses.'

In a long series of vacation journeys, Scott saw the country in which the heroes of his poems and novels were shortly to move. Travelling from house to house of his legal friends in one early vacation, he met at Tullibody an old laird who had been received by Rob Roy 'in a cavern exactly such as that of *Bean Lean*'; with the laird of Cambusmore he saw Loch Katrine, and made the first of those 'merry expeditions' which were always associated in his mind with the scenery of 'The Lady of the Lake'; Craighall in Perthshire was the original of Tully-Veolan in 'Waverley'; from Meigle in Forfarshire he visited Dunottar Castle, and in the churchyard met Peter Paterson, 'Old Mortality.' Stopping at Halgards in Tweed-dale, in a vacation of 1797, 'he had his first and only interview with David Ritchie, the original of his Black Dwarf.' Thence he went on among the English Lakes, and with Gilsland as centre saw 'Skiddaw's dim and distant head,' 'Helvellyn's cliffs sublime,' 'Glaramara's ridgy back,' 'Red Penrith's Table Round' – the scenery of 'The Bridal of Triermain.' Among the party at Gilsland, Scott found the lady, Charlotte Margaret Carpenter, whom he was to make his wife before the end of the year.

SCOTT

In the summer after their marriage, Scott and his wife took
a cottage six miles from Edinburgh, at Lasswade on the Esk,
in a neighbourhood full of friends and of friends to be. A year
later, 1799, Scott was appointed Sheriff-depute of Selkirk-
shire. This office gave him yet another centre, the inn at
Clovenford on the road from Edinburgh to Selkirk. Thus he
could learn Ettrick Forest, the vales of Ettrick and Yarrow,
St. Mary's Lake and Roslin. He made friends there with
William Laidlaw and his wife, of Blackhouse on the Douglas-
burn, who helped him, says Lockhart, to the greater part of
the characters of Dandie Dinmont, his wife and their house at
Charlieshope. Through Laidlaw Scott met James Hogg, who
had been shepherd for ten years to Laidlaw's father. Hogg
was to detect Scott's hand in 'The Black Dwarf' when he
read a word for word repetition in it of a discussion in 1801
on long sheep and short sheep. Scott was now beginning a
first draft of 'The Lady of the Lake,' with Loch Katrine and
its neighbourhood for the scene of it.

'I took,' says he, 'uncommon pains to verify the accuracy
of the local circumstances of this story. I recollect, in particular, that, to ascertain whether I was telling a probable tale,
I went into Perthshire, to see whether King James could
actually have ridden from the banks of Loch Vennachar to
Stirling Castle within the time supposed in the poem, and had
the pleasure to satisfy myself that it was quite practicable.'

But 'The Lay of the Last Minstrel' was to precede 'The
Lady of the Lake.' It was written at the Lasswade cottage
where John Stoddart paid him a visit and repeated passages
from Coleridge's unpublished 'Christabel,' which gave Scott
the hint for his narrative metre. Wordsworth came there in
the autumn of 1803, and Scott read aloud for him the first
four cantos. Scott's knowledge of men, Nature, history, and

tradition, went blithely into the story, and Wordsworth, like all the world, was delighted. The scene was his own country. He must have ridden the same paths as William of Deloraine, from Teviot side to where

> 'Old Melros' rose, and fair Tweed ran.'

Few bards could have exclaimed, other things being equal, with less untruth than Scott, through the lips of his last minstrel:

> 'O Caledonia! stern and wild,
> Meet nurse for a poetic child!
> Land of brown heath and shaggy wood,
> Land of the mountain and the flood,
> Land of my sires! what mortal hand
> Can e'er untie the filial band
> That knits me to thy rugged strand!
> Still as I view each well-known scene,
> Think what is now and what hath been,
> Seems as to me, of all bereft,
> Sole friends thy woods and streams were left;
> And thus I love them better still,
> Even in extremity of ill.
> By Yarrow's stream still let me stray,
> Though none should guide my feeble way,
> Still feel the breeze down Ettrick break,
> Although it chill my wither'd cheek;
> Still lay my head by Teviot Stone,
> Though there, forgotten and alone,
> The Bard may draw his parting groan.'

But the success of this poem set Scott free to exchange the servitude of law for that of literature. Already in 1804 – the 'Lay' appeared in 1805 – he had settled at Ashestiel, on the

Upper Tweed, in wilder country, only thirty miles from
Edinburgh. There he wrote 'Marmion' and the introduction
beginning:

> 'November's sky is chill and drear,
> November's leaf is red and sere:
> Late, gazing down the sleepy linn,
> That hems our little garden in. . . .'

There he could mingle writing, entertaining, and coursing,
by means of rising early. And when the lease of Ashestiel was
out in 1811, he could afford to buy an estate a few miles lower
down the river, and the greeting of 'laird of Abbotsford.'

Thenceforward he was giving out almost as much as he
received. His life was mostly either travelling by hill and
water, or sitting still with a pen; his recreations, 'the musing
ramble among his own glens, the breezy ride over the moors,
the merry spell at the woodman's axe, or the festive chase of
Newark, Fernilee, Hanging-Shaw, or Deloraine; the quiet
old-fashioned contentment of the little domestic circle, alternating with the brilliant phantasmagoria of admiring, and
sometimes admired, strangers — or the hoisting of the tele-
graph flag that called laird and bonnet-laird to the burning of
the water, or the wassail of the hall.' He had begun to live
and to write at Abbotsford (in 1812) when there was only one
room habitable, and that surrounded by masons working.
Planting, buying more land, 'completing' the house, receiving
tourists, while he worked and his children grew up, he lived
here chiefly until his death, but kept on until 1826 the house
at 39, Castle Street, Edinburgh, which he had taken in 1802,
soon after his marriage. But his books flowed mainly out of
those old 'raids' on the Border. Over and over again we can
see the particular receiving which corresponds to the particular giving out. For example, there was an alarm of French

invasion while Scott and his wife were at Gilsland on holiday. He, being a quartermaster and light-horseman in the Volunteer Cavalry, rode hard to join his troop at Dalkeith. It was a false alarm. The result was 'The Bard's Incantation':

> 'The forest of Glenmore is drear,
>   It is all of black pine and the dark oak-tree;
> And the midnight wind to the mountain deer
>   Is whistling the forest lullaby. . . .'

He called upon the 'minstrels and bards of other days,' the 'souls of the mighty,' to sing a mighty strain against 'Gaul's ravening legions,' and had the answer from 'the dread voice of other years':

> 'When targets clash'd, and bugles rung,
> And blades round warriors' heads were flung,
> The foremost of the band were we,
> And hymn'd the joys of Liberty.'

In 'The Antiquary' he used over again the same incident. Another case is the description, in 'A Legend of Montrose,' of the steep pass up into the Highlands from the Lowlands of Perthshire. 'The beautiful pass of Lessy, near Callender, in Menteith,' says Scott's footnote, 'would in some respects answer his description.' This way, where Montrose met Dugald Dalgetty, Scott himself must have gone more than once. But Scott did not use photography. Dick Tinto expressed quite another view from Scott's own when he said that 'Description was to the author of a romance exactly what drawing and tinting were to a painter; words were his colours, and, if properly employed, they could not fail to place the scene, which he wished to conjure up, as effectually before the mind's eye as the tablet or canvas presents it to the bodily organ.' All that Scott did was to set down the most vividly remembered points of a scene in the order in which his memory, when worked clear, presented them, trusting that readers with some knowledge of the same world would have something, according to their different powers and interests, to set their minds towards a scene as near it as possible. Moreover, he had greatly simplified the earth. He saw it as beautiful or sublime or tame, and if he loved a thing it had or came to have one of those qualities in a high degree. Thus, St. Mary's Lake had elements which at once endeared itself to him as a typical romantic water. He knew it well. In the introduction to the second canto of 'Marmion' he recalls it to a friend with whom he had hunted:

> 'Up pathless Ettrick and on Yarrow,
> Where erst the outlaw drew his arrow.
> But not more blithe that silvan court,
> Than we have been at humbler sport;
> Though small our pomp, and mean our game,
> Our mirth, dear Marriott, was the same.
> Remember'st thou my greyhounds true?
> O'er holt or hill there never flew,
> From slip or leash there never sprang,
> More fleet of foot or sure of fang.
> Nor dull, between each merry chase,
> Pass'd by the intermitted space;
> For we had fair resource in store,
> In classic and in Gothic lore:
> We mark'd each memorable scene,
> And held poetic talk between;
> Nor hill nor brook we paced along,
> But had its legend or its song. . . .'

With the aid of memory, and of legend and song, he made St. Mary's Lake the model for a crystal lake where,

> 'Abrupt and sheer, the mountains sink
> At once upon the level brink;
> And just a trace of silver sand
> Marks where the water meets the land. . . .'

But, as Andrew Lang pointed out, the water is peaty brown; there is no sand, but a 'white margin of dry stones, ordinary stones'; and 'there are no mountains, nothing is "abrupt," nothing is "sheer"; green, grassy slopes descend placidly to the loch on one side, the other side is a plain, to which hills fall easily.' He transmuted it as Jefferies did Coate Reservoir. He was not imitating or rivalling the works of Nature, but stamping his own image upon the offspring of a union between Nature and the Lady of the Lake —

> 'Sole sitting on the shores of old romance.'

He had not the pedantry to look at hills with a yard-measure, and be obliged to condemn Hindhead because it is so much smaller than Ben Lomond. Thus, if his country is Scotland, it is no duplicate of that ancient kingdom. The two exist together separate, yet hardly independent of one another. Nor can their union cease to be fertile until there are no more heads, upon 'the shores of old romance,' where it can be celebrated afresh.

R. L. STEVENSON

*

STEVENSON's country was Edinburgh and the Pentlands. He was born at Howard Place, Edinburgh; 17, Heriot Row became seven years later the home of the family, and for thirty years continued so. Edinburgh gave him his school and University. When he was seventeen, and for fourteen years after, his father rented Swanston Cottage, five miles away at the foot of the Pentlands; and there and thereabouts, so long as he was in Scotland, he spent his best leisure thenceforward, reading, writing, and seeing men and Nature.

In early childhood, the suburbs of Edinburgh, as Mr. Graham Balfour has told us, gave substance to the words of the twenty-third Psalm, ' "the pastures green" being stubble-fields by the water of Leith, and "death's dark vale" a certain archway in the Warriston Cemetery.' The essay 'A Penny Plain and Twopence Coloured' describes his pleasures at the age of six, when he had the company of his cousin, R. A. M. Stevenson, and of Skelt's Juvenile Drama, bought at a shop 'which was dark and smelt of Bibles,' and 'was a loadstone rock for all that bore the name of boy.' The cousins 'lived together in a purely visionary state, and were never tired of dressing up.' When he was in Samoa, he could still hear the bugles at Edinburgh Castle, 'those strains of martial music that she goes to bed with, ending each day, like an act of an opera, to the notes of bugles. . . . It is the beautiful that I thus actively recall: the august airs of the Castle on its rock, nocturnal passages of lights and trees, the sudden song of the blackbird in a suburban lane, rosy and dusky winter sunsets, the uninhabited splendours of the early dawn, the building up of the city on a misty day, house above house, spire above spire, until it was received into a sky of softly glowing clouds, and seemed to pass on and upwards, fresh grades and rises, city beyond city, a new Jerusalem, bodily scaling heaven.' In his letters of the 'seventies he shows how much his eye was turned on Edinburgh and the surrounding earth and air, and on his impression of them. They are in varying stages of execution, but never done without some thought of the morrow. Here is one, belonging to 1873:

'I was wakened this morning by a long flourish of bugles and a roll upon the drums – the *réveillé* at the Castle. I went to the window; it was a grey, quiet dawn, a few people passed already up the street between the gardens, already I heard the noise of an early cab somewhere in the distance, most of the lamps had been extinguished but not all, and there were two or three lit windows in the opposite façade that showed where sick people and watchers had been awake all night and knew not yet of the new, cool day. This appeals to me with a special sadness: how often in the old times my nurse and I had looked across at these, and sympathized!'

And another of a day's end:

'Every now and then as we went, Arthur's Seat showed its head at the end of a street. Now to-day the blue sky and the sunshine were both entirely wintry; and there was about the hill, in those glimpses, a sort of thin, unreal, crystalline distinctness that I have not often seen excelled. As the sun began to go down over the valley between the new town and the old, the evening grew resplendent; all the gardens and low-lying buildings sank back and became almost invisible in a mist of wonderful sun, and the Castle stood up against the sky, as thin and sharp in outline as a castle cut out of paper. . . .'

Day after day he had his eye on the object and on his writing-paper.

But Stevenson's happiest early memories were of his grandfather Balfour's manse at Colinton, beyond the suburbs. He used to stay there often in bad health.

'Out of my reminiscences of life in that dear place,' said he, 'all the morbid and painful elements have disappeared. That was my golden age: *et ego in Arcadia vixi*. There is something so fresh and wholesome about all that went on at Colinton, compared with what I recollect of the town, that I can hardly, even in my own mind, unite the two chains of reminiscences together; they look like stories of two different people, ages apart in time and quite dissimilar in character.'

Manse and garden made an ample playground for his feet and his imagination. There he could meet cousins, witches, or antelopes, according to his need and mood, and always the silver hair and beautiful face of his grandfather. He has written of house and garden and people in 'The Manse':

'. . . A place in that time like no other: the garden cut into provinces by a great hedge of beech, and overlooked by the church and the terrace of the churchyard, where the tomb-stones were thick, and after nightfall "spunkies" might be seen to dance, at least by children; flower-pots lying warm in sunshine; laurels and the great yew making elsewhere a pleas-ing horror of shade; the smell of water rising from all round, with an added tang of paper-mills; the sound of water every-where, and the sound of mills — the wheel and the dam singing their alternate strain; the birds on every bush and from every corner of the overhanging woods pealing out their notes until the air throbbed with them; and in the midst of this the Manse. . . .'

Other holidays in better health and in lively company he spent at Peebles and North Berwick. He and his cousin R. A. M. both rode, one a pony called 'Hell,' the other 'Purgatory.' Above all, they 'crusoed,' 'crusoeing' being 'a word that covers all extempore eating in the open air: digging, perhaps, a house under the margin of the links, kindling a fire of the sea-ware and cooking apples there.' The rest is written in 'The Lantern Bearers.' You see there the rocks, the grey islets, the 'spit between two sandy bays,' the 'easterly fisher-village' itself, and the 'endless links and sand-wreaths, a wilderness of hiding-holes, alive with popping rabbits and soaring gulls.' Later on the sand-hills, the 'promontory between two shallow bays,' the islet, the rabbits and the gulls, reappear in 'The Pavilion on the Links.'

When he had left school and was nearing eighteen, he spent July at Anstruther, August and part of September at Wick, as he told his mother in letters, and the world in 'Random Memories.' Those letters to his mother in 1868 were among his first exercises in precise description of this kind:

'Wick lies at the end or elbow of an open triangular bay, hemmed on either side by shores, either cliff or steep earth-bank, of no great height. The grey houses of Pulteney extend along the southerly shore almost to the cape; and it is about halfway down this shore – no, six-sevenths way down – that the new breakwater extends athwart the way.'

You see him studying the storm, watching to see if it would throw the big stones at the wall, and then remarking that to appreciate a storm 'requires a little of the artistic temperament of which Mr. T. S., C.E. [his father] possesses some, whatever he may say.' He concludes that he cannot look at the storm practically – that is, as an engineer.

Two years later he was at the Isle of Earraid, off the coast of Mull. The people on the ship and the scenery of the shore were a whole, said he, that 'would have made a novelist's fortune'; and he was himself twice in later years to make use of the isle. It was the scene of David Balfour's shipwreck in 'Kidnapped.' It had the essay, 'Memoirs of an Islet,' to itself. At the beginning of that essay he tells us what we should otherwise have had to discover for ourselves, how he treated his experience.

'Those who try to be artists,' he says, 'use, time after time, the matter of their recollections, setting and resetting little colouried memories of men and scenes, rigging up (it may be) some especial friend in the attire of a buccaneer, and decreeing armies to manœuvre, or murder to be done, on the playground of their youth.'

He speaks of memories being 'pleasant spectres' which can be 'laid' by use in a book:

'I used one but the other day: a little eyot of dense, fresh-water sand, where I once waded deep in butterburs, delighting to hear the song of the river on both sides, and to tell myself that I was indeed and at last upon an island. Two of my puppets lay there a summer's day, hearkening to the shearers at work in riverside fields and to the drums of the grey old garrison upon the neighbouring hill. And this was, I think, done rightly: the place was rightly peopled – and now belongs not to me, but to my puppets – for a time at least. . . .'

There is, he continues, another island in his 'collection,' the memory of which besieges him:

'I put a whole family there in one of my tales, and later on threw upon its shores, and condemned to several days of rain and shellfish on its tumbled boulders, the hero of another. The ink is not yet faded; the sound of the sentences is still in my mind's ear; and I am under a spell to write of that island again.'

This was Earraid.

But by that time, since May, 1867, Stevenson's head-quarters were at Swanston. This also, after his manner, he used three times in writing: first in letters; second in 'Picturesque Notes on Edinburgh'; lastly in 'St. Ives.' It is on the main slope of the Pentlands:

'A bouquet of old trees stands round a white farmhouse, and from a neighbouring dell you can see smoke rising and leaves rustling in the breeze. Straight above, the hills climb a thousand feet into the air. The neighbourhood, about the time of lambs, is clamorous with the bleating of flocks; and you will be awakened in the grey of early summer mornings by the barking of a dog, or the voice of a shepherd shouting to the echoes. . . .'

They were six hundred feet above the sea in a climate that had done little towards clothing the garden by May.

Here Stevenson may be seen at work and play, inter-mingled, writing long letters; talking to John Todd, 'the oldest herd on the Pentlands,' or Robert Young, the old Scotch gardener, or the military beggar who asseverated that Keats was a fine poet; walking, skating, fishing, canoeing, reading behind the yew-hedge. While he was at work on 'John Knox' he was describing a storm and his sensations at Swanston:

'. . . But the quaking was not what put me about; it was the horrible howl of the wind round the corner; the audible haunting of an incarnate anger about the house; the evil spirit that was abroad; and, above all, the shuddering silent pauses when the storm's heart stands dreadfully still for a moment. O how I hate a storm at night! They have been a great influence in my life, I am sure; for I can remember them so far back — long before I was six at least. . . .'

Nor was night only solemn. It was, he said, 'very solemn to see the top of one hill steadfastly regarding you over the shoulder of another'; he 'never before to-day fully realized the haunting of such a gigantic face, as it peers over into a valley and seems to command all corners.'

This was written when Stevenson was twenty-three. But at the end of the year – 1873 – he was ordered South, and did not revisit Swanston till the following May. His wanderings had begun. He was much in London or Paris. He yachted on the west coast of Scotland; he canoed through Belgium. He walked in England and in France. He returned to Edinburgh and Swanston for visits of a few months, sometimes alone, sometimes with friends. Henley and he finished 'Deacon Brodie' there. But travel had schooled him to write where he found himself, at Swanston, at Pitlochry, at Braemar, at Kingussie. He became something of an epicure in scenery by the time he had crossed America and settled in Bournemouth; and, what with the refining influences of his style on whatsoever it touched, it can hardly be said that he had a country, except that he knew best and remembered most affectionately Edinburgh and Swanston, and that as subjects they are more conspicuous in his writing than other places. When to go himself was impossible, he asked his nurse to sprinkle the turf of Halkerside, above Swanston, with water from the spring where he used to 'sit and make bad verses.' It was 'Ille Terrarum' of the poem in 'Underwoods':

> 'An' there the auld housie beeks an' dozes,
> A' by her lane.'

INDEX

*

303

INDEX

INDEX

307

INDEX

INDEX

INDEX

INDEX

INDEX

EDWARD THOMAS

Edited by

R. *George Thomas*

It is astonishing to realize that all of Edward Thomas's poetry was written in only four years: between 1914, when at the age of thirty-six he wrote his first poem, and 1917, when he was killed at the Battle of Arras. Collected in chronological order in this definitive edition, with fascinating background notes, the poems allow the reader to appreciate the distinctive character of this major war poet – an introspective and often despondent man, particularly sensitive to the world of natural and living things, who stubbornly refused to abandon the search for a truth that lies behind our everyday experiences. Edward Thomas's illuminating War Diary, covering the last three months of his life, is also included as an appendix.

EDWARD THOMAS: THE LAST FOUR YEARS

ELEANOR FARJEON

This book, which was first published in 1958, is a double memoir. Eleanor Farjeon describes her meeting with the self-conscious, unfledged poet Edward Thomas and the subsequent development of their deep friendship. But by weaving into her narrative the letters Thomas wrote to her between 1913 and 1917 she also offers a detailed record of Thomas's life and a unique account of his development as a poet, for it was during these 'last four years' that he wrote all his poetry. Another dimension to this book is its eye-witness account of the First World War, for after 1915, when Thomas enlisted in the Artists' Rifles, many of his letters to Eleanor were written from army camps and, finally, from the battle-fields of Europe.

THE AUTOBIOGRAPHY OF
A SUPER-TRAMP

W. H. DAVIES

With a Preface by George Bernard Shaw

This is the classic account of the poet W. H. Davies's adventures as a young man travelling around America and England at the turn of the century. His spare, evocative prose gives raw power to his experiences among tricksters, down-and-outs, and itinerant labourers, and makes the characters he encounters – New Haven Baldy, the Indian Kid and Boozy Bob – unforgettable.

GUIDE TO THE LAKES

WILLIAM WORDSWORTH

Complete with illustrations, notes, and a map, this is the best-selling guide to the part of England that inspired one of its greatest poets.

'... the archetypal book for the Lake District connoisseur ... a classic of committed prose about a passionately loved landscape' *Melvyn Bragg*

STILL GLIDES THE STREAM

FLORA THOMPSON

Like her well-loved trilogy *Lark Rise to Candleford,* this book depicts the vanished life of the countryside which Flora Thompson knew as a child in the 1880s. Cast in a fictional form, it is an enchanting portrait of an Oxfordshire village and its inhabitants around the time of Queen Victoria's Golden Jubilee.

'... reading it is a perfect pleasure' *Benny Green*